June 7, 1991

To Manuel,
Thanks for all you do
to keep America strong!

All the Best,
Capt. Don Peterson

★ ★ ★

# DRES
# GRA

★ ★ ★

# A
# WOMA
# AT
# WEST
# POIN

★ ★ ★

## CAPTAI
## DONNA
## PETERSO

★ ★ ★

**EAKIN PRESS** ★ Aust

Dear Mom and Dad,

This book is dedicated to you. Without your constant support, unwavering faith in me, and unconditional love this book would never have been penned, for it would never have been lived. You're the greatest!

I Love You.
Donna

# Contents

*"It doesn't hurt so much to pay taxes when I look at all of you."*

— Bob Hope, during an address
to the Corps of Cadets

# Introduction:  The Appointment

The handsome blond man in spic-and-span West Point uniform stepped up to the petite young woman approaching the entryway. He saluted sharply; she saluted timidly in return.

"Miss, may I touch you?"

As she gazed into his deep blue eyes her thoughts raced from *Oh, please do!* to *I thought you'd never ask!* Her heart beating excitedly, she replied, "Yes, sir." However, she heard the breathy words drone to disappointment as he touched her hand and adjusted her salute.

I was once that timid young lady, and this is my story.

In 1976 the world came to an end. Just ask any male graduate of the nation's oldest and most prestigious military institution. The tombstones of Lee, Grant, Eisenhower, and Patton cracked as they felt an American institution begin to crumble: Women would soon be setting foot *inside* West Point. Yes, women would finally know the secret rituals and rites that bound the men of the Long Gray Line. Not elaborate elements, just secret ones. Things these men didn't even tell their wives.

I cannot imagine a place on earth that wanted me less. Yet I went, of my own free will, knowing it could not be easy.

I entered the United States Military Academy on the day before my eighteenth birthday, 6 July 1978. On 26 May 1982, I took off the sparkling silver saber I carried at my side and handed it to my father, the symbolic gesture of a job well done. In between, I was harassed, threatened, and betrayed.

1

When I kept my eyes and ears open, and my mouth shut, I survived extremely well. But I was perpetually a witness: I listened to the bitter stories the first class with women relayed with frightening hostility; I sensed the failing pride and battered egos of the "last all-male class" struggling to reverse the fate of an American institution; I saw the first female cadet in U.S. history receive her diploma *and* be selected a Rhodes Scholar; and I was there when the first female cadets were dismissed for homosexual behavior. Personally, I suffered the pain of being a pioneer and later felt the disappointment that, in 1990, the acceptance of women into this cloistered world had still not occurred. And I lived in fear: Afraid that I would be unable to live up to the time-honored title of "West Pointer," afraid that I would never get the chance to obtain the title, afraid that I would leave West Point as less of a woman than when I entered.

Modern history has recorded two instances when women have, en masse, completely ceased to have monthly menstrual cycles for an extended amount of time: the Jewish concentration camps and the induction of women at West Point. This condition, known as amenorrhea, is brought on by a combination of extreme stress and exaggerated physical conditioning. In some women, it leads to an inability to conceive children. For me, it was just one of the many hidden costs of being a pioneer.

Before 1976, I wanted to become a heart surgeon. I had planned to go to Baylor College of Medicine, then relocate to nearby Houston to perform with the world's greatest heart specialists. The publicity surrounding the introduction of women to the service academies changed all of that. Because I enjoyed flying and had won the Aviation Award in high school, I applied to the U.S. Air Force Academy. And because I loved the history of America, I also applied to West Point. I had no thoughts of a military career; I knew nothing at all about military life. My father had served four years in the navy, but that was long before I was born. I just wanted to attend West Point: to be a part of history, to walk the halls where warriors and legends were created, to live in a moral, disciplined environment under an internalized Honor Code where a person's word is his bond and patriotism is a rallying point. Five years of military service after graduation from West Point was the bill the U.S. government would hand me for that opportunity.

When I received appointments to both of the service academies, my parents gifted me with a "prospective candidate" visit to each, during spring break of my senior year in high school. My mother and I flew to New York first. As the bus from the airport curved around a mountainside and I saw West Point, nestled in the valley under a blanket of snow, it looked like a beautiful picture postcard. I let out an uncontrolled gasp, as did most of the passengers on the bus that afternoon. Even the newest buildings were old. West Point took pains to ensure that the historical charm of the gray stone buildings was retained forever.

As I walked around the Academy with my cadet guides that weekend, other cadets would pass by and yell, "Don't come!"

"It's a beautiful place," I'd say.

"They never give you a chance to look at it," came the foreboding reply.

After my visit to West Point, I really never gave the Air Force Academy a fair chance. Its buildings were concrete and glass; they had no souls. Actually, its cadets were friendlier, but much more arrogant. "We work with our brains," they'd say. "Let the army cadets get their fingernails dirty!" The Air Force Academy admissions officers spoke to me about flying (I was a "pilot qualified" candidate) and about the Air Force astronaut program. I knew going to West Point would mean the end of my flying. It would be a small price to pay.

In Texas, women didn't get appointments to service academies every day, let alone two appointments. After all, Texas breeds a majority of the world's beauty queens, not female army officers. As a tribute to my dual appointments, the Beaumont Rotary Club hosted a luncheon and placed me in the spotlight. After the club president rattled off a list of my qualifications for appointment he announced, "And she has chosen West Point!"

The crowd went wild. My parents looked stunned. I just smiled. I hadn't "chosen" anything yet.

My parents whisked me away as soon as the luncheon ended, before the media had an opportunity to ask me about my decision. We sat down in a small Irish pub across the highway from where the luncheon had been held, beside a crackling fire from an old stone fireplace. I knew it was time to decide. After all, I was holding two appointments. And just as I had held my breath, waiting and hoping for those appointments, so too was some other deserving young man or woman waiting for me to release one of those appointments.

"You're not even considering Air Force are you?" My mother's voice was sad. "You know it's better for the women there. You'll be fighting much less tradition by going there. And they want you to fly." She was almost pleading.

"I can't, Mom," I answered. "I know it'll be tougher, stricter, but my God, Mom, it's West Point! How many young women get an opportunity like this in life — to experience a part of history? Besides, they've got the most rigid Honor Code, and you know how much that means to me." I had made my decision.

Several days later, the local papers carried the news about the "First Woman from Southeast Texas to Attend Military Academy." I wrote to Senator John Tower, thanking him for my nomination to West Point and vowing to keep him abreast of my progress.

I had expended an enormous amount of energy working for my nomination, but I never really thought I had a chance. Why would Senator Tower choose me over some Houston or Dallas oil millionaire's son? Wouldn't it be smarter to nominate the child of someone who could be politically advantageous to the senator? I wasn't deaf to the rumors that no one could get an appointment to West Point without "connections" of some sort, and I had none. What chance did I have? Receiving the nomination from Senator Tower and the subsequent appointment to West Point made me believe that qualifications *do* matter after all; that it's not always who you know that counts. I wrote: "Because you have given me this tremendous opportunity, I would vote for you for God, if you were running!" I suppose that comment stemmed from the emotionalism that goes along with being not quite eighteen years old. But today, having survived four years at West Point and having been able to appreciate what a marvelous opportunity John Tower gave me, I still mean it.

My entire family was on hand to say goodbye at the Beaumont airport. No tears, I told myself. If I cried, my family would cry, and I might not leave. Besides, what was there to cry about? My parents' child was leaving home to become a West Pointer! What parent would cry about that? I vowed to be strong. I had already decided that, no matter what, I was not going to cry while I was at the Academy, and I might as well start being strong right then.

I hugged and kissed the members of my family, waved goodbye, and boarded the plane. Then I cried all the way to New York.

## CHAPTER 1

# Welcome to West Point!

*"By entering this Academy, and becoming the recipients of the thorough instruction here imparted, you have incurred the most weighty and solemn of obligations: You no longer have the privilege of common citizens to live and die in obscurity."*
— Ashbel Smith, address to Corps of Cadets, 1848

I have often thought that if corporations could harness the organization and efficiency of those first ten hours at West Point, on what is known as "R-Day," they could easily make a fortune. Groups of new cadet candidates begin arriving at about 9:00 A.M. By 5:00 P.M., 1,400 civilian teenagers have been fed, outfitted, taught to march, moved into living quarters, had their hair cut, and "militarized" enough to accept the oath of induction at a parade ceremony on the Plain in front of several thousand family members, officers, West Point personnel, and photographers. I didn't realize until years later, when my class became seniors and were ourselves in charge of the R-Day operation, what a tremendous feat it really was. For the candidates, however, this phenomenal day can only be described as trying to take a drink from a firehose.

I arrived by bus from New York City at about 9:00 A.M. All of the new cadet candidates were shuttled into the bleachers of the stadium for a "welcome briefing." This is the last time that family and friends (who accompanied very few of the new cadets) would see us for at least several weeks.

A cadet in a perfectly tailored white and gray uniform stood before us. As he stepped up to the microphone, his brass gleaming in the New York sun, the crowd of several hundred hushed.

"New cadets! I'd like to welcome you to the United States Military Academy at West Point," he began. I could hardly believe that I was among those he was addressing. Randy Odom, one of several candidates I'd met at the Barbizon Plaza Hotel the night before, sat next to me in the stands. He was the perfect "boy-next-door" with dazzling blue eyes. I felt safe when I looked into them. We squeezed hands and stared at each other in disbelief. We were so excited!

The cadet continued. "During the next eight weeks you will undergo some of the most grueling training on the face of the earth." There was no doubt in our minds that this spit-and-polish cadet meant every word of his carefully rehearsed speech. He concluded by again welcoming us and telling our friends and relatives to say goodbye, then he moved us down from the bleached-white concrete stands. Parents who could stay for the parade that afternoon were treated to marvelously well-organized, cadet-guided tours, which included lunch in the fascinating West Point cadet mess hall, while new cadet candidates were shuttled into the tunnel beneath the stadium, out of view of "John Q. Public." There, long tables lined with paper tags and pencils awaited us. We were told to stand beside a pencil on the table. As we stopped, I set my baggage down.

*"You!"*

I looked up to see what was the matter. My God, the cadet was looking right at me!

"No one told you to put your bag down. Pick it up. From now on you'd better learn to do what you're told — *only* what you're told — or you'll be out of here as fast as you came in."

I stared at the cadet as I quickly picked up my bag. Every hair on my arm was standing on end, ready to sense any activity in this new, strange environment.

We finished tagging our bags just as the bus pulled up. The poor new cadet candidate at the head of the line tried to step on board before our cadet guide told him to do so. It was five minutes before the cadet got through with that guy, and we hadn't even gotten to the barracks area yet. It was amazing, I thought, how a person can reduce you to dust without even raising his voice.

Once on the bus, it seemed only logical to believe that we might never again see the friends we'd made in New York City the night before. So, we tried to exchange names and home states with each other. Then one of our group of six said, "You know, they say that one out of every three of us won't make it." I'm sure that all of us believed the young man because our group got very silent. We just sat there, looking each other over, wondering which two of us would be the first sacrifices.

It was only a five-minute trip from the stadium on the hill to the huge West Point gymnasium complex adjacent to the cadet barracks. As we got off the bus we were paraded through a series of stations where we signed papers, stepped on weight scales, had our heights measured and the number of pull-ups we could do recorded. The entire process reminded me of the way cattle are shoved through chutes and prodded at every juncture at the stockyards in East Texas. After that, each of the "signed, sealed and delivered" candidates was seated in one of eight separate sections in one of the smaller gymnasiums, according to the Cadet Basic Training (CBT) company to which they would be assigned.

As I sat in the Second Company bleachers, I looked around for Randy. After only about ten minutes he was paraded in and sat in the company bleachers next to mine. We both moved over to the tape that divided our two sections, oblivious to the signs posted across the gym walls: "SILENCE" and "NO TALKING." I smiled for the first time in hours and we started talking, smiling, blushing a little, and . . .

"Hey, you two! Can't you read?" the cadet asked as he pointed over our heads to the signs we missed the first time but would not miss again. Nothing more was said, and Randy and I sat in silence until a cadet came by to march each of the collected groups of candidates to their new companies. Randy left first, in a small group that looked strangely like the Seven Dwarfs marching off to work. I watched until the little group was out of sight, feeling like I'd lost my only friend in this new world. At least I knew what company he was in. *Maybe,* I hoped, *when things settle down I can look him up — if they don't wash him out before I have a chance to say goodbye.*

"Hey, Miss!" a cadet shouted in my general direction. "Get your head out of your ass and get down here!" I had been so busy watching Randy leave that I failed to hear a cadet calling out my company number. Only two hours had passed and already I'd been yelled at twice. At that rate I thought I'd never make it through the day, let alone through four years. As the cadet marched a group of six of us to the Second CBT Company, I decided that I would not be yelled at again — at least not for an hour. To do that I'd have to stay alert, watch the mistakes that others made, and not make the same ones. It sounded good in theory, anyway.

The company "area" was a huge, black-topped space about the size of three basketball courts, surrounded by five-story "barracks" buildings which housed the cadets. This was the first big moment in a new cadet's history. Each of us would report to "The-Man-in-the-Red-Sash" for our "personal" welcome to the Academy. It was our official introduction to the eight weeks of basic training known as "Beast Barracks." I was fourth in line.

"Get your feet off my line!" the cadet with the scarlet sash barked as the first candidate moved in front of him. "I said step up *to* my line, Mister. Not *on* my line, not *over* my line, but *to* my line. Are you hard of hearing or just stupid? Shut up! No one asked you to speak!"

I decided I was going to put my toes so close to that line you wouldn't be able to squeeze a hair between them. I wondered how the next candidate would do.

"I said *drop* your bags, Mister! Not *set* them, not *place* them, *drop* them! Do you understand English, or did the doctor drop you when you were born? Now pick up your bags and try it again!"

When the third, extremely nervous candidate stepped up, it was obvious that he'd been doing the same thinking I had: He placed his toes within a hair's breadth of the line and dropped his bags with a thud when the cadet commanded. But guess what? This was West Point, and I had just learned the first rule of this place: there are no steadfast rules. It just depends upon the mood of the person in authority at the time.

"I said *drop* them, not knock a hole in my concrete! You want to *buy* that concrete? Then show a little respect. Try it again."

By this time it was obvious that the only chance I had was if this guy got hoarse before he got to me.

Suddenly, it was my turn. I took a deep breath and stepped forward, my toes just kissing his thin yellow line. I looked up, saluted, and reported: "Sir, New Cadet Candidate Peterson reports to the Man-in-the-Red-Sash." And then I froze.

He was gorgeous: tall, blond, tanned, with muscles that teased at the seams of his starched white shirt. I stood there for what seemed like five minutes, staring into those cool blue eyes, feeling like a Cinderella whose prince had arrived before she'd had a chance to put on her makeup and change into her gown. So mesmerized was I that it hadn't dawned on me that no one was yelling at me. All I could do was stare and try to keep my heart from pounding out of my chest. The cadet saluted sharply in return, then spoke in a deep, crisp voice: "Miss, may I touch you?"

*God does answer a young girl's prayers after all!* I thought. As I gazed deeper into those blue eyes, answers raced across my mind: *Oh, please do! . . . I've been waiting eighteen years for a man like you to ask me that!* My heart beat excitedly as I replied, calmly, "Yes, sir." Instantly, the reality of the situation grasped me as he merely touched my hand and adjusted my enthusiastic but improper salute. Then the Man-in-the-Red-Sash completed his well-rehearsed speech about how I was to act, where I was to live, and what the Academy expected of me. But I missed most of it. I was resolving to be much more specific in my future prayers to God!

I picked up my bags and moved quickly into the barracks, the smell of his after-shave lingering in my nostrils. Yes, the United States Military Academy had normal, healthy, eighteen-year-old women in attendance. *This place might not be that bad after all . . .*

The daydream was over quickly. At the top of the stairs on the third floor of the barracks was a line of new cadet candidates waiting to meet the first sergeant and learn our "four answers." These were to be the only allowed responses to any questions or comments made by the cadet cadre (the cadets in charge of basic training) and any upper-class cadet during the entire first year. They were: "Yes, sir," "No, sir," "No excuse, sir," and "Sir, I do not understand" (the latter to be used more than any other during the first eight weeks). As luck would have it, the line to the first sergeant's door was so long that, by the time I got to the head of it, I had all the answers memorized, thereby escaping a third tongue-lashing. Soon I found myself sitting on a bare mattress in the barren room which would quickly become home.

Too afraid to even move, I just sat there for about ten minutes until another cadet pushed open the door and ordered me to get in line behind the other new cadets he was leading, Seven Dwarf-style, back to the gymnasium. There we were paraded through "issue points" where we received T-shirts with the West Point crest on them, black and gold athletic shorts, black dress socks, and black leather military shoes. This would be our uniform for most of the day. We hardly looked like the cadets in the movies about West Point. To top it off, they pinned long paper tags to our shorts and, rather than ask us if we'd been to eat lunch or gotten our uniforms fitted, they'd simply stop us and grasp our tags to see if the item was checked off. We were too "low" to even have to speak to.

We returned to our barracks, dressed like geeks, each with two green laundry bags carrying everything from combat boots to Crest toothpaste and yellow Dial soap. Everything we would need for the next eight weeks was contained in those two cotton bags. Males were allowed to keep their razors brought from home; women, their bras and cotton underwear. Some were smart enough to keep (and hide) an alarm clock. You weren't allowed to use it — they woke you when they wanted you up — but you could keep it under your pillow and hope you heard it if you needed to get up early. The key was to get back in bed before they came around to wake you. (Watches with alarms weren't popular in 1978 like they are today. What a challenge it must be now for the cadre to monitor those alarms!)

Our civilian luggage was taken from us and locked away. They would give it back to us when we left CBT. I kept my clock and pocket camera. One female several doors down kept her curling iron. She got caught trying to use it one weekend and really took some grief from the cadre. Our cadre was made up of "the last all-male class" at the Academy, and the use of curling irons during field training was not a concept those macho guys could easily accept. Frankly, I could never figure out where she found the time — or the hair — to use it.

The rest of that first afternoon was hectic but not too difficult. The hardest part for most of the candidates was learning to march before the 5:00 P.M. parade. I had been the drum major for my high school band, so I spent little time on this activity, which left me ample time to prepare my room and try on the "real" cadet uniform we would wear in the parade. The hardest part of the day for me was a forced trip to the barber shop.

You see, for as long as I could remember, I had long hair. I usually wore my hair long and straight, down to my waist, cut evenly across the bottom. During my junior year in high school, I was convinced by a smooth-talking barber to allow my hair to be cut into a trendy "Farrah Fawcett" style. When my girlfriends found out that I had to cut my hair short in order to attend the Academy, they were more upset than I was. Trying to sound brave, I explained that, though it would be rough at first, my hair would always grow back, and it was a very small price to pay for the experience. Still, the female freshman cadets I stayed with during my visit to West Point as a "prospective candidate" had warned me about the lack of quality haircutting skills at USMA: "Get it cut before you get here, whatever you do!" So I did, about a week before reporting to the Academy. Nevertheless, the cadre was sending me to the barber shop. I thought I'd be butchered.

The barber shop looked like an assembly line for sheep shearing. There were four rows of barber chairs, about fifteen in all, and eight long lines of geeks, standing at attention, moving one at a time closer to the slaughter. Mounds of multicolored hair lay around the floor, the barbers being too busy to sweep on that day. At the head of the lines were cadre members who evaluated the haircuts of the candidates and signed off the tags hanging from our shorts as we departed. I was terrified. Before I could experience my first regulation haircut, however, the cadre member evaluating my section stepped back to my place in line.

"Hi. I see you made it." A friendly voice! It was Pete, the squad leader for the women I stayed with when I visited the Academy back in March.

"Yes, sir," I said, allowing the right corner of my mouth to turn up just a bit (and hoping Pete wouldn't mind).

"You wouldn't listen to us, would you?" He was smiling, and it was the nicest smile I'd ever seen. "You look great, even with short hair." Then, signing off the block on my tag that indicated I'd been to the barber shop, he winked and said, "I don't think you need to go any further. But try to get back here in about a week. Your hair's a little bit long, and you don't want to be yelled at. Hang in there, Donna."

I held back all but the one long tear that escaped from my right eye. There was so much I wanted to say to him but so little I should say. I was pleased with my effort as I heard a quiet "Thank you" leave my lips. He read the appreciation in my eyes.

Back in my room, I was greeted by two women I would never forget: my roommates. Two more opposite people never shared the same living space, of that I was certain. Claire was a large-boned girl with a heavy Midwestern accent and sandy brown strawlike hair. She wore thick black military glasses that fit improperly, causing her to have an annoying habit of pressing her middle finger to the bridge of her nose in an attempt to push up her continuously slipping glasses. The barber shop had not been kind to her. She had a bowl-cut hairstyle which looked as if the proverbial lawnmower had driven over it. Our squad leader would often beseech us to "take her to the barber shop and see if you can get her fixed somehow." We tried, but experienced failure. The other roommate was to become my best friend. MaryAnn Bates was a pert blond with twinkling blue eyes, a cross-country runner who quickly became the best female runner the Academy had seen up to that time. She was the first female in the prestigious "Black" running group, named for one of the three school colors: black, gold, and gray. The "Gray" running group is where most of the new cadets found themselves. I started out there, but spent most of my time in the infamous "Gold" group, for new cadets who needed remedial help in running.

There was little opportunity for chit-chat that first afternoon. Soon my roommates and I were dressing for the parade. Our squad leader (the cadet in charge of our ten-person group) ran in and out, supervising and delaying our endeavor. Finally fully dressed, the three of us took turns surveying our efforts in the small mirror above the sink, jumping into the air to catch a glimpse of any part of ourselves below the waist.

*Funny thing,* I thought, disappointedly. *I'm wearing the historic gray uniform of a West Point cadet, but I don't look like a West Point cadet.* What I didn't know then was there there is so much more to looking like a cadet than just putting on the historical uniform. It's the combination of body carriage, presence, and a sense of self-assurance that creates the "look" of a West Pointer. But at least we didn't look like geeks anymore.

Our squad leader led us downstairs and outside to our first formation, where the company commander gave any of us the chance to depart the Academy, for the last time, before we took the induction oath. I couldn't believe my eyes when I saw several young men step out of the formation — after all it took to get here!

There was no time to think about them now, however. The huge block formation of 170 of the country's freshest and most frightened military recruits was being called to attention. Then we marched through the stone archways (known as sallyports) leading from the area to the front of the barracks, and onto the Plain at West Point, where we joined the seven other company blocks to receive the oath. We swore allegiance to West Point and promised to do our best to be our best. Now we were officially "new cadets."

After the parade, most of the evening was spent meeting our

"squad-mates" and finding out what our squad leader, and West Point, expected of us. We were handed a *CBT Barracks Guide* which diagramed in specific detail the exact method of setting up a cadet room, and were told to have our rooms "looking like that" by the next night. This guide was remarkable in its detail. For example, the tooth-brush was stored, clean and dry, with bristles facing up, head on the right, straddled across the two ends of the toothbrush holder which were placed with the open-ends facing the back of the chest. The same detail was used for soap, underwear, socks; even the wooden hangers in the closet had to be an equal distance apart and canted toward the door of the cadet room. But, for all of its detail, the guide neglected to cover one essential item: women's bras. Where in the underwear drawer were they to be located, and how were they supposed to be folded? After a short discussion about which one of the occupants of our room would ask our squad leader for guidance in this matter, we decided that all three of us would ask.

I had been at the Academy for only one day, but I had come to view the cadre as strong and stalwart men. The man who swallowed his gum when we asked this question did not fit that description. He took a deep breath and picked up one of the bras from the dresser top.

"Well, uh, you just fold it in half," he said slowly and methodi-cally. My roommates and I could "hear" the gears of his mind grind-ing. MaryAnn nudged me on the arm. We knew better than to laugh. There was a brief pause, then our squad leader placed the bra back on the dresser and, regaining his composure, said gruffly, "Just be sure they look neat and that all three of you do it the same way!"

"Yes, sir!" we chimed in unison (well almost, Claire was always a little late) as he left the room.

MaryAnn and I waited for several seconds before we went to the door to listen to the commotion in the hallway.

"Jim! How in the hell do you fold those things?" our squad leader asked an unsuspecting classmate of his in the hall.

"What things?" the second cadet asked.

"Girl things . . . bras and stuff." Our squad leader was having a hard time spitting out his words.

"How the hell should I know? Hey, John!" Now a third cadet was added to their state of confusion. "You have sisters . . . how do you fold a bra?"

"Yeah, I have sisters," the cadet said irately, "but I don't go through their underwear drawers! Give me a break!"

Finding no solutions in the mix of great minds gathered around him, my squad leader volunteered the one he had just relayed to us. "Hey, that's great! We'll tell the CO and put it out to the squad leaders tomorrow as SOP [standard operating procedure]," came the enthusiastic response. As the proud group dispersed, MaryAnn and I closed the door and smiled at each other. America's most superbly molded combat leaders still had the modesty of young men. I was glad.

Around 2100 hours (9:00 P.M.) we were told to don our prescribed "shower uniform" consisting of bathrobe, shower shoes, towel folded neatly over the right forearm (which is extended perpendicularly from the body), and clean Dial soap in a clean, dry soap dish, carried in the outstretched right hand. We would be inspected in this uniform each night before showers by our squad leader, who would check for hygiene problems and blisters — two common problems due to the excessive amount of physical activity during the hot, humid New York summer. After the inspection we were told that we would have five minutes — no more — to be showered and standing again with our squad-mates in the hall. "And absolutely no talking, at any time during the eight weeks, while you are in the latrine," was our squad leader's last command as we scurried off.

All of the female new cadets on the floor used the same latrine and shower facilities. When my roommates and I got into the latrine we found five other women already in there, and only four shower spigots! Now, traditionally, men are much less self-conscious about baring themselves in front of total strangers than women are — and especially if those women must share the same shower spigot! The women in the latrine that night were very self-conscious, very nervous, and very afraid that they'd be late returning to formation. So we made do the best we could.

"Excuse me, I'm Donna. Could I share your shower?" I couldn't believe I was saying this.

"Yeah, I'm Karen," came the less-than-enthusiastic response as she modestly turned her back to me. Within moments all of us were showering and talking, trying to make each other feel at ease in an awkward situation. Suddenly, another of the female new cadets came into the shower area in her robe.

"There's a cadet out here who says you all have fifteen seconds to get out of the shower and into formation." What was she talking about? A cadre member outside the door? At first we thought she was joking, and did nothing. Then she returned. "You don't understand. There's a *female* cadet out here, *in* the latrine, who wants you out now!" We scurried out of the shower, soap still clinging to our bodies, shampoo suds dripping from our hair. I stepped out mostly because of curiosity. There were no female cadre members in our company, and I was finally going to meet one of the actual female cadets I'd read about in the admissions brochure. Well, I met her all right. The cadet lined us up — some naked, some wearing only towels — and chewed our butts!

"I don't like having to come to another CBT company to police its female new cadets," she spouted as she strolled back and forth in front of us, both hands clasped behind her back and looking remarkably like George C. Scott surveying the troops. I recognized her. It was Claire Kirby from the first class with females, daughter of Colonel Kirby, the professor in charge of the Department of Geography and Computer Science at West Point. "If anyone has to come and get me again because of you ladies, heads will roll! Do I make myself clear?"

I had been so caught up in finally encountering one of these great ladies that I hadn't realized what had actually happened here. She had stood us at attention, while we were naked, among total strangers, and had yelled at us! How degrading, not to mention embarrassing! She left the latrine and we quickly, and silently, finished showering, then dressed and returned to formation in the hallway. The male members of our squad were already waiting for us. Our squad leader looked at us knowingly as we slipped, quietly, into formation.

"When I say something, ladies, I mean it," was his comment.

Well, he didn't have to worry about me. I was never going to speak again after that incident! I'd heard the women in the other two classes — when I visited the Academy as a candidate — talk about embarrassing situations they had been in, but they never relayed anything like this. Then again, there were no upper-class women in leadership positions for them to have to deal with. This was really bad luck. For my class, the two classes with leadership positions would be the "last all-male class" and the "first class with women." I could tell we were in for hell.

My roommates and I returned to our room, turned out the lights, and slipped into bed, too embarrassed to speak or even say goodnight. Before I dozed off, I remembered something my mother told me: "Years from now you'll look back on all this and laugh." God, I hoped so.

The next morning our squad leader woke us at 5:30, what is known as "O-dark-thirty." We had fifteen minutes to dress and be standing in formation prepared for our first morning PT (physical training). Although we didn't know it then, fifteen minutes to dress was a luxury. In the future we would have far less time to perform tasks like these.

The unforgettable strains of "Patton's Theme" blared from the Academy's loudspeakers as we marched across the blacktop area between the barracks and headed for the concrete apron bordering the parade field. We stretched, exercised, and ran as a company group. This gave our cadre an opportunity to evaluate our running abilities for breakout into running groups later in the week. While MaryAnn and my squad leader landed in the fast "Black" running group, the rest of my squad ran in the "Gray" group, at least at first. I would soon find myself running with the "Gold" group.

I came to the Academy unprepared for the running challenge. In most of the admissions literature the running standards were listed as "be able to run two miles in sixteen minutes." That was no problem. I'd put on my shorts, tie my hair back with a ribbon, and take off on a warm, sunny Texas day. Two miles later, I'd stop and check my watch: sixteen minutes. I thought I was prepared. At the Academy, however, cadets run in formations, at 6:00 A.M., calling cadences as they run up and down hills, rain or shine. I was 5'4" tall, with short legs, requiring me to take two steps for every one that most of the men took. I ended up running twice as far, just to finish. I always finished the runs, but rarely with the rest of the formation. I'd usually straggle in, accompanied by a cadre member who had to "fall out" of the running formation to follow me, several minutes behind the main group. My greatest joy was felt on those mornings when, by the grace of God, I was standing in the area with the rest of the group as the leader yelled, "Quick time, march!," meaning "Stop running."

By the end of Beast I made my way back to the Gray group. Still, to look at my face at the end of the run, it was obvious I'd given tremendous effort to stay up with the group. On one occasion, standing at a wobbly attention and feeling particularly proud that I'd finished with the entire group, I heard one cadre member remark to another, "Do you think she's okay? Maybe we should get a doctor . . ." I shook my flushed face and said, "No, sir. I feel great!" (When you look like you're going to die, they let you get away with saying more than just your "four answers.")

Actually, quite a few new cadets enter the Academy improperly prepared for the running challenge. Whether male or female, overweight or thin, short, tall or very tall, the only way to prepare for the tremendous amount of running required at West Point is to *run*. It was not until the beginning of my junior year, when my roommate and I were running five to ten miles per day, that I shed the label of a poor runner. For now MaryAnn's heart went out to me. She wanted to help, but there was nothing she could do except lend moral support when the going got tough.

During those first eight weeks, MaryAnn and I grew especially close. We complemented each other and seemed to be a "team" well liked by the cadre. MaryAnn could run and offer me moral support in that area. My strong suit was being able to memorize easily the mountain of information, or "poop," that each new cadet was required to know. I was usually a week ahead in "passing off my knowledge" (reciting the required information) to my squad leader, which gave me time to assist MaryAnn with her memorization. Sometimes we'd lie in bed at night after taps and work on it. Since I had it memorized already, I could lie there in the dark, without benefit of script, and check her memorization. We tried to be the best support system to each other that we could possibly be.

MaryAnn also got along well with our first detail company commander, a situation that was rather unorthodox. Cadet Forrester was also blond-haired and blue-eyed, so he and MaryAnn were kindred spirits. When MaryAnn would get into trouble and have to report to the company commander for what was known as a "special inspection" (SI), this blond Adonis would stand her at the position of parade rest while he would lie on his bed, strumming his guitar, and say "Miss Bates, what's the name of this song?" and "Miss Bates, who sings this song?" This would continue for about thirty minutes, after which he'd tell her to try harder militarily and send her back to our room. She is reportedly the only new cadet who ever enjoyed special inspections. When Claire had to go to SI she'd be gone for an hour and would return frazzled after being raked over the coals. In the meantime, MaryAnn and I would have to shine her shoes and clean her weapon to prevent her from getting into more trouble. Because of the extra time she had to spend at SIs, she couldn't complete her other duties, which made her fall even further behind and get into even more trouble. MaryAnn and I tried to pick up the slack.

I was one of the lucky few new cadets who never attended an SI session. In fact, I can remember only one occasion during my entire

Beast experience when I actually felt "hazed," but I remember it vividly.

I developed shin-splints about two weeks after I entered the Academy. It was actually more annoying than painful, until, because of the continuous running and constant fast-paced walking, I developed a slight stress-fracture. I returned from "sick call" (seeing a doctor) one morning, having been diagnosed with this condition. The doctor gave me crutches, which was quite common for cadets during their four years at USMA, and told me to use them as much as possible in an attempt to rest my leg for the next three days. The other new cadets in my company had not yet returned from a briefing they were attending. The company seemed deserted, but I couldn't be sure. Because it was not a good idea to get caught doing nothing while my classmates were busy, I began delivering some bundles of laundry (one of many of the new cadet duties), one at a time, while maneuvering on my crutches.

After delivering a bundle at the end of the hallway, I turned the corner to find a cadre member seated at a desk reading a newspaper. He was the designated cadet-in-charge-of-quarters, or "CQ," the cadet who watched over the barracks while all of the other cadets were away. I greeted him with a "Good morning, sir" and hobbled as quickly as I could down the hall, feverishly working my crutches.

That was when it began. He waited for me to get completely down the hall and turn the corner toward my room before he spoke: "Miss! Get back here!" It was the coldest voice I can remember.

I hobbled back to his desk and was put at the position of attention. For a solid forty-five minutes he stood me there, with my crutches, calling me everything but a human being, venting all of his frustrations and anger about women being admitted to "his" academy. He tried to get me confused and flustered. When I didn't oblige him, he got even uglier and crueler with his tongue-lashing. Toward the end of this sadistic tirade a single tear fell from one of my eyes. It was just what he had been hoping for. He lit into me with a furor.

"Oh, that's great! That's the answer to everything! When you can't stand the heat because you're so goddamned inept, you just cry and the men are supposed to fall down around you and make it all better! Is that what you're going to do when the bullets start flying? Maybe if you cry enough they'll stop the war for you, huh?"

Then he paused and took a deep breath. The voice that slid from his throat when he began again was bloodlessly calm.

"So, tell me, Miss Peterson, just how much money did your daddy have to pay to get you in here?"

Pay? How degrading! I had worked harder than many of the other cadets for my appointment. I didn't know anything about getting a West Point nomination. My parents were hard-working, middle-income Americans struggling to raise a family of four children. What did this cadet know about what I had to do to get here?

"You really think it's fair that you took the place of some *deserving* young man just because your father could pull a few strings?" he continued. "But that's just your style, isn't it? Let a man do all your work for you. That's your style."

My arms ached from the weight of the crutches, and the muscles in my back were tight from standing in an awkward position for such a long time. *If I shift my weight or adjust my stance now,* I thought, *this cadet will leave nothing but a smoking hole where I'm standing!*

As he continued his verbal assault, my mind began to wander to 1976, when I was a sophomore in high school . . .

My mother and I were sharing the newspaper one Sunday — she in the big easy chair, me sprawled comfortably on the floor — when she asked, "Did you know that Congress has decided to allow women to attend West Point?"

"West Point, Mother?" I asked, looking up at her in disbelief. "Robert E. Lee's West Point?"

She assured me that they were one and the same. From that moment on, I read all I could about this historic remodeling. It wasn't difficult to keep up with the latest outcries on the situation as they were chronicled almost daily in the local papers and in the majority of women's magazines.

One day I saw a postcard insert about "Army Opportunities." I pulled it from the magazine, wrote on it, "I would like information about West Point," and mailed it in. Imagine my mother's surprise when the card was returned in the mail with an accompanying note that read: "You've contacted the wrong people. Write to: Director of Admissions, USMA, West Point, New York."

"Do you want to go to West Point?" my mother queried.

I nodded my head affirmatively, yet almost embarrassed to admit that I had thoughts of being good enough to make it into a place like West Point. My mom and I talked for almost an hour about the pros and cons of what I was considering. But, like a true proud mother, she never said I couldn't make it once I got to West Point, only that she hoped that she and my father could help me get there in the first place.

The first correspondence I received from West Point stated that I had applied for admission too early. The first class with women were entering in the summer of 1976, and West Point had their hands full dealing with the changes that accompanied their introduction. Therefore, they could "not prepare admissions packets for women in any succeeding classes, at this time." All I could do was wait.

By Christmas of 1976 I had received a second packet of materials. It was a copy of the admissions literature for the second class to include women, the Class of 1981. The Academy still had no packets prepared for my class (1982); however, they did have academic and athletic data on the progress of the first women at West Point. From all indications, it appeared the women in the Class of 1980 had attrited from the Academy at only about a thirty-five percent rate during the first seven months, and were exceeding the carefully researched physical standards required of the women. I felt sorry for the women whose pictures graced the pages of the admissions brochure. Everyone seemed to want them to fail. So many pairs of eyes were watching, analyzing, and criticizing them through every waking moment, and yet they were succeeding. I thought they must have felt so very alone.

Finally, just before the end of the school year, an admissions packet for "Women in the Class of 1982" arrived. The packet contained several questionnaires and a booklet listing the required steps in the nomination procedure. Some forms had to be filled out and sent to the official from whom the nomination was being requested, while others had to be returned to the admissions department at West Point. On one pre-printed form a candidate was required to darken the blocks that corresponded to the sports and activities in which a candidate participated. Selections included Student Government, Honor Society, Band, Boy and Girl Scouts, Sea Explorers, High School ROTC, Boy's and Girl's State, UIL, and Varsity Athletics, to name only a few. There was very little a candidate could participate in that this form did not cover. In addition, there was ample space to add comments about activities that were not listed.

As I filled out the form, I marked blocks for tennis, gymnastics and judo, honor society, band, twirler, drum major, church youth group, church choir, and Girl Scouts, then referred to the fill-in section to include a small business that I operated raising and selling registered poodle puppies to earn spending money (since my activities left no time for a job with regular hours) and I included the fact that I was responsible for the care and feeding of my two horses. It was obvious to me that West Point was looking for young men and women who were well-rounded — a "total man concept" where a candidate did many things, and did them well, rather than excel in only one area. Diversity seemed to be the desired quality.

Once all the forms were filled out and returned to West Point, the candidate was scheduled for a medical evaluation and a physical aptitude test. I received "orders" to report to Fort Polk, Louisiana, for the first complete physical I had ever been given in my life.

My mother and I drove to Fort Polk and waited outside the old World War II wooden barracks with the red cross painted on the building's side for the "hospital" to open. At 0700 hours the physical process began. The biggest problem, however, was that my paperwork required a "service academy physical" and no one seemed to know what that entailed. So the soldiers who manned the hospital proceeded with a regular physical until the doctor arrived at 0830 hours and explained that this was the most thorough routine physical exam the military gives: it even included reading aloud from a prepared text to be certain a candidate did not have any speech impediments. I spent most of the morning moving from station to station, from giving blood to checking blood pressure and from testing hearing to counting fingers and toes. The entire time I was seriously doubting I was doing the right thing. Did I really want to go into the army?

I looked around at what was supposed to be a hospital and saw an unshaven orderly with a skin condition under his beard, yellowing tile that was cracked and peeling up from the floor, and overhead air ducts and metal water pipes hanging from the ceilings by makeshift wire hangers. The building had a rotted-wood smell to it, musty and rank. A roach crawled across the floor while I waited to be called into my eye exam. The young private just walked over to it and smashed it with the toe of his boot, then calmly returned to his desk, leaving the carcass stuck to the floor in front of me. *So this is the army,* I thought. So far, I didn't like it.

Enter an old army colonel who didn't like the idea of women attending West Point. Better still, make him the gynecologist for a young girl's first physical exam, and you can imagine how the rest of the experience went.

The gynecology nurse was very helpful. My mother had called

ahead to the clinic to be certain that the doctor knew I had never had sexual intercourse or a gynecological exam before in my seventeen years. When I walked through the doors of the clinic, all of the women in the waiting room turned to look at me.

"Are you the one?" the nurse asked sweetly.

"Yes, ma'am. I'm Donna Peterson," I replied.

The next thing I knew, she rose from her desk, put her arms around me and said, "You poor thing. Don't worry. It'll be okay." As I looked around the room I had the definite feeling that she had enlightened the entire waiting room as to my "situation."

The nurse spoke to me as I undressed for the exam. I was so nervous that she had to help me with the buttons on my blouse. I had always imagined how things would be the first time I was touched by a man — loving and warm, and very tender, not cold and clinical. It was hard to convince myself that I had nothing to be nervous about. Millions of women live through this every year, right? Actually, I was able to hold myself together fairly well until the doctor walked into the room. He had thin, graying hair and a pox-marked complexion, and wore a slightly soiled white hospital coat over his faded fatigues. Worn loosely on his feet, laces dangling as he walked, were a pair of dirty, road-worn combat boots.

I began to cry silently.

"So you want to go to West Point?" he said without lifting his eyes from my medical file.

"Yes, sir," I was barely able to squeak from my mouth between tears. The doctor looked up.

"Is that what you're gonna do when you get in front of your troops — cry?" he asked, loudly enough for the patients in the waiting room to hear every syllable. "What do you think they'll think of their leader then?" After a short pause he continued. "Oh, come on. Cut the tears. Nobody is gonna kill you. How the hell do you think you'd last in combat if you can't even stand a physical exam?"

I was really crying now. The nurse had said she would stay with me but he told her to leave. "She doesn't need anyone to hold her hand. She's not a baby. She wants to be a leader of men!" he said sarcastically after asking her to leave.

I couldn't wait for the exam to be over. It was just as horrible as I had imagined, made so by Dr. Compassionate himself. As I left he muttered something about my remembering what he'd told me, but all I could think of was canceling the nomination process. I desperately wanted to attend West Point, but not if it was going to be like this.

I spoke to several people at West Point the next day who assured me that Fort Polk was not the standard for the army.

"I can't believe they sent you there," a major in the admissions department said. "You should have taken your physical at NASA in Houston like all the other cadets in your area. Someone made a mistake in sending you to Polk."

I decided to finish the admissions process after all. The next step was to write a letter to my congressman or senator requesting that I be considered for a nomination. Some candidates with military backgrounds or parents who were disabled combat veterans or war heroes needed only to apply to the Academy itself and the nomination process was taken care of for them. Also, the sons (and now daughters) of Medal of Honor recipients were granted automatic appointments to West Point, provided they could meet the minimum qualification standards. While I was at the Academy, the Episcopal priest was a West Point graduate who had received his appointment while still in his mother's womb. His father was World War II hero Colin Kelly, who died before the future cadet was born.

For most cadets, though, the process is one of applying to an elected official, either senator or congressman. Since I thought I had a better chance of getting into a less prestigious school, I applied to my congressman for an appointment to the Air Force Academy (I had to fill out a separate admissions packet for the Air Force, but they accepted the physical I had already taken), and I applied to Senators John Tower and Lloyd Bentsen of Texas for appointment to West Point. Part of this procedure required filing, with each of their offices, copies of all the forms I'd sent to West Point, writing an essay about "Why I Want To Attend West Point," and sending in three letters of recommendation (from community, church, or school leaders).

I labored for more than a week on the single essay I sent to all three elected officials, and I began asking for letters of recommendation. Because I believed I was an underdog in the fight to receive a precious nomination to a service academy, I felt that I had to do something extra to give me an advantage. So I went back to the people who were subscribers on the paper route I had operated more than seven years before and asked them for letters of recommendation to West Point.

I had been the first female paper carrier in my hometown, at a time when Texas did not allow females to have paper routes. But my older brother had taken a route and decided he no longer wanted it, and my parents let me finish delivering his route until the end of the month. Since I seemed to be able to handle it, my parents allowed me to keep it. There were two problems with this arrangement, however. First of all, as I said, females could not have paper routes at that time. Secondly, I was only ten years old (I looked about eight), and carriers had to be twelve years old. So, I left the route in my brother's name and just told his customers that I was "helping my brother" on the route.

It wasn't very long before the paper company realized what was going on. To my surprise, however, they never admitted they knew. They couldn't afford to. This was the downtown route, where the carrier had to get off of his bike and go into the businesses, the City Hall, the fire station, and the Chamber of Commerce to hand subscribers their papers. I even had to get into an elevator to deliver the paper to the president of a local bank. The newspaper company had a hard time getting young boys to take this route. On most other routes, the boys could deliver twice the number of papers in half the time, without ever stopping their bicycles. I could hardly complain, since I was delivering the route illegally anyway. The company did nothing to stop me because they needed someone to deliver the route, and I was doing a good job. In fact, my customers kept nominating me for "Carrier of the Month," and the publisher of the paper found himself continually having to explain that as soon as they gave me the award they would have to take the route away from me!

That route is probably the major reason for my getting into West Point. My subscribers were all successful people in their own right and their signatures on letters of recommendation were rather impressive. Though many of these people seemed surprised when I approached them (because no one from our area had ever attended West Point), they all remembered me, and no one refused. The mayor wrote, the city attorney wrote, as did the executive director of the Chamber of Commerce and the fire chief. As the community, school, and church leaders returned the forms I'd given them, I made copies of them and sent them in batches to each of the elected officials. In the end I had sent them each sixty-two letters!

While I waited for the nomination process to work (some officials require extra testing and interviews to make their selections, some do not) I was scheduled for the physical aptitude test, this time correctly, at NASA. The day before the test, I was sitting in the classroom at my high school when the principal interrupted an afternoon class with this announcement: "I am pleased to announce that Donna Peterson has just received a nomination to the United States Military Academy at West Point! Donna, please come to the principal's office." My parents had received the letter in the mail and had driven up to the school to share the news. The next day, at NASA, the eight other male candidates and I were talking about the admissions process. One was boasting about how he was a "sure-thing" to receive Tower's nomination. I didn't say anything until another candidate asked me who I'd applied to and if I'd heard anything. When I told him, he just looked sick.

"Well, I might as well go home," he said. I never did see him at the Academy.

I was fortunate. I did very well on my physical aptitude test that day and received nominations and subsequent appointments to both of the schools to which I had applied. Senator Tower told me, after I'd become a cadet, that he gave me the nomination just so I wouldn't send him any more letters of recommendation.

"Your file was three times the size of all the others!" he said.

I don't necessarily recommend my method of getting an appointment, but it worked for me. Actually, one of the best things a cadet can do is to obtain a letter of recommendation from a graduate of the service academy he or she chooses to attend. The feeling at an academy is that a graduate's judgment about his own school and a candidate's qualifications for attendance at that school is a better marker for success. And, of course, I made certain to meet both my congressman and senator during the nomination process.

*Sixty-two letters,* I was thinking to myself, nearly smiling at my ingenuity, when I heard a resounding, "Smirk off, new cadet!" ring in my ears. Back to reality. The CQ had still not finished with me.

The smile vanished quickly from my face, and I searched his athletic shirt with my eyes until I found the monogram above the Academy crest and memorized it: KEY. I knew that it was a name I would never forget. Cadet Key was everything in a cadet that I did not want to be, and I wished him every horrible thing in life that could possibly happen to a person.

I have no doubt that this charade would have continued indefinitely had a cadre member not returned early from the briefing.

"Key! What the hell do you think you're doing?" the cadet

screamed at my assailant. "Miss Peterson, return to your room. Your classmates will be returning any moment now." I responded with a "Yes, sir" and headed for the sanctuary of my room. As I made my way I could hear my savior reprimanding Cadet Key and threatening him with severe action should such behavior occur in the future. I was glad that I would never forget Tom Key; sometimes examples of what we never wish to become provide our best role models.

That was not the first time I had shed a tear during Beast, though it was the only public display. On the fifth night I was at the Academy, I remember tears falling on my pillow for several seconds before I fell asleep. Before then, I was probably too tired at night to stay awake long enough to cry. Many of my classmates, however, were not that lucky. Claire cried herself to sleep the very first night, and I sat on MaryAnn's bed comforting her two nights later. I really didn't understand why they were crying. *This place isn't that terrible,* I thought. But I must have been wrong, because a great many new cadets shed tears those first few days, male and female.

The second night of Beast, just after bed-check, I heard sobbing coming from the other side of the wall. It was obvious that someone was lying in bed crying themselves to sleep. The next morning I saw the young man with puffy eyes walk out of his room. I was astonished: this place even caused males to cry. Many times that first week I'd walk into a male classmate's room and find him in tears. Five or six new cadets spent time in our room, in tears, during the next eight weeks. Some of them, I think, just needed some comforting from a female. Others were moved to tears by the fear that they would not survive eight weeks of Beast. But mostly, despite all of the qualifications and high school accomplishments of the members of my class and all of the accolades and awards that had been showered upon us during our young lives, we were still just eighteen-year-old kids, living away from the sanctity and security of the homes we had known all of our lives. And this new world was a scary place.

As the weeks passed, however, the routine became familiar, and the only time I saw a male new cadet's eyes fill with tears was after he'd gotten a "Dear John" letter from his hometown sweetheart. This always made me mad. Here were some of the most outstanding, decent, good-looking young men in America, going through absolute hell to become the very best adults and military leaders they could possibly be, and their women were dumping them. I wondered if the women were crazy or just cruel. Their timing certainly couldn't have been worse.

"It's her loss," MaryAnn and I would tell our young classmates. "Someday she'll kick herself for throwing away a guy like you. After all, you can always get another girl like her, but where is she going to find another West Point cadet?"

My heart ached for them.

What surprised me more than the number of male cadets who received letters of this type was the number of female cadets who had *not* received those letters. In fact, I never knew of any female cadet who had been rejected by her hometown boyfriend. It seemed that most of the women had (wisely) either ended their relationships with their boyfriends before leaving home or sent their own "Dear John" letters after entering the Academy.

Of course, the female cadets would have plenty of time to experience their share of heartaches over the next four years. For now, however, my roommates and I would have easily traded away a boyfriend for an extra couple hours of sleep.

# CHAPTER 2

# Beast Barracks

*"Only the Corps of Cadets has for 150 years received the heritages of the past, molded them to the present, and carried them forward as traditions for the future."*

— Gen. Lucius D. Clay, 1952

After two exhausting weeks of twenty-six-hour days in a hostile, strange environment — without a single break — I was ready for our first "privilege weekend." Actually, "weekend" was the cadre's term for it. In reality, those cadets who had earned the right to have privileges were allowed an afternoon respite during our second weekend at the Academy. Though I am extremely proud to be one of the group of Texas cadets at the Academy, for a few moments, when our privileges were announced, I wished I had been from Connecticut, like my roommate MaryAnn.

Since privileges were announced unexpectedly, all MaryAnn had to do was phone her parents, who lived only a two-hour drive away from West Point, and they would be able to meet her. My parents couldn't even drive to the Houston airport in two hours! We worked feverishly to get Claire ready for privileges. Our squad leader's policy was that "all make privileges or none do." She had to report to him four times in order to be considered eligible for privileges, but finally

28

— no, miraculously — she made it, and the three of us left the barracks. Claire headed straight for the PX to buy food. MaryAnn and I made a beeline for the soccer field.

When MaryAnn's parents and two brothers came to visit her that weekend, I was invited along. It wasn't the same as having my own parents visit, but, by the end of the visit, it seemed pretty close. The Bates family was waiting for us at the soccer field. After a tearful greeting and a few introductions, Mr. Bates dropped the tailgate of his car and asked, "Is anyone hungry?" I couldn't believe it. Inside that station wagon was enough food to feed an army! It was fabulous! The two elements of the "real world" that cadets seem to miss the most are kindness and food, and the Bateses brought both. They fed us and listened to our tales of torture with great compassion. Even their departure after six hours was kind: they sent us back to our room with food.

MaryAnn's father drove a delivery truck for a company that sold individually wrapped blueberry pies. We took them back to our room and plotted our next move. We'd have to be careful not to let our third roommate, Claire, know about the food. New cadets were not supposed to have any food after privilege hours. All food had to be given to the squad leader for "safekeeping." Actually, once you handed it over to your squad leader you never saw it again. But those were the rules, and we knew Claire would never let us get away with it if she knew it. MaryAnn hid the tiny pies in a bureau drawer and we waited for nightfall.

"Claire?" MaryAnn questioned softly. "Are you awake?"

No response.

"Hey, Claire!" I added in my loudest whisper.

Still no response.

"Okay, let's do it!" MaryAnn began, whispering her excitement. But as she swung her legs out of the bed a loud squeak filled the room. She snuggled back into bed just as a cadre member opened the only partially closed door to our room and asked, "Everything all right in here?" Only the sound of breathing and Claire's light snoring could be heard. It seemed like hours before MaryAnn woke me.

"Ready to try it again?" she whispered.

"Yeah. What time is it?"

"About eleven-thirty. Still hungry?"

Was she kidding? New cadets are always hungry, and I was no exception. We sat on MaryAnn's bed, trying hard not to crinkle the plastic as we unwrapped two pies each and began to savor a sorely missed slice of life. We talked and even giggled, quietly, stopping only to hold our breath when our other roommate shifted in her sleep. I doubt I've ever appreciated a meal more than those little pies. After hiding the incriminating wrappers in our underwear drawer until we could dispose of them secretly in the morning, MaryAnn and I said good-night and slipped back into bed. As I closed my eyes and licked my lips one last time, I smiled. I don't even like blueberries.

MaryAnn and I slipped out of bed after taps quite a few times during Beast, usually to accomplish much less enjoyable tasks. You see, the Academy realizes that it assigns tasks to the cadets which cannot all be completed in a normal day. The new cadets do not realize this. The challenge for these young cadets is to devise a way to accomplish everything, by time management and priority determination. The cadets' struggle to do so disciplines and educates them. This educational process often found my roommates and me hidden in the open area under our desks, stamping our names on our laundry. Each new cadet was issued a name stamp and ink pad during R-Day issue and was told to mark everything, including every piece of clothing. But when our clothing was returned from the laundry each week, the stamp had washed off and we had to restamp each item all over again. Since stamping the laundry was a simple process, it was easily accomplished in the dark after taps, with the aid of a small flashlight placed in an athletic sock to dim the beam. My roommates and I would freeze in place and hold our breath as cadre members walked past our door. I'm convinced they knew what we were doing; they had done it themselves as new cadets. Still, new cadets were not allowed out of their beds after taps, and the cadre often checked, so my roommates and I were as careful as possible. To this day, whenever I smell the chemical aroma of an ink pad, I'm reminded of my experiences in Beast Barracks.

The cadre delighted in giving new cadets every opportunity to develop creative solutions to the problem of time management. Each night the company first sergeant wrote the schedule for the next day on the chalkboard in the hallway just outside of his room. Often, though new cadets could not be out of their rooms after taps, the first sergeant wouldn't post the schedule until taps was sounding. This was a problem since we had to have the schedule by 0530 the next morning.

The male new cadets had an easy solution to this one: When all of the lights were out and they were certain that all of the cadre were asleep, they would slip out of their rooms and head for the latrine. The first sergeant's room was located directly across from the men's latrine, and the males could copy down the next day's schedule by standing inside the latrine and opening the door just enough to allow the light from the latrine to illuminate the board. Their only worry would be that a cadre member might need to go to the bathroom in the middle of the night. But since the women's latrine was not so perfectly located, our solution to this dilemma had to be a little more creative.

Not long after taps, while the lights were still on in the hallway, I'd put on my soft slippers and robe and head out the door with a small pencil and piece of paper tucked in my pocket. Since I had to pass the first sergeant's room en route to the women's latrine, I simply cut my eyes toward the board as I passed it and tried to memorize the first several lines. Once in the latrine, I would take out the paper and pencil and write down what I remembered. I would reverse the process on the return trip, writing down what I could remember when I returned to my room. Then I'd hand the paper and pencil to another roommate and she'd make the same trip, followed by the other roommate, if necessary. If we were caught, we would simply say we were on our way to the latrine, and the cadre member would bark something about "better prior planning in the future" and let us go. This worked like a charm, except for the time the cadre turned the hall light off while we were in the middle of our mission! Win some, lose some.

New cadets were inspected on a daily basis, but the Saturday morning inspection (SAMI, pronounced "Sammy") was the ultimate inspection for the week. Our room had made it, rather successfully, through two of these inspections already and we were determined that the third would be our finest showing yet.

For this inspection all drawers and doors had to be opened and the contents displayed; all hangers had to be an equal distance apart in the closet and canted at the same angle; all clothes had to be hung and buttoned per SOP; beds had to be tight and wrinkle-free; and, of course, no dust could be found. The inspectors wore white gloves. The uniform each of us wore had to be at its best too. Each cadet had two pairs of trousers. One pair went to the wash each week, and the fresh pair was brought out on Saturday morning for this inspection. Once you put them on, you couldn't sit down or you'd get a wrinkle in the crease. The last action before the inspection was to put on your pants and white gloves.

During our last inspection, try as he might, the inspector could find nothing to reprimand us about. Well, almost nothing. But he had to really dig for this one. On each of our desks was one dust-free picture and a clock. Our error? The time on each of the three clocks was one minute different.

As the three of us stood poised for the third week's inspection, our hearts pounding frantically every time we heard footsteps in the hallway, we remembered those darn clocks! All three read the same time, but did they match the time on the clock in the main hall? And what could we do about it now anyway? Any second now they'd pound on our door and begin the inspection. And none of us wanted to move for fear we'd wrinkle something or ruin our "dress-off" — the smart crease that laid our white shirts flat against our backs.

"Okay," I said. "We'll match-out to see who has to check the clock in the hall." Now this little arrangement really wasn't fair. You see, MaryAnn and I were tired of Claire's mess-ups and had talked things over beforehand so that she and I would match "even" and Claire would be the "odd man out." It worked like a charm.

"All right, I'll go," she said in her heavy Midwestern accent. With that she proceeded to the door, opened it, leaned her upper torso far out into the hall to see the clock, then snapped back and closed the door with a thud. Her face was ghost-white and she was trembling all over.

"Claire, what's wrong?" I asked.

"*Oh,*" she said. "There was someone out there!"

"Did they see you?"

"I don't know. I hope not."

"Claire, if you got us in trouble again . . ." MaryAnn began, shooting Claire a look that could kill. But her words were cut short by two loud knocks at the door.

"Oh, shit!" MaryAnn whispered. "Enter, sir." (MaryAnn had the dubious responsibility of answering those types of knocks and reporting to the person behind the fist because she was the alphabetically ranking cadet in our room.) As the door opened, my mind raced. *Oh, God, is our squad leader going to be mad. What if he has our platoon leader with him? Whatever happens, please don't let it be our company commander!*

As the cadet entered the room, all I remember seeing was an eight-foot nametag that read "Knowles." None of us had ever seen this man before, but we knew the name well. Cadet Capt. Danny Knowles held the title "King of Beast." That meant that he was the number-one ranking cadet at the Academy that summer. Everyone answered to him. And now my roommates and I were about to do the same.

I wanted to cry. MaryAnn wanted to strangle Claire — and would have after they left if I hadn't pulled her off. Not only did Cadet Knowles show up, but every officer in our chain-of-command as well, down to and including our squad leader. There were so many people in that room there wasn't room for any air!

"Which one of you was it that I saw in the hall?" this tall cadet with the fiery red hair asked.

Claire had a habit of not answering when she did things wrong, but this time she was too afraid not to answer. "Here, sir." The words choked her throat upon exit.

"Why did you slam the door in my face?" he asked calmly. I knew then we were not going to live through the next two minutes. I had seen cadets of much less importance tear new cadets to shreds for having a water spot in the sink. Yep. We were dead meat.

"No excuse, sir," came the reply. Then Claire tried to explain, in her usual run-on-sentence-never-take-a-breath manner, how our only fault the week prior had been the mismatched clocks and how we'd matched out and she'd lost and, because she was nervous and in a hurry, she hadn't taken the time to properly enter the hallway, make the correct facing movements, check the time and return to the room, according to SOP. At this point, the man with the eight-foot nametag had to turn his head to conceal the smile which would turn to laughter as soon as he left our room. It was obvious that the entire group was having a hard time hiding their laughter.

Without saying a word, as the rest of the group held their breath, Cadet Knowles moved around the room, putting his white-gloved finger in the most difficult dust spots: under the bed frame, behind the upper closet door, under the marble window sill. Then, coming up white-glove clean, he smiled.

"I came to this room because your chain-of-command spoke so highly of your performance at inspection. I can see they were correct." Addressing MaryAnn and me alone, he added, "You two should keep a better eye on your roommate. She'll get you all in trouble."

As the entourage followed him out the door, some of the cadets shot us glances that should've turned our blood to stone. Others smiled and shook their heads.

The three of us stood frozen for ten minutes afterward. We knew that when word spread of this, every cadet from every company was going to come over and haze us. So we waited. I would've preferred instant death. Dying six or eight times in one hour can really ruin your day. But, luckily, no one came.

"I think it's safe to move now," I offered after about ten minutes of standing at a stiff parade rest. MaryAnn never said a word. She flung her body through the air and had her hands on Claire's throat before I could blink. I gave MaryAnn several good seconds to get out enough anger for both of us before I stepped in and helped Claire off the floor.

Not one demerit. Our best inspection ever, and our last under this group of cadets.

Cadet Basic Training, or "Beast Barracks," lasts eight weeks and is divided into two "details." At the end of four weeks the cadets who make up the leadership for the second detail arrive and the first detail cadre take their summer leave.

The night before the change-of-command was very emotional. In a letter to my mother I wrote: "MaryAnn and I sat in our windows and watched the detail of men who'd stripped us of our identity and our spirit, as they scurried around moving out of their rooms and positioning their 'Firstie' cars for a speedy exit at dawn's light, and we cried. I told MaryAnn that it was because we had come to feel safe with these people after four weeks and we were just suffering from a 'fear of the unknown,' a.k.a. the second detail cadre. But in my own mind I honestly believe we've grown to care about the people who took us through this initiation and changed our lives forever." We didn't discuss it, but I'm certain that MaryAnn felt it too. After all, there wasn't even a rule against sitting in the window and looking out because it was such an unacceptable thing to do! And yet, there we sat, tears streaming down our cheeks, as the cadre wheeled their loaded barracks carts along the road behind the mess hall. We'd wave or say goodbye to a cadet from our company and he would look up in disbelief, then wave in return and smile. There had to be a bond there somewhere. Getting to sleep that night was difficult.

The next day, after the change-of-command, I was sitting at my desk when the door flew open without a knock. Standing there was one of the first detail cadre, a tall, red-headed man.

"MaryAnn, can I write to you?"

*Mary Ann?* I thought. *Whatever happened to "Miss Bates" and a proper "fourth-class system" relationship?* This was my first live glimpse of fraternization. I thought to myself, *If he's going to break the rules this flagrantly, I'm not even going to bother to stand up!* I pointed to the floor in front of the closet where MaryAnn was sitting.

He looked around the corner as MaryAnn said, "Yes, sir," then he smiled and closed the door. About two weeks later he sent her some sweetbread from Hawaii.

Our first in-ranks inspection during second detail was rained out. This meant that, rather than cancel a scheduled inspection (they only canceled two during my entire four years), it was held indoors.

As we stood at attention, being inspected by our squad leader, a voice bellowed down the hallway: "Where's Peterson?"

I snapped to attention and stuck out a closed fist. "Here, sir!" I stated.

"Peterson, if I ever see that bed made like that again I'll smoke you like a cheap Havana cigar! You got me?"

"Yes, sir!" I replied. I had no idea who the man was, but I could tell by my new squad leader's wide eyes and throbbing temples that he must be important.

"Peterson, do you know who that was?" my squad leader asked in a deep country-boy twang.

"No, sir," I answered.

"Well, Peterson, thanks for embarrassing the entire squad in front of the new company commander!"

*Ugh!* Cadet Cuccolo. I had memorized the name, but I didn't know the voice. What a way to meet the new company commander. This incident just confirmed my suspicions that the second detail cadre were not going to be anywhere near as good as the first detail cadre. And, by the way, what was wrong with my bed? I left it in perfect shape!

As soon as the inspection was over, my roommates and I returned to our room. I went straight to my bed. It looked like an elephant had stepped right in the middle of it. The blanket was wrinkled, and there was a sagging hole in the center. Through squinted eyes I glared at Claire. "What did you do?"

"Well," she began, "I had to get the wrinkles out of my pillow before the inspection and there wasn't time to use a chair to reach the top bunk so I just stepped on your bed a little bit. I tried to fix it. I didn't think anyone would notice."

For the first time in our five-week acquaintance, I yelled at Claire. "You're so incompetent! You say you came to West Point because God told you to. He probably wanted you to go to a convent but he was afraid you'd screw that up too! I'm sick of it! I had to take the demerits when you left a hanger out on *my* bed, and I had to take the hit when you hung your gloves *out the window* to dry. I aged ten years because you couldn't even handle checking the clock in the hall correctly. And how about the time that MaryAnn and I had to clean your weapon and shine your shoes so you could be on time for a formation and you were *still* late and the entire squad had to take a hit?"

I was on a roll now. "We have to sit and listen while you read us letters from your *cat,* and instead of getting ready for a formation that you're already late for, MaryAnn and I find you crying because your cat misses you and you think he'll be permanently affected by it! Well, if you don't get your act together *you* will be permanently affected, I'll see to that! I should've let MaryAnn beat the crap out of you last week!"

She just sat in her chair, wide-eyed, scared half to death, I think. This was completely out of character for me. As she opened her mouth to speak, I continued. "Just shut up! I'm not interested in you or anything you have to say. Just shut up." Even MaryAnn was being quiet at this point.

After MaryAnn and I left the room, she told me how concerned about me she was. "I've never seen you like that. Are you okay? It's normal for *me* to react that way, but not you."

She was right, that wasn't me. I had no respect for people who had to resort to anger and violence to get their point across, and I didn't like myself very much at that moment. There isn't any excuse for hurting someone's feelings unnecessarily. I'm certain I could've gotten my point across to Claire without the cat comments and without announcing her shortcomings to the entire world. I later apologized to her for being so unkind. I never recanted what I said — just the way I said it. Claire was definitely unique, and I had to believe that a system which produced Robert E. Lee, George Patton, and Douglas MacArthur would rid itself of those who were not up to the challenge, just as it had for 176 years. I *had* to believe . . .

Our squad leader told me he felt sorry for MaryAnn and me, but he didn't have the time to square Claire away and we would have to pick up part of her load. CBT is tough enough when you're trying to survive yourself, let alone trying to survive while carrying someone else. But survive we did — somehow. Of course, not before Claire got a chance to strike a few more times.

Because Claire had a knack for always being late to formations, our squad leader required us to be at all formations five minutes early. During CBT there is barely enough time to get to the formation on time because they pack the schedule so tight, let alone arrive five minutes early. But that was our penance for having Claire in our squad. One afternoon the entire squad was in formation, minus Claire.

"Miss Peterson, I get so tired of asking this: Where is your roommate?" our squad leader asked as he sighed heavily.

"Sir, when New Cadet Bates and I left the room she was right behind us," I offered.

"Both of you go back into the barracks and find your roommate. Now!"

When we got to the room we found her turning circles as if she were looking for something, and she was crying. She was looking for her gloves, but she couldn't find them because she couldn't see anything — the tears had fogged up the thick, black-rimmed military glasses she had to wear.

"You had your gloves on when we left," I stated.

"I know, but I had a spot on one so I came back to change it and I couldn't find a clean one and I started crying and then I got so confused!" she blabbered as she pushed her glasses higher up onto her nose and began to cry harder.

"Jesus Christ, Claire. Here," said MaryAnn, offering Claire one of her gloves and hoping it would fit Claire's larger hands.

"Now just stop crying. It won't help anything," I said soothingly as I dried her tears with my handkerchief and wiped her smudged glasses. "Now let's go, or we'll be late!"

"Wait!" Claire stopped in the doorway. "I need a dress-off."

"There's no time now, Claire," I began, as I smoothed the wrinkles the best I could on the way out the door.

Once in formation, all seemed to be going well until the platoon leader remarked about Claire's lousy appearance. "Who gave you that dress-off?" he asked.

Instead of volunteering that she hadn't gotten any dress-off at all, she responded boldly, "Sir, New Cadet Peterson gave me this dress-off." MaryAnn nudged me with her elbow. My mind was racing. Yes, I heard. She knew it was a lie. Maybe we could get her kicked out on honor. The platoon leader called me everything bad he could think of in one minute, never offering me a chance to explain.

Once back in the room, Claire said she honestly believed I'd given her a "sort of dress-off" and she hadn't wanted to lie to the platoon leader and tell him that she hadn't gotten one at all!

My mother had told me that, perhaps, God was preparing me for something later in life. After all, if I could hold up under the strain of Claire, I could certainly handle raising three or four kids!

As things turned out, Claire left West Point shortly after the academic year began, saying God had "told" her it was time to leave. Although I understood that Claire had fared well academically, she had a hard time adjusting to the stressful West Point lifestyle. It isn't for everyone. The first eight weeks of Beast are designed to weed out the weakest very early, and, in this case, the system worked. Of course, once Claire had departed the Academy, MaryAnn and I spent many hours recanting — and actually laughing about — our many experiences with this unique gal. MaryAnn had one favorite story to laugh about.

During the first detail, the three of us returned to our room with barely enough time to change our clothes before dinner formation. It was laundry day and, like all good new cadets, we had sent one pair of our trousers to the cleaners and had one pair remaining to wear. I reached in my closet for my pants and found — surprise! — none were there.

"MaryAnn, what could've happened to my pants?" I asked.

Slowly, a sick look came over Claire's face. "You know what?" she said innocently. "I must have sent out your pants instead of mine. I wondered why I still had two pair of pants in my closet."

"You did *what?*" MaryAnn yelled. "I can't believe how stupid you are, Claire!"

"Never mind that, Mary Ann," I said. "What am I going to do for pants? I can't wear her extra pair, they're four sizes too big! I guess I'll go tell our squad leader. There just isn't anything else to do!"

I'll never forget the look on his face when I told him. He said he had expected to run into many crises as a CBT squad leader, but could never have imagined this one. He'd never even heard of this happening in the entire 176-year history of the Academy. The only solution, since no other female new cadets would have a second pair of trousers either, was to borrow a pair of my squad leader's pants (thank goodness he was small and slim) and pin them at the waist. Actually, they didn't look that bad, except that men's trousers had opposite zippers from women's and the pants were bunched-up at the waist. Holding a proper dress-off was impossible.

After about three minutes in formation, it became obvious to my squad leader that he would have to stay somewhere in my vicinity to ward off the numerous cadre members who had a number of questions about my appearance.

"Just let it go," he'd tell his classmates. "It's something beyond her control. I'll tell you about it later."

The cadre would give me a disbelieving look and would turn away from me very slowly, but I'll bet they couldn't wait to find out the rest of the story. When the platoon leader noticed the situation, however, my squad leader ended up telling him the entire story, and suddenly Claire was the object of a great deal of attention.

I have no idea what "Miss Space Cadet," as she was dubbed by the cadre, is doing today. Given life's little ironies, MaryAnn and I wouldn't be surprised if she's performing brain surgery somewhere and going home at night to a house full of cats.

Problems with Claire took up a great deal of my time that summer, but so did everything — from field training, road marches, and swim tests, to classes on proper etiquette, military orientation, and academic placement testing. Despite the hectic schedule, I often thought about my friend from New York City. In fact, I even got bold enough to pay him a visit one weekend.

Randy Odom was in First Company. I knew that because he sat with that company when we got in trouble for talking in the gym on R-Day. First Company was located only one floor beneath Second Company.

On Saturday, during the second privilege weekend, I took a few deep breaths and headed down the stairs. I scurried along the first-floor hallway. Since all new cadets lived three or four people per room, while cadre members lived by themselves or with a maximum of one roommate, I moved along the wall using only the movement of my eyes to find a room with three or more nametags on the door. Eureka! I made a sharp facing movement to the left, stopped smartly at the door, and quickly knocked.

"Enter, sir," I heard the male voices reply. I opened the door and slipped in, and just as quickly slipped back out, standing at attention with my nose pressed against the door. They weren't completely dressed! As I waited outside for them to finish dressing, hoping they'd be able to tell me where Randy's room was, a cadre member who had witnessed this brave attempt made his presence known.

"Miss, are you lost?" He was surprisingly calm. There weren't very many cadre members around on this afternoon. They seemed to enjoy their time away from us as much as we enjoyed our time away from them. But one upperclassman was all it took for trouble to find you. And it had.

"No, sir!" I replied confidently.

"Well, then, why are you standing out in the hall?"

"No excuse, sir." When you are allowed only four answers, that's the most logical of the four in response to most questions of this sort. And besides, it's the only one the cadre want to hear. There is never any excuse for anything at this place when you're a plebe (freshman cadet).

"You learn well, Miss Peterson," he began again, glancing at the shiny black nametag on the chest of my pressed white shirt. "But I really want to know what's going on. You aren't from this company, are you?"

"Sir, I am in Second Cadet Basic Training Company," I replied curtly. "I came to see New Cadet Odom." Sweat was pouring down my back. It's hard enough to get caught by the cadre in your own company, but in someone else's company . . .

"Odom, eh?" He paused. "Come on, I'll show you his room." With that I followed him down the hallway. I had missed the right room by about four doorways. He knocked on the door, then opened it as I stood at rigid attention in the hall. "Hey, Odom. Someone here to visit you. She's pretty squared away, Odom. Can't imagine what she wants with you. Don't embarrass the company, Odom." Turning to me, he said, "I know your company commander pretty well. Maybe I'll tell him that his company isn't quite as bad as everyone says it is." He was referring to the fierce rivalries that the cadre foster between companies. Then he walked away. I barely had time to comprehend that someone had been nice to me when I saw Randy's eyes, sparkling blue and glad to see me.

Randy and I made several more trips to see each other before the eight weeks were over, and we met at dances during our plebe year. He was sweet and a little shy when it came to girls, I thought. We'd go for walks around the scenic Trophy Point area or make the steep climb up to Fort Putnam, which overlooked the Academy, and we'd tour the restored fortifications. He was the first true gentleman I had ever been close to, and I savored every moment we spent together. We were well into plebe year before he even tried to kiss me, ever-so-delicately, and I enjoyed that too.

I thought the trips Randy and I made to each other's companies that summer were the most courageous activities I'd heard of a new cadet attempting during the first eight weeks, until I observed my roommate MaryAnn on our overnight trips to the woods.

Each company scheduled several overnight trips to the field during Beast. On these bivouacs new cadets learned to pitch tents, eat C-rations, qualify-fire with weapons, maneuver obstacle courses, complete road marches, and perform "rifle PT" (exercising with rifles in your hands for added weight). For esprit building there were squad competitions (I learned that I could carry a 160-pound man out of a burning building), the bayonet obstacle course (I learned that exercising while breathing in gas and yellow smoke burns your lungs), and assault and survival training (I learned that the taste of blood and dirt, separated or mixed together, really can't kill you). The days were filled until darkness, blessed darkness, sent us into transitory sleep. All, that is, except MaryAnn.

Each night, after body count and weapons count, MaryAnn would sneak away. "Where are you going?" I'd ask. "I'll be back," was all she'd reply. I suppose I thought she was going to the bathroom. In the absence of portable toilets, most women tried their best to wait until darkness to perform certain bodily functions. Besides, I didn't care where she was going. Being the smallest of three women sleeping in a two-person pup tent (women were not allowed to stay alone in a tent, though many males did), I had to sleep straddling the pole that held up our tiny covering. Between our gear, our rifles, and ourselves, there was little room left for anything. Any extra room, for any reason, was welcome.

It wasn't until our third overnight exercise that MaryAnn finally confessed the nature of her evening reconnaissances: she had a boyfriend. She'd meet him each evening after bed check at a designated tree. How they ever found their way without getting caught, let alone finding a specific tree in the darkness of the woods, still dumbfounds me. I have no idea what they did when they got there (how could they even talk without being overheard?) or how long they stayed (I was never awake when she returned).

To this day, when asked about it, all MaryAnn will say is that she still bears the scars from running into boulders and low-hanging tree limbs en route to their rendezvous. The things people will go through for love . . .


By the second detail the new cadets were fairly comfortable with their daily routine. Get up early, go to bed tired, with little room for any personal pursuits in between. At least that's the way things worked until one humid August night.

The day had been stiflingly hot and the Academy barracks were not air-conditioned, so a cool shower and soft bed were welcome experiences. I don't even remember falling off to sleep, but I do remember waking up to a piercing alarm bell and the sounds of activity in the halls.

I sat up in bed. It was pitch dark. A cadre member flung open the door just as the hall lights came on. "Get outside, *now!*" I grabbed our robes and my roommates and flew out into the stairwell, the three of us dressing as we fled. Chaos surrounded us. People were running everywhere, yelling confused commands to startled, half-sleeping new cadets: "Don't square corners, just move! Don't run! Stand in formation on the apron! Move, move, move!"

When we got outside we saw cadets filtering out of every exit and entranceway of the barracks. Then we heard them — firetrucks. My senses were piqued: no smoke, no flames, no burning smell. Could it be a false alarm? I guessed, instead, that they did this on purpose, to test us.

My roommates and I were among the first new cadets on the apron. As I stood there under the bright spotlights, new cadets and cadre in all shapes, sizes, and modes of dress filtered into the formation. Squad leaders took quick accountabilty and seemed just as confused about what we were all doing standing in formation after midnight as we were.

After about ten minutes, it became clear that there existed no threat to life or limb and, standing there, fear and confusion turned to excitement. After all, this was the first time since I set foot on the Academy that the rules weren't strict. The cadre let fly the rules in the interest of safety, and the slight relaxation felt good. It also gave the female new cadets a chance to see the cadre out of their staunch cadet attitudes and starched cadet uniforms! We thought many of the cadre looked great in their uniforms, but some looked even better in other attire. MaryAnn, Claire, and I stood there smiling as we watched one particularly stunning cadet move around the formation. He was tall and dark-haired, with a distinctly Italian look about him. I wondered how a man could look that fabulous after being awakened from a sound sleep, but I was unconcerned about the answer.

"He's even better-looking than Cadet Forrester," remarked Claire. It was the most correct statement I had ever heard Claire utter.

"Oh, I only hope there's another one like him somewhere at the Academy," said MaryAnn.

"I'd settle for anywhere on this planet!" I whispered. "Oh, I envy the lucky lady that gets next to that," I added with personal regret, as my roommates nodded their heads in agreement.

Soon we were shuttled back to our company and to sleep. The next day I was surprised (though I really shouldn't have been) to find out that the primary topic of conversation among the twelve or so females in the company was our handsome new company commander. So that was Cadet Cuccolo! When he yelled at me during the inspection, I never really got a chance to see his face.

"Compared to him," one of the females in another squad offered, "Tom Selleck is an eight!" Not one of us argued with her.

That night I fell asleep, as I suspect many of my fellow female classmates did, dreaming about a ladies' man and wishing he and I could've met under different circumstances.

By the end of Beast it became clear to me that Cadet Cuccolo had become my role model. He was the epitome of what I thought a cadet should act like, think like, and, yes, even look like. It wasn't difficult to learn a lot about him; everyone seemed to respect him and like him. Mentally, emotionally, morally, and militarily, this resplendent man was the best of West Point personified, and he was everything I wanted to be — the perfect West Pointer. His impact on my career, and my life, was almost immediate, and ineradicable.

The end of CBT was marked by a weeklong bivouac at Lake Freddrick on the West Point reservation. Though we lost many of the new cadets during the seven-mile march to the site (they were picked up and transported by jeep), all 1,200 of the new cadets remaining in the class at the end of the eight weeks collected at Lake Freddrick. During the early part of the week, some movie cameras appeared in order to catch a glimpse of this enormous field exercise (over 800 tents on one hillside) for a public relations film to be shown to prospective West Point candidates. My squad and I were performing "manual of arms" drill with our rifles in the middle of this "tent city," and the cameras came by to capture some of it. But the closer the cameras moved to my roommates and me, the more nervous we became. Soon we were grinning and giggling. "Smirk off!" commanded our squad leader, with little effect. After a few moments, my roommates were able to get themselves under control, which left only me to ruin our squad's chance for immortality on film with my smirking. The cameras finally decided to leave, when I saw Cadet Cuccolo move into view. He was standing, with one hand casually on his hip, about twenty feet away, observing.

"Why don't you try it one more time?" he called to the crew. "I have a feeling it'll be just what you're looking for." His voice was neither harsh nor commanding. Instead it had a suggestive, knowing quality about it. This man was confident of the effect he had on people: Cadet Cuccolo gave people the strength to do the correct thing, to choose the proper course of action, in any given situation. I did not smile at all during that final take, and a year later I was able to obtain a copy of that film while working with the Public Relations Council and the Admissions Office. What for me had been twenty grueling minutes of squad drill ended up as only five seconds of film after final editing.

The first part of our weeklong exercise was spent training and preparing for a "squad competition" at the end of the week. The weather was typical of sweltering New York in the summer, and the training was "real army" training, so it was particularly important that it be learned well. Despite the intense heat, concentrating on the training was not too difficult for most new cadets. Of course, most new cadets did not have to babysit Claire.

She was on the loose again. Why, Lord, did I have to be her partner at the grenade-throwing range? We practiced for several hours: 1) hold the grenade in front of your chest, one hand on the grenade, one hand on the pin; 2) pull the pin; 3) hand the pin to your instructor and throw the grenade. It couldn't have been simpler.

Claire got confused. She was so nervous when it came time to throw the real grenades that she pulled the pin and threw it, handing the grenade to the instructor. The instructor yelled and shoved my face into the dirt. He threw the grenade into a pile of tires, and rubber flew like fireworks on the Fourth of July. The cadre descended on us like locusts. Their hands were all over me. "Are you hurt? Are you cut? Are you bleeding anywhere?" they asked. My squad leader said he knew the moment he heard the commotion that Claire was once again earning her reputation. MaryAnn came running over.

"Goddamn it, Claire!" This was becoming MaryAnn's most used expression. I sat down on a nearby log and began picking dirt from my eyelashes and rinsing grit from my mouth with water from my canteen. I wasn't even shaken by the experience — mad, but not shaken. Somehow I expected this sort of thing from her. I was blowing dirt from my nose for the rest of the week. I thought for certain they'd release me from my misery after the attempt on my life, but Claire was still there the next morning.

One of the training exercises we were supposed to do was the disassembly/assembly of the M16A1 rifle. Since cadets carried the wooden M14 model rifles during ceremonies and parades, we were unfamiliar with this lighter weapon and, therefore, were being taken through the instruction step by step. Our squad was seated crosslegged on the ground with a diagram of a disassembled M16 rifle in front of us. Because there were not enough of these diagrams for each individual to have one, the instructor required the new cadets to share. Claire and I were partners. I had a bad feeling about this.

I gave Claire the majority of the diagram and a slight shove, saying, "Don't sit so close."

The instructor motioned for us to take off our fatigue caps, since we were seated in the shade, and began his presentation. "First I will show you what to do, then I will tell you to do it yourselves," he began. "Do nothing until I tell you to do it." He even repeated these instructions twice. I suppose Claire's head was in the ozone because before I knew it, she had her weapon in her hand. "If you push this pin out the weapon will 'shotgun' into two pieces," the instructor continued, "but don't do it until I tell you because it may shotgun and hit your neighbor in the head."

*Clunk!* The next thing I knew I was on the ground.

"Claire!" MaryAnn was screaming. "Don't you ever listen?" My classmates were snickering as they helped me back to a seated position. I'm sure that if my head hadn't been bleeding I would've been laughing too. I sat there holding my head in my hands. The instructor was fighting to keep from laughing himself, and was losing the fight. I turned my face toward him and said, very slowly and matter-of-factly, "She's trying to kill me, you know." MaryAnn burst into laughter.

I poured a canteen of water on my head and the instructor attempted to finish the class. During the rest of the week cadre members would walk by me, snickering, and say, "Now be sure you don't push this pin," or ask "How's your headache, new cadet?"

This time I wanted revenge, and the pugil stick training seemed to be the perfect opportunity for it.

The pugil sticks were used to prepare officers to fight with bayonets and rifle butts when bullets were strategically or logistically not the best alternative. Of course, at West Point it seemed as if the primary purpose of this training was to rid cadets of any timidity — to give them guts. For training purposes, these weapons were fashioned from four-foot sticks with huge pads on each end. The new cadets wore football helmets and individually fitted mouthpieces to minimize injury during the training. Head blows, body blows, thrusting, and countering were the desired objects of the fight. And the cadre loved watching us beat each other up.

Two squads were used to form a circle. Each squad leader stood behind his troops spouting orders. "Smith!" my squad leader would yell. "Johnson!" the other cadet would yell. Then both Smith and Johnson would step into the center of the circle and begin exchanging blows until one of the squad leaders gave the order to cease. Most of the new cadets were very timid, so the fighting was rather boring.

My squad leader must have been sympathetic to my tribulations because I heard him yell my name and Claire's. MaryAnn nudged me with her elbow. It was difficult to smile while wearing my mouthpiece. I entered the ring and, after three blows, Claire was on the ground at my feet. My squad leader made her get up and continue. I danced around for a few seconds and, as soon as she tried to strike a blow, I countered with a shot to the head, then twisted for a shot to the legs and she was down again. The cadre called the match off and I returned to my place within the circle while another pair was selected to fight.

This had not been our first experience with pugil sticks. We were originally trained on the soccer field, near the football stadium. Today, however, we were going through actual competition and fighting, not training. It was obvious to the cadre that MaryAnn and I were some of the best fighters in the platoon, male or female. We weren't afraid to scrap, and we were fast movers. This was probably because MaryAnn grew up as the only sister among three brothers, and my parents ran a Boy Scout troop and I often participated when the boys played games. Whatever the reason, the cadre decided to use us to spice up the competition.

As several of the cadre members gathered around, my squad

leader yelled, "Bates and Peterson." We looked at each other but did not move. Again he called our names, but we refused to move. Us? How could he do this? He knew we were best friends. They all knew how close we were by now.

"Either the two of you move or I'll come in there and fight with both of you myself," he said in a low growl. MaryAnn and I stepped slowly from the circle into the ring. For about the first minute the padded stick ends bounced softly off of our helmets and hips. We weren't fooling anyone.

"I think your classmates would like to go for a swim in the lake this afternoon," my squad leader began. We had been waiting for a cool dip in the lake all week and he knew it. "Now, we are going to stay here, all afternoon if necessary, until the two of you fight, while the rest of the company gets to swim. Understand?"

The cadre incited our classmates to begin yelling and cheering us on.

"I'm sorry," I said to MaryAnn

"I'm sorry, too," she replied.

Blows were flying left and right. Parée. Thrust. Head butt. My head was ringing, MaryAnn's eyes looked glassy, but both of us remained on our feet. *When are they going to stop this?* I thought. It seemed as if we stood in that ring for a half hour, but it must have been only a few minutes before our squad leader broke things up.

"You okay?" I asked MaryAnn between breaths.

"I hate this place," MaryAnn countered, removing her partially bloody mouthpiece.

We stepped into line and marched back up the hill to our camp and a bath. Since field shower facilities were scarce, a swim in the cold Lake Freddrick water would serve that purpose just as well.

The next day, the squad competition continued. Members of each squad were required to perform tasks for points which would, by the end of the week, determine the best squad at Lake Freddrick. I was selected to assemble/disassemble the .45-caliber pistol and to demonstrate medical survival techniques. When I arrived at the medical station, three cadre members I did not recognize were acting as scorers. A young black new cadet lay on the ground. The cadre led off with a list of symptoms. "Well, what are you going to do?" they taunted. It was obvious that the "victim" was unable to breathe, probably due to a blocked windpipe. I spouted the exact course of action as recommended in the medical survival manual.

"Don't tell us, show us," a cocky, curly-haired cadet ordered.

I knelt beside my classmate, tilted his head back, simulated removing the obstruction from his throat, pinched his nostrils shut and announced the intervals and the duration of the resuscitation procedure I would perform.

The three cadets began to excitedly, almost angrily, shout commands. "Well, do it! I don't see you doing anything! Your classmate is dying! C'mon, do it!" I looked at them in disbelief, then at the floor, the walls, anywhere for guidance. I had given the procedure perfectly, even demonstrated it as clearly as I could. Was this a trick? They had to know that it was dangerous to perform resuscitation on someone who was not in need of it. Maybe they were testing me to see if I knew that. Or perhaps they were just trying to get their kicks for the afternoon by seeing me squirm: It was obvious I had no intention of placing my lips on those of someone I did not know. I looked at my classmate on the ground. His eyes were wide and he was not smiling. *Buddy*, I thought, *if you're in on this little game of theirs, I'll strangle you!* I turned back to the three cadets. "Sir, it is dangerous to perform . . ."

"Never mind, never mind. He's dead. Your classmate died, new cadet. How does it feel?" they jeered, not desiring an answer. "Get out of here. Zero points."

As soon as possible, I notified my squad leader of my failure. "Could this cost us the competition?" I asked anxiously. "Don't worry, it'll be fine," my squad leader offered. Still, I had to know if I'd done the correct thing.

I spoke briefly to Cadet Cuccolo later in the week and carefully explained what had taken place.

"Do you know who the cadre members were?" was his first question of me. I gave the only name I remembered. "You did the right thing, Miss Peterson. And don't worry, your squad will get the points." I don't know what happened with the situation after that. I didn't care about the points, except that it could hurt the squad total. Certainly, if the cadet had actually been in need of medical intervention, I would not have hesitated. I only cared that I'd handled the situation correctly.

There were several instances during my four years at West Point when I knew that attending the Academy had been the right thing for me. One of the more poignant of these instances occurred the night before we left our "tent city" bivouac to return to the garrison of West Point.

On this night, after the field training and competitions of the week were over, the new cadets displayed their dramatic talents in what is traditionally known as the "Colorline Show." The flatbed of a tractor-trailer truck served as the stage, and one spotlight was rigged along the side of the hill for effect. The last eight weeks had been grueling and hectic; guitar players hadn't picked their guitars, singers hadn't warbled any tunes, and dancers had confined their steps to the beat of called cadences rather than dance rhythms. Not surprisingly, then, the Colorline Show has never had the reputation for being a top-quality production — just a chance to relax a little before the next stage of cadet development.

As my classmates and I lounged in the grass on the side of that hill, our muscles stiff from the inactivity of the evening and dampness of the ground, the darkness tugging at our eyelids, the last performer jumped down from the platform. The show was over and the new cadets were commanded back to their tents for the night. As we rose, a voice softly crooned from somewhere in the depths of the crowd, and our group stood motionless, at attention, as choral strains of "God Bless America" began echoing around the mountainside from 1,200 throats. Patriotism and faith had replaced strain and fatigue in the country's newest young soldiers. The cadre members stood speechless.

"You guys are going to make fine West Pointers after all," I heard one senior remark as we headed back up the hillside to our tents.

*Yes, we are,* I thought silently. And at that moment I knew, despite all the hassles and all the pain, I could never be as happy anyplace else.

Just as the new cadet companies had marched *out* to Lake Freddrick, so too did we have to march back. It was beastly hot and the route of march was about twelve miles long. We stopped about one-half mile short of the entrance to the West Point garrison for a brief rest. We were told to spruce up: brush off our boots, change our socks, comb our hair, dust off our fatigues, and drink water. We had to look good going in the gate.

This was typical of West Point training: West Point could *be* tough; it just wasn't supposed to *look* it to the Great American (taxpaying) Public. The GAP wanted and needed us to be the West Pointers from the history books, the ones who face adversity with smiles and never dirty their uniforms and never sweat.

On parade days, when the Corps of Cadets, 4,000 strong, filters from the great stone sallyports which are named for famous battles fought, it is a breathtaking and unforgettable experience for the viewers seated in the stands. My parents, and so many of the thousands of visitors to West Point each year, have attested to feeling renewed after viewing the cadets. Bob Hope, during one of several visits to the Academy, told cadets that viewing the perfection of a cadet parade "restores my faith in life." More than a decade later, while filming one of his television specials at the Academy, Mr. Hope looked into the cadet crowd assembled for the performance and remarked, "It doesn't hurt as much to pay taxes when I look at all of you."

What the public does not see, however, are the cadets' prayers to the medieval God of Rain for the parade to be canceled. "Odon!" cadets cry from their windows during the hours before a parade.

Once on the parade field, the cadets stand perfectly still, 4,000 shining Spartans. But inside the formations, upper-class cadets are hazing plebes, telling tasteless jokes, singing never-before-heard-of lyrics to the military marches played by the Army Band, or "checking out the babes" spattered throughout the parade onlookers standing five layers deep along the fringes of the Plain. These antics are not frowned upon by the Academy administration. They know these things go on, because the administrators participated themselves when they were members of the Corps. As long as the public doesn't see them, which it doesn't, there's no need for concern. After all, it's supposedly harmless, stress-inducing fun. But just let a cadet mess up noticeably during the parade ceremony and the cadets themselves will give him hell when the formation returns to the barracks.

The public was waiting for us as we marched through the gate from Lake Freddrick that day. Hundreds of people from the families of officers, professors, government employees, and enlisted personnel stationed at West Point lined the roads to welcome us back. The commandant of cadets and the superintendent of the Military Academy were there as well. We had no problem staying in step, chanting loudly, and looking fit. The new cadets had no idea all this was awaiting us; it was inspiring. The onlookers held banners, and somewhere along the route each company was named specifically: "GREAT JOB SECOND COMPANY . . . RUN WITH THE PACK [our motto]."

I was proud to be passing in front of the crowd, feeling part of the West Point spirit. Much has been written about the communal atmosphere of West Point. Nowhere else in the world is the belief in the "military family" ideal so firmly ingrained or so beautifully exemplified. You never meet a stranger at West Point, only friends and family — officers, cadets, or civilians. I wanted to shout: "Thank you for letting me be here!"

Back in the barracks we showered quickly and went to lunch. I was famished. I had made a lot of friends during field problems because I gave away most of my C-rations, except for the canned tuna, which I rarely got anyway, and the crackers and cheese. I couldn't wait to sit down to this meal, despite all the hassles and duties mealtime brought with it. At least it was real food.

But what I saw before me were fishburgers — probably the summertime meal I disliked the most. It didn't matter. I was hungry, and the cadre made us eat it anyway. "Be sure you get plenty of salt so you don't cramp up," the cadre reminded us. Good advice. I had been awakened on more than one occasion by the screams of a roommate clutching a cramped leg muscle in the dark of the night.

A few days prior to our weeklong bivouac at Lake Freddrick, the new cadets had been assigned to the regular companies they would belong to during the academic year. Cadet Cuccolo and several of his classmates in Second Company lived in Company B4. Not surprisingly, most of the new cadets wanted to be assigned to B4. As they posted the company assignments, MaryAnn and I smiled hesitantly. We had not gotten our wishes: we were not assigned to B4 and we were not in the same company. But we *were* in the 4th Regiment; MaryAnn in A4, myself in G4. Since the regiments paraded and took classes together, we felt certain we'd see each other, and Cadet Cuccolo, often.

There had been tears that afternoon as we packed our belongings and moved them to our new companies, where plebes would be outnumbered three to one. As the company commander said his goodbye, he sounded almost tearful. "If you see me walking around during the year, don't be afraid to say 'Hi' or even 'Run with the Pack.' " Cadet Cuccolo had probably heard that motto hundreds of times during that year. I'd pass by him, striking my most military posture, and spout a professional "Run with the Pack, sir." It never mattered what he was doing, or who he was with, but he would always turn and reply with a smile, "Run with the Pack, Miss Peterson." That was part of his charm. He was strict and tough, but he made us feel like people instead of animals. He always referred to us as "Miss" or "Mister," and never said it like he was spitting out spinach or some other foul-tasting

food. He was a man's man, he was a ladies' man, and one of the finest
West Pointers I have ever known.


    The end of Beast was marked with another ceremony, a parade
and induction ceremony where we would lose the title "new cadets"
and officially become "plebes," or freshmen (fourth-class). Webster's
offers the definition of *plebian* as a "member of the lowest social class."
At West Point, however, it took us eight weeks of stress and labor to
work our way up to attaining the rank of "plebe."
    West Point has developed a way of making a cadet appreciate the
very smallest of rewards or achievements. The Academy also knows
that the harder someone works toward a goal, the more the achievement, no matter how small, means to them. We were finally "cadets";
not new cadets or new cadet candidates, but real live (though bruised)
cadets. And it felt wonderful.
    Back in our new barracks, the upper-class cadets were playing
games with the new freshmen.
    "New Cadet, halt!" I heard one command.
    As I stopped, I recalled some sage advice from the plebe women
I'd stayed with during my initial candidate visit to the Academy:
"Watch out. They'll try to trick you by calling you a New Cadet, and
see if you react. Just ignore everything they say unless they specifically
call you 'Cadet'."
    I quickly started walking again. Too late. They were all over me
like flies at a picnic.
    "So, you're not proud to be a cadet, huh? You'd rather still be a
new cadet, where you're babied and taken care of? Well, this is the real
West Point. You'll tow the line here or you'll be out. Understand?"
    "Yes, sir!" I responded loudly. But the upper-class cadets just
stood there. What did they want?
    "Sir, may I pass?" I asked the cadet who stood directly in my
path. I wanted to get out of there, and I was tired of this strange game.
    "Hypothetical situation, Miss Peterson," the cadet began slowly,
after reading my nametag. "Two minutes to go in the second quarter,
Army has the ball . . ." He was going to test my knowledge of football. Was he in for a surprise. I love football, and I know the game better than many men do.
    The hypothetical situation game had been tried on the new cadets
during Beast. The cadet gives you a football situation to analyze. Since

the ultimate goal of the game is for the plebe to be able to "pass," they start out by giving you situations where the correct play is to pass the football. Just when the plebe gets used to responding, "Sir, I would pass. That is where cadets with little knowledge of football get messed upper-class cadets throw in a curve where the correct response is not to pass. That is where cadets with little knowledge of football get screwed up. But these guys were not going to have their fun with this plebe.

The cadet continued with his story: "The score is tied, it's fourth and seven, ball on their forty-yard line. What do you want to do?" He was smiling slyly at his buddies. They looked like drooling coyotes encircling an easy prey.

"Sir, I would punt," I announced confidently. Their mouths dropped, and they just stood there, having been outsmarted by their "dinner."

Then the other two cadets each took a turn. Again I answered correctly. Finally, the cadet that started this game gave me a second scenario for which the answer was, "Sir, I would pass."

"Wrong!" he delighted in announcing. "I said this was the ARMY team. You wouldn't get very far if you tried passing with our quarterback. You'd better run, if you hope to gain any yards at all." He was laughing, enjoying his coup.

Just when you think you have another aspect of West Point figured out, these cadets come up with another angle so that even when you're right, they find a way for you to be wrong. Cadets were masters at it.

As I made my way up the stairs to my room on the third floor, I realized how glad I was that they played the scenario game. West Point takes football very seriously. Upper-class cadets have tested underclassmen's knowledge of this great sport for generations. In addition, plebes have to memorize the names and jersey numbers of all of the Army football players, and God forbid that you don't know the name of the coach! The Army team certainly wasn't the ranked team of yesteryear during my four years, but the history of the team in its glory days still thrived.

Of course, now that women were in attendance at the Academy, the male cadets thought they had perfect pawns for their game, since women stereotypically are much less enthusiastic about male-dominated sports, especially football. I, however, lived in a family that was crazy about weekend football, and we always watched the best. We were Green Bay Packer (in the Lombardi days) and Dallas Cowboy fans. And I hadn't missed a school football game since I became a baton twirler in the seventh grade.

I was glad that school would be starting soon, because that meant the start of the football season. There was one other important personal event: my mother would soon be coming to visit, for Labor Day, and I needed to see her. It would have been ten weeks, and I wondered how she'd react. I left home a young girl, and I'd meet her at the Hotel Thayer as a proud West Point cadet.

It was a perfect West Point day. The sky was crystal blue, the sun warm and yellow, the air hot but not too humid. The walk from the barracks area to the hotel was only about a mile long, but I don't remember most of it. I was remembering my first phone call home . . .

It was after two weeks at the Academy. New cadets who had earned the privilege were permitted to make a phone call home. Our squad leader inspected our uniforms for perfection ("After all, you're going out in public") before we left our area of the barracks. I bounced down the steps and headed for the basement where the phone booths were located. I can remember standing at a rigid position of parade rest, with one hand placed in the small of my back, the other hand cradling the "Bugle Notes" I was studying, for over two hours while I waited in one of many long lines that had formed for a phone. Just as the new cadet in front of me stepped into the booth, a senior cadet, who had been surveying the operation, made an announcement.

"You people are dicking all over your classmates. You don't need to spend thirty minutes on the phone. Your classmates at the ends of the lines won't get to make a phone call until sometime next week at this rate! Cooperate and graduate, people. That's the name of the game here. I want all phone calls limited to fifteen minutes. The next person in line will monitor the time and tap on the booth when your time is up. Does everyone understand?"

"Yes, sir," responded a chorus of cracking voices. Since no talking was allowed, except in your own room, none of the new cadets had spoken a word for hours. Instead of being upset, however, that I had waited several hours for what would now be only a fifteen-minute phone call, I was excited because I knew that in only fifteen minutes I would be on the phone to my parents.

I tapped on the glass door at fifteen minutes. I tapped harder at twenty minutes. By twenty-two minutes after, I was ready to kill! As five of us knocked on the glass in unison, the new cadet emerged from the booth. It should not have surprised me that everyone in line was now monitoring the time limits of the callers ahead of them.

As I stepped into the booth, I prayed: *Dear God, please let them be at home!* My parents had no knowledge that I was going to call, and this was a Saturday afternoon. With each ring of the phone, my hand gripped the receiver tighter. Just after the third ring I heard, "Hello?" It was my mother.

"Mom?" I questioned, my voice breaking.

"Donna! Oh, my God! How are you? Hey, everybody, it's Donna! I love you!"

"I love you too, Mom," I managed to choke from my throat, before I began to cry. For the next three minutes my family heard only sobs from the other end of the phone lines. My mother continued to talk, with the entire family on every extension phone in the house, offering support and encouraging words. The more she spoke, the more I cried.

"If it's that bad, we'll come up and get you," she said. Now I had to speak. I didn't want them to panic, and they were beginning to get scared. After all, they send their daughter to West Point, they don't hear from her for two weeks and, when they finally do, all she does is cry.

"Mom, it's hell!" I said, as I stopped myself from crying. Then I pulled the white cotton handkerchief (which all cadets were required to carry) from the back pocket of my pants, blew my nose, wiped my eyes, and managed to carry on a conversation for the ten minutes that remained. As the next new cadet in line tapped on the glass I said, "Mom I have to go." The protests on the other end of the phone made me smile. "Really, I have to. We have a fifteen-minute time limit. I don't know when I'll get to call again. Next time I'll try to cry less and talk more."

Again my mom came to the rescue. "You can cry all you want when you get on this phone," she said.

I said my "I love yous" and was rewarded with a chorus of "I love yous" and "I miss yous." I left the phone booth feeling drained, yet strangely rejuvenated. I was lucky to have loving and very supportive family members, one of whom I was about be reunited with.

As I strode briskly toward the hotel, feeling the warm sun on my face, I sang to myself:

> *"Shine on me sunshine, walk with me world*
> *It's a skippedee-doo-dah day.*
> *I'm the happiest girl, in the whole USA!"*

Suddenly, I realized I had arrived at the hotel. My heart beat excitedly as I climbed the steep incline up from the street. *What if something happened and she didn't get here?* I wondered. *Would I even be able to hug her, or does the regulation against public display of affection cover daughters and mothers as well? What if . . .* Too late to wonder anymore. I opened the great glass doors and stepped inside. Though I made the trip to the hotel with the pace of a rabbit, I was now climbing the marble lobby steps like a snail, my eyes closely surveying the lobby.

There she was! She was seated on a huge leather chair in the exact center of the lobby, before the great stone fireplace. She was dressed like a ray of sunshine, in a pale yellow dress with a bright yellow jacket, her blonde curls pinned up on her head to gain some relief from the heat, and a big yellow button she'd purchased from the hotel gift shop which read "GO ARMY" pinned to the pocket of the jacket. She must have been watching the entryway for hours, for she saw me immediately, jumped up, and stretched out her arms. "Donna!" The sound of her voice was music to my ears.

"Mom!" I said as I threw myself into her arms, smiling. Lost in the familiar safety of her arms, I began to cry. "I love you, Mom. God how I've missed you!" She soothed me and sat me down beside her. It soon became apparent that the entire lobby of visitors was involved in our reunion. Several couples squeezed hands as they waited for their own cadets to ascend the lobby stairs; smiling, teary-eyed women reached into their purses for tissues. Remembering how important public perception was at this place, my mother and I quickly moved to a more secluded corner of the lobby to continue our reunion. I saw the tears well up in her eyes, and we hugged for at least ten minutes. Then we stepped outside to the lawn and patio area behind the hotel. We sat together on the iron lawn chairs, admiring the beauty of the scenery and taking pictures of each other. Though my mother had accompanied me on my initial visit to West Point during March, she had never seen the Academy in the summer.

"I've got so much to tell you and show you!" I told her.

We had lunch in the restaurant and I took her to meet MaryAnn and her parents, who had also come to visit for the three-day weekend. We talked, laughed, and visited for hours. I tried to educate my mother about the lifestyle of a plebe as quickly as possible. She, like most parents, was eager to learn and help in any way.

Later that afternoon, I walked back to the hotel with her. Along the journey our path crossed that of many of the upperclassmen, some with dates, some returning from the hotel alone or with other cadets. If they were upperclassmen, I was required, as a plebe, to offer a greeting, such as, "Good afternoon, sir," to each of them. As my mother and I walked and talked, her eyes telescoped the horizon. "Get ready," she'd say nervously as a cadet approached, "this one has stuff on his shoulders." Plebes had no gold braid on the epaulettes they wore with their white summer dress shirts; all upperclassmen did.

"Good afternoon, sir," I'd offer, and my mother would relax a little.

"This is nerve wracking," she'd say. "And you have to live like this every day?"

It really wasn't difficult once you got used to it. The problem on this sunny day was that the gold braid was often difficult to see on a cadet's shoulders. The cadet brass, worn on the gray class uniform, made class delineation much easier to detect. Several times that day I offered a greeting to one of my own classmates, and several offered one to me, the idea being that it was safer to embarrass yourself by saying "sir" or "ma'am" to one of your own classmates than to suffer the consequences of not saying it to an upperclassman. Even with the outstanding efforts of my mother to assist me, I still missed one. Thank goodness the second classman ("cow") was walking with his girlfriend at the time and, not wanting his girlfriend to see the "other side" of him, he simply shot me a deadly glance with his eyes and continued walking with his girl on his arm.

"He had stuff!" my mom said.

"I know," I replied, as the hair on my neck stiffened and I waited for the cadet to change his mind and scream at me.

"But you didn't say anything!" My mother was slightly bewildered. I assured her, however, that, even if he hadn't been walking with his girlfriend, he would not have been as "unkind" as I had written her that upper-class cadets could be. You see, to a West Point cadet, the most sacred entity on earth is a mother, and no one would have embarrassed me in front of mine, unless I had really done something horrendous.

"So that's why every one of the cadets we've passed has said hello to me," she reasoned.

"You'd better believe it. In fact, the upperclassmen think nothing of pulling a cadet's privileges, even if you have a date coming to visit. But if your parents are coming, they'll tell you to enjoy your visit, and they'll deal with your punishment later."

Parents are revered, and they belong to everyone. If my parents were visiting, every cadet I knew felt like they had a set of parents visiting. We just kind of "shared" parents. And the parents loved it. Those who lived close to the Academy found their homes filled with cadets on the weekends, even if their particular son or daughter wasn't one of them. They wrote to and received letters from their cadet's classmates, and would respond anytime they heard someone call "Mom" or "Dad."

Several times during the day my mother had inquired about my physical health; she detected a slight limp. Each time I would say it was "nothing" or "I have a blister" and, given the excitement of the day, she dismissed her worries. When we returned to the hotel, however, I found that a mother's worries weren't forgotten that easily.

"Donna, that's more than just a slight limp from a blister. Let me see your feet." Under protest, she moved me into a vacant ballroom just off the hotel lobby, sat me down on a long row of chairs, and took off my shiny black shoes. "Oh, my God!" She cringed as she turned her face away from the oozing, multicolored mess that had once been smooth size-seven feet. There were bruises and blisters in every stage and color of development and healing.

"Oh, my God," she kept repeating, tears rolling from her eyes, as she held my feet in her lap and sobbed. "What have they done to you?"

"It's not so bad, Mom," I protested meekly. "Don't cry. It doesn't hurt much. You get used to it. Please, Mom." As we sat in that empty ballroom, our sobs echoing, we were sharing our pain. No mother wants to know that her child is suffering, even for the best of causes, and for me, every tear that I dared not cry during the last ten weeks was freely falling on the safe shoulders of a parent.

It wasn't that I had neglected my feet. Rather, the Academy is a very physical place, and there is no "down time," so to speak, for physical recuperation. Add to that the fact that women had been improperly fitted with combat boots, and the results for many of the female cadets were feet that resembled my own. At that time, it seemed that the military's thinking was that women's feet were just like men's, only smaller, so they issued smaller men's boots to the women, rather than boots specifically designed and sized for women. To compound the problem, I had been issued a pair that were too large: size six, men's. The boot shop's response was that I should've known they didn't fit properly. But how would I know if a combat boot fit correctly? I'd never even seen one before I got to West Point, let alone had a pair on my feet. To solve the problem, we women began swapping boots around until we found pairs that did fit. A female cadet in another regiment traded her boots to one of my roommates, and my roommate traded hers to me, size four and a half, men's! Other women who couldn't find boots to trade would borrow boots when necessary, and when they found a size that fit they would purchase new boots at the cadet store. Today, when a female goes to a military clothing store to buy boots, she buys boots specifically made and sized for females. Progress takes time.

I thoroughly enjoyed my mother's visit. There had been very few upperclassmen to contend with as most of them took advantage of the three-day weekend to travel away from the Academy, so I felt more relaxed than I had since I first set foot on the Academy grounds more than two months earlier. I showed my mother some of the reasons why the Military Academy is one of the most popular tourist attractions in the nation, and told her all of the history and trivia I had learned about the Academy so far. I took her to Sunday brunch in the cadet mess hall and introduced her to the people who were the most important to me in this new world. MaryAnn and her folks sat with us in the restaurant of Eisenhower Hall on Sunday afternoon, eating ice cream and laughing hysterically about the events of the past eight weeks. The worst weeks of a four-year cadet career were over, and already we were able to laugh at some of it.

It was my mother who changed the tone of the conversation, however, when she asked, very innocently, "So, when am I going to get to meet Cadet Cuccolo?"

MaryAnn and I looked at each other, wide-eyed, then broke into laughter.

"Mother," I said patronizingly, "you don't just 'meet' Cadet Cuccolo."

"No," MaryAnn finished for me, "you fall in love with him!" She was laughing and pointing at me, knowingly.

My mother was smiling too. I had written her about this Italian soldier of the Gods, and of his impact on my cadet career and my heart. We filled in MaryAnn's mother about Cadet Cuccolo so that she too could poke fun at me for the rest of the day. My mother was particularly enjoying the teasing I was receiving because I had never been a boy-crazy young woman, never read teen magazines or hung posters of teen heartthrobs around my walls. If I needed or wanted a date, I had one. The rest of the time I was very busy with myriad high school activities, and I loved spending time with my adorable younger sister and brother. To see my heart doing flip-flops now, over a man I could never have, was a new experience for my mother.

"Oh, c'mon, MaryAnn, tell the truth," I challenged. "You know you felt the same way about him. All the women did. Besides, I know I don't stand a chance with him, but it doesn't hurt to admire beauty, does it?"

"Is that what you're doing?" she chided. "Hey, kid," her voice was the most serious it had been all afternoon. "It wouldn't surprise me to find out that the two of you did get together someday, knowing your perseverance. As for me," she leaned back in her chair and crossed her arms in front of her, smiling like a Cheshire cat, "I actually preferred Pat Forrester, with his blond hair and blue eyes." It was obvious that she was quickly leaving the present for a far more fascinating dream world. I leaned over the table and snapped my fingers in front of her face.

"Earth to MaryAnn. Earth to MaryAnn. Let's talk reality here, dear. After the grueling, and I do emphasize the word *grueling*," I said for the benefit of the parents who were listening intently, "special inspections you had with Cadet Forrester, I'm not surprised that you get a rosy glow to your cheeks when you think about him." I held her chin in my hand and turned her face left and right to show off the glow. She swatted my hand away and joined in the laughter. It felt so good to laugh and relax.

The weekend was over too soon. My mother had planned to leave on the 2:00 P.M. bus on Monday. She was packed and ready to go, but as the bus pulled up to the Academy gate, we both began to cry. Suddenly she turned and asked the driver, "When is the next bus to the airport?" Another bus would be arriving in an hour and twenty minutes. We went back inside the hotel to change my mother's plane reservations and take advantage of the reprieve. I desperately did not want her to leave. After all, I did not have to be back in the barracks until 7:00 P.M. and I wanted her with me as much as possible. When the next bus drove up, she and I walked stoically to the bus stop. As we stood there embracing, I began to cry.

"I love you," I managed to sputter as she walked across the street to catch the bus. I lost sight of her as she walked around the other side of the bus to board. I continued to watch until the bus pulled away. There stood my mother! I went running to her.

"The driver said that there is a 6:30 P.M. bus, but it's the last one

I can catch and still make the last flight to Houston, so I have to be on it!" she said, smiling.

This was great! We sat on the stone wall at the bottom of the ramp to the hotel and watched three more buses depart for the airport before my mother's arrived. It was a good feeling to watch those buses depart and still feel my mom's hand in mine as they drove out of sight. Finally, the time came, and so did the 6:30 bus. The last four hours had given me a chance to get used to the idea of her departure, and I did have to be back in my barracks soon, so this farewell seemed much less traumatic than the first two I'd experienced that day.

As I walked back to the barracks area, my mind had ample time to return to the requirements of life as a plebe. My pace quickened and my body returned to the rigid form of a new plebe. I bounced up the stone stairs and stepped into my company barracks.

"Hey, Miss! Are you gazing around?" I heard in a familiar tone. *Gee, it's good to be home . . .*

CHAPTER 3

# Plebe Year

*"It is nice to know there are still teen-agers who can agree on something."*

— Bob Hope, observing a cadet parade, 1968

B y the end of Beast, we had been at the Academy for two months and still hadn't attended a class. The summer training made us "cadets"; the academic year would now make us "college students." The harassment that had permeated every waking moment of our lives would now be concentrated into pockets of time — between classes, at formations, while performing plebe duties — so as not to interfere with class schedules or mandatory study time in the evenings.

Besides academic classes, plebes always look forward to a new cadet uniform: the gray "class" shirt over gray trousers (or skirt for women) with the crescent-shaped "garrison cap" for headgear. After wearing the white-over-gray or fatigue uniforms for eight weeks, this is an exciting event. In addition, plebes get their first interaction with cadets from the next two classes, known as "yearlings" (sophomores) and "cows" (juniors). I disliked yearlings (or "yuks") immediately.

Having spent the summer being told to "smirk off," I had finally learned to control my facial muscles. Now these immature yearlings would goad me, in the most serious of situations, to smile. "Come on,

Miss Peterson, lighten up. Smile, there aren't any seniors around."
There were *always* seniors around.

After living through the summer under the direction of the
staunchest cadets at the Academy, these yearlings did little to impress
me. In fact, they made me mad. Some of my other classmates played
along with the yearlings, but I never did. I didn't see anything funny
about trying to get plebes to break the rules on purpose. We broke too
many of the rules without even trying!

Cows were the cadets with the most direct control over the cadets;
they were our squad leaders, upon whom we relied heavily for guidance, information, and to save our butts when the seniors applied too
much heat. This was the Class of 1980, the troubled class that survived
the disruption of having the first female cadets within their ranks. The
class, as a whole, did not seem to receive respect from the members of
the Class of 1979, probably because the men in the Class of 1979 had
witnessed the chaos created by the media, which continually surrounded and hounded the class because of the presence of the first
women, and they did not like the results. Said one member of the Class
of 1979, "The Academy was not certain what the women could do
when they arrived, what standards they could meet. So, the Class of
1980 floundered for a time, until experiments [tests] could be performed and adjustments could be made." The 1980 graduates were
touted as less military than the other classes in attendance at that time.

Being the first class to incorporate women was their cross to bear.
If they seemed less military, perhaps it was because they had suffered
more. I was told by an officer in the admissions department that many
men due to be admitted to the Academy with the Class of 1980 declined attendance, knowing that women would be standing beside
them in ranks. Others, who accepted their appointments, were passed
over by television cameras and journalists who came from all over the
world to capture this historic event, in favor of pictures and interviews
of women in the class. These men, who had worked equally as hard at
earning an appointment to West Point as the women of the class, were
overlooked as insignificant. The hometown newspapers printed proud
credits on their behalf, but the *New York Times* ran stories of the
women. After all, men at the Academy were not news. The feelings of
these men would continue to be trampled on throughout their four
years. Perhaps because of all they'd been through, I found the cows to
be a very patient group of cadets, much more so than the seniors.

The academic year also brings the opportunity to be "recognized." Normally, plebes are recognized only at the end of year, during graduation week. However, if a plebe was previously known by an upper-class cadet, that cadet can ask the plebe's squad leader for permission to "recognize" him. This simply allows the upper-class cadet to establish a personal relationship, by the use of first names, with the plebe, providing the names are not used in public. This is especially helpful in situations where siblings attend the Academy at the same time, as was the case with one of my new roommates.

Karen and Debbie were my roommates in Company G4. Karen had a sister in the Class of 1980. About three days into the academic year, her sister knocked on the door. Debbie (alphabetically ranking) saluted and reported. I stared at the upperclassman's nametag: the last name was the same as Karen's. She had never told us she had a sister there! We were told to "go about our business" (we had been seated at our desks, studying) while she allowed Karen to stand at parade rest. She then began asking her questions about Beast, whether she'd run into any of her sisters' friends yet, and other small talk. This went on for about ten minutes until Karen's sister put out her hand and said, "Brennan" (her name). Karen shook her sister's hand and said, "Karen." I watched this stoic display (from the corner of my eyes) and thought how I would be on the phone to our mother as fast as my legs could carry me, complaining: "Mom, you wouldn't believe how my sister acted!" If that was my sister, especially knowing first-hand how difficult it is for women at this place, I'd have my arms around her two seconds after I walked in the door! And I'd probably hug her roommates too, just for good measure. At least I'd *talk* to them! After the handshake, the two embraced, and Karen relaxed for the first time since her sister stepped through the door.

Several weeks later, much to my surprise, someone came by to recognize me. It was Sunday, 9 September 1978. I met MaryAnn for brunch and, afterward, we stopped by her company to get her books before returning to my room to do some studying. After about an hour, someone knocked four times on the door. Since two knocks is the signal for an upperclassman, I assumed it was one of my classmates, remained seated and said, "Enter." It was Dave! I stood up. MaryAnn stood too. My heart was racing. He was even more gorgeous than when I first met him as a new cadet candidate. His shoulders were broader, summer training had bronzed his skin and, since he was now a yearling, his hair was slightly fuller and longer than he had worn it as a plebe. Latin blood coursed through his veins, and he looked remarkably like a young Burt Reynolds.

"Hi," he said.

"Hello, sir," I replied meekly, smiling.

Dave smiled too and fumbled with the white dress hat he carried in his hands. "I see you made it through Beast in one piece," he said. "I can't believe you cut your hair. It looks good, it just takes some getting used to."

I introduced MaryAnn to him, then she sat down and continued reading her history.

"Please don't call me 'sir' anymore, Donna," he said as he offered me his hand. "It's Dave. I spoke to your squad leader, and he said it's all right." I shook his hand, and we talked for another five minutes or so before he had to leave. "If you need anything, don't hesitate to ask, okay? I'm in Company G1." I nodded, and he left.

After the door closed behind him, I found it difficult to move. I don't know if it was because I felt cared about, having just been recognized, or because I've always loved the smell of Aramis cologne . . .

Dave and I met, originally, in March 1978, during my visit to the Academy as a prospective candidate; I visited his Saturday morning calculus class. As a plebe, he was arrogant and very forward. He finished putting his math problem on the chalkboard then asked the professor for permission to talk to me. He came over and sat on my desk, telling me how "kindred" we were since he was also from Texas (San Antonio). After the class he ran down the hall screaming for his best friend, Chuck, to see the "beautiful blonde" he'd just met. He was a bit pushy for my taste. We spoke again before I left West Point that weekend, and he called once during the summer to see if I had decided to attend. Technically, that's all that was needed for Dave to be able to recognize me. And, despite my initial feelings about his pushy attitude as a plebe, I was very attracted to the quiet arrogance with which he carried himself as an upperclassman.

We corresponded throughout the rest of the academic year, often studying together in the library or, on Sundays, in Dave's room in his company. I finally got to meet Chuck and the rest of Dave's friends in Company G1. I was even assigned guard duty at his company one night, purely by accident. "The gang" and I would often sit together at football games or concerts, providing they didn't have dates visiting. I was uneasy when his yearling friends began calling me by my first name, however.

"You have to understand, Donna," his friend Burt (one of the DJs for the West Point radio station) said. "Throughout our summer training at Camp Buckner the mysterious 'Donna' was all Dave talked about. We feel like we know you!"

I was flattered, but a bit uneasy.

During the rest of my plebe year, Dave and his friends were always available. If Dave couldn't come and get me to "walk me" to his company (many upperclassmen did this so that there was less possibility of the plebe getting into trouble in an unfamiliar company), one of his friends would meet me and escort me to Company G1. It was a good thing too. Dave lived in the newer barracks on the other side of the corps. These barracks were set up differently from the ancient barracks in which I lived. Plebes in all companies had to "square" all corners when walking in the hallways, and in Dave's company the walls had small indentations and telephone booths sat in the hallways. On my first visit there, in late October, I was by myself and got caught "spazing," confusedly trying to square all those places. When Dave and his friends heard all the commotion, they stepped into the hallway. They were shocked when they saw that I was the object of all the negative attention! Dave smoothed things with the seniors, and from then on, someone walked me to the company whenever necessary.

Though Dave was allowed to officially recognize me, we were not allowed to date. Upper-class dances and functions were held at a four-story, multilevel building known as Eisenhower Hall, which overlooked the Hudson. This fairly new building had several ballrooms, a "student union" restaurant, the offices of the cadet hostesses, and a 4,500-seat auditorium, praised as the finest auditorium in the East, next to Radio City Music Hall. Plebes socialized in a majestic three-level building located about half a mile away from "Ike" (Eisenhower Hall), known as Cullum Hall (formerly the Cadet Activities Center). Visitors to the Academy recognize Cullum as the huge white building with "Beat Navy" painted on its copper roof. During Army-Navy football week, cadets painted this roof so often (with perfect white block letters) that the Academy finally decided it was cheaper for the Academy, and safer for the cadets, to simply leave it painted there.

Plebe dances were held in the second-floor ballroom each weekend. I attended the dance every Saturday night. Only a handful of female cadets attended dances regularly. Some felt uncomfortable dancing in uniform, others preferred to dance in skirts but disliked the style and cut of the cadet skirts, while some just didn't like going to

dances. But the dances were great fun. West Point spared no expense
in providing cadets with fabulous social and recreational opportunities
throughout my four years, and these dances were just one example. At
least two were held each weekend — one for the upper-class cadets, at
Ike, and one for the plebes, at Cullum. Often the tables in the Ike restaurant were pushed aside to accommodate a dance floor and stage for
a band or DJ (a DJ booth was installed by my senior year to provide
record music in the restaurant every weekend), and, on special weekends, any formal dances were held in the Main Ballroom at Ike. As a
minimum, the cadet hostesses — civilian women who were "second
moms" to the Corps — always provided nonalcoholic beverages and
finger foods, while a DJ spun records or, once a month, a local band
performed. The entertainment was varied (pop, rock, country) and
usually enjoyable, though you could get an "off" band occasionally.
One of the cadets' favorites was a German "oompah" band that played
for the upper-class as well as plebe dances three or four times a year.

The female cadets who attended dances never lacked for attention
from male cadets. My dance card was always filled. I made some great
friends from opposite areas of the Corps whom I never would have met
if it weren't for these dances. My male classmates never acted like it
bothered them to dance with the female cadets. In fact, I'd get asked
during the week: "Donna, are you gonna be at the dance Saturday?
Good, I'll be there too." I'd often hear some of my female classmates
lament the fact that they'd like to attend the dances, but they didn't
want to suffer the embarrassment of being rebuked by our male classmates, in favor of the civilian women in pretty dresses. I would assure
them that as soon as the cadet girls step off the dance floor with one
cadet, another would take her back onto the floor. The next week these
women would show up and often they had a good time.

I usually met Randy Odom at these dances. We shared our first
kiss on the balcony, shaded from view by the shadows of a full Hudson
moon. Sometimes, however, Dave showed up. He was a Hop Committee representative, and sometimes he was scheduled to work the plebe
dance. We'd talk or drink punch, he'd watch me dance with my classmates, I'd watch him dance with the civilian cadet hostesses. Dave was
a fabulous dancer. Secretly, each of us longed for the opportunity to
dance together. But for the time being, it was enough just to get to see
him wearing his red sash!

Despite the lack of female cadet participation, the male cadets
didn't lack for dancing partners. Another "tradition" at the Military

Academy, one which most male cadets have laughed about for decades, is the busing of women from local towns and colleges to the dances. The cadet hostesses coordinate with local girls' colleges to provide busloads of women for the cadets to socialize with at these dances, known as "cattle calls." (Male cadets often "moo" quietly as the girls are "herded" off of the bus.) In all, however, this practice works very well, at least for the upper-class cadets. Girls prefer to attend the upper-class dances, where there are older cadets with more money and privileges, and less time before graduation. To say that many of these women attend the dances with the express purpose of finding a West Point husband is no exaggeration. Therefore, fewer busloads of women attend the plebe dances, and many who do are visibly unhappy about their drop-off location. Frequently they take out their frustrations on the young males.

"No, thank you. I'm dancing with her," the woman will say when asked by a cadet to dance, pointing to the girlfriend standing beside her. Each time I saw the broken looks cross these young men's faces, I hated those college women.

One night, I watched a charade like this until I could tolerate it no longer.

"Why do you even come here?" I said to one group of women who continually rebuked the male cadets. "You volunteer to come to these dances. If you're not going to dance with them, stay home. They certainly don't need the likes of you to help crush their egos. This place does that well enough seven days a week, twenty-four hours a day." The women responded by turning their backs on me and continuing their conversation.

I gave up counting the number of times these women would check under the bathroom stalls, to be certain a female cadet was within earshot, to say, "No self-respecting woman would ever attend West Point," and "*Uck!* Have you seen how *ugly* those female cadets are? No wonder these men are so hungry for real women."

Imagine how we felt: So many of the male cadets didn't want us there, the male graduates and officers had gone on record objecting to our presence, the women members of the first class with women were rude to us, and now so were the civilian women who came to visit. I wondered why we didn't just take our toys and go home. Even a civilian male visiting the plebe dance one weekend took his turn at putting us down.

"I guess it must be pretty hard for you, huh?" he inquired, walking me off the dance floor after a three-record set.

"I'm not sure I know what you mean," I replied.

"I mean, hard for you to compete, you in that uniform and all these civilian women in their fancy dresses."

This comment really didn't bother me. I liked wearing the West Point uniforms, and I was proud of what it took to be able to wear them.

"I don't have to 'compete'," I said, shooting him a what-rock-did-you-crawl-out-from-under glance. "I have plenty of dresses like those at home in my closet. And if I didn't, I could walk into any store in the world and buy one. But *they can't buy* what I'm wearing!"

I had expected resistance to women at West Point. But throughout my four years as a cadet, and even as recently as the last Army-Navy football game I attended, the blatant rudeness of cadets, graduates, wives and girlfriends of graduates, and even general officers toward females at West Point astounded me. I got my first sample of such confrontations during the homecoming football weekend of my plebe year.

This was my mother's second visit to the Academy, my father's first. My dad, an ardent history buff (and former navy submariner), had just been converted into one of the greatest Army football fans of all time. To celebrate this conversion, he was "buying out" the gift shop at the Hotel Thayer. My mother and I were waiting for him in the foyer near the lobby doors. Quite a few graduates who had returned for their twenty-five-year reunion were gathered in the foyer as well. I was smiling and talking to my mother about the remainder of our plans for the weekend, when a group of about twenty or so "old grads" noticed me. They took the opportunity to express, loudly, their unhappiness about the Congressional Order of 1975. These "gentlemen" turned from their group to face my mother and me, wrinkling their noses and distorting their mouths as if reacting to a repulsive odor, to remark, "It's disgusting. It's just not natural. She looks ridiculous."

I was so hurt. How could they be so cruel in front of my mother? These men were some of the country's military and economic leaders. They were company presidents, general officers, and millionaires. I knew how these men felt about women at their alma mater, but I expected them to be the gentlemen that the country assumed they were. I turned my back, and my mother, away from them. My mother was visibly shaken.

"It's okay, Mom. Don't let it get to you. It happens sometimes,"

I said, trying to smile and pretend that their actions didn't bother me.

"Are you sure you're all right?" my mother asked as she pulled me closer to the corner of the foyer and farther from the remarks of these surprisingly unkind men. I nodded that I was and began to continue our conversation about our weekend plans. Since we were facing the corner of the lobby, neither my mother nor I noticed that a man had removed himself from a second group of alumni standing in the foyer until he maneuvered himself into our corner and positioned himself in front of us, with much effort.

"Cadet Peterson, how are you today? Is this your mother?" It was General Goodpaster, the superintendent of the Military Academy!

"Yes, sir," I replied shakily, and made the appropriate introductions. He chatted with us for several minutes, inquiring about our plans for the weekend and telling my mother, in a voice purposefully loud enough for all of the graduates in the foyer to hear, how very proud the Academy was to have such fine young women as her daughter in attendance. "We're really fortunate," he continued. "These young women certainly could've had their pick of any of the finest colleges in the country, yet they chose to come here."

I'll never be able to express my appreciation to him for what he did that afternoon — not only because he subtly reprimanded those graduates, but because he went out of his way to be kind to my mother and to make her feel at ease after a bad experience.

I realize that, as the superintendent, he had to espouse the "party line" whether he agreed with it or not. That was his job. But the person who joined my mother and me in the corner that day was the father, the grandfather, the patriot, the West Point graduate, the gentleman, and the sensitive, caring man inside the green uniform with the stars on the shoulders. At that moment I understood why this respected officer and advisor to presidents on military and world affairs had come out of retirement, where he held the rank of four-star general, and took an active duty position as the three-star general in charge of the Academy. He did it for his beloved West Point, to help it through a difficult transition period filled with "bad press" after the cheating scandal of 1976, and the introduction of women to the Academy during the summer of that same year; and he did it because it was asked of him. Despite his retirement and recuperating health, the leadership of the army (and the country) felt he was the best man — the only man — who could lead the Academy, as well as members of the Long Gray Line who were panicking in all corners of the globe, into the future with confidence. He put the needs of the nation ahead of his own personal desires, just as he learned to do while a cadet at West Point, and earned the respect of presidents during his illustrious career. His wise leadership is responsible for keeping the Academy together during that difficult transition.

Many of the cadets at the Academy during General Goodpaster's tenure felt that they could not relate to him. Actually, they chose not to relate to him because he reminded them of their grandfathers. "He's not 'with it'," I'd hear them say. "He's old. He doesn't understand our needs." At the same time, many of the general officers who were passed over for the position of superintendent in favor of this "old man" wasted no time, after his retirement in 1981, in saying that he had "loved the cadets like a grandfather" instead of "commanding them like a military leader," insinuating that he was too lenient on the Corps. And yet, there existed a third faction who formed opinions about this man: a group comprising cadets, officers, graduates, and statesmen who united to voice unyielding adoration and tremendous respect for a great American.

Generally, cadets have very little opportunity for personal interaction with the superintendent. Truthfully, very few cadets *want* any personal interaction with him! My second "opportunity" to meet the Supe occurred one Saturday afternoon during the latter portion of my plebe year. I was alone in my room when I heard two knocks on the door. Because it was a weekend, and upperclassmen usually did not go out of their way to hassle plebes when they could be enjoying privileges, I was not too worried about the consequences of the two knocks. Still, I stood at attention and voiced, "Enter, sir!" I brought my hand to my forehead and prepared to report as I watched the CQ open the door for an officer.

"Thank you," I heard the Supe remark to the CQ.

"Sir, Cadet Peterson reports!" I heard myself say. I stood at my most perfect attention as he asked about the whereabouts of my roommates and commented about the condition of the room, even noticing that I had shined the brass handles on the windows. Then he authorized me to stand at parade rest while he told me the reason for his visit: Being the Supe gave him a lot of "perks," to include visiting the room he had lived in as a cadet! He told me that, years ago, all of the companies in the Corps (which consisted of only two regiments) were sized according to height. Because he was one of the taller cadets, he was in L2, which, at the time, was assigned to the old barracks near the gym, now known as the "Lost Forties" (43rd through 49th divisions). Suddenly, I was very glad that I had taken the time to clean the soap dish, crease the towel hanging beside the sink, Windex the chrome, Brasso the brass, and wipe the doorsill with Lemon Pledge to give the room a fresh smell when people entered, despite all of the razing I took from my roommates for going "above and beyond." Of course, after they found out about my afternoon visitor, they stopped complaining about my meticulous cleaning.

Except for the few run-ins I had with graduates of the institution, I never felt particularly unwelcome at the Academy during my first year. The seniors could be extremely rude, but firsties (first-class senior cadets) were rude to all plebes, so I didn't feel singled-out because I was female. In fact, my plebe year was the only year in which I did *not* feel like an unwelcome minority, perhaps because I had been too busy to notice.

A typical plebe day begins at about 5:30 A.M. and runs like a freight train until taps (from 11:00 P.M. to midnight — it changed several times during my four years). Of the cadet duties to be performed before breakfast formation, one includes the delivery of a *New York Times* newspaper to every room in the company. In my company one plebe was assigned to deliver the papers to each of the three divisions — five stories of rooms, with four rooms and one bathroom per floor. This was not a very difficult chore on a weekday, but on Sundays, when each newspaper was about two inches thick, I had to make several trips. I'd carry enough papers for one floor, deliver them, then return to the first floor for another load. I'd continue this way until I had delivered to all five floors.

Since most of the upperclassmen remained asleep until the "minute callers" woke them ten minutes before the formation, this duty had to be performed quietly. It was difficult enough to "bounce quickly" up the metal barracks steps, as plebes were required to do, while carrying an armload of heavy newspapers, let alone do it quietly. Somehow I managed to accomplish the entire mission on tip-toe, without evoking the wrath of sleeping seniors. Often, though, I would meet upperclassmen in the dark hallway as they were headed for the latrine. Sometimes these dazed cadets would speak to me as I offered a soft "Good morning, sir" when our paths crossed; sometimes they couldn't be bothered. I simply went about the accomplishment of my assigned task.

Of the three divisions that housed the almost 120 cadets that made up my company, only one carried any special distinction. The 49th Division was still all-male, three years after women had been admitted to the Corps. The men fought to live in that division, proclaimed the "last all-male bastion of the regiment," then strutted like peacocks, proud of this minor coup over Congress and the Academy. And they were not happy when I was inadvertently assigned to deliver papers to that division one week.

I had no idea that there would be a problem of any kind; I'd just deliver the papers as I had delivered them in the other two divisions. What I did not realize was that these men were trying to keep the "old Corps" alive in this division: they all ran around naked! So when I delivered the papers, quietly, and they'd walk out of their rooms to go to the bathroom, they were completely nude. The first time this happened it caught me off guard, but, without breaking stride, I just passed by as if I hadn't noticed a thing. The upperclassman didn't seem bothered by it in the least. He just continued to the latrine as if I didn't exist, not even trying to cover up in any way. I decided that if they were going to be rude enough to just stand there nude, I was certainly not going to offer them a greeting. So I never did, and I never got in trouble for it. The men were just mad that a woman had ruined their comfortable world. After the third morning, enough men were upset enough that they tried to get me removed from delivering newspapers to that division. And they succeeded.

"It's nothing against you, Cadet Peterson," one of the cows told me. They just did not want to change the lifestyle that only they were still perpetuating within the company. And they didn't have to — for the time being. Imagine my surprise when, during my yearling year, my roommate and I were assigned to the 49th Division.

"There must be some mistake," I said to the company commander.

"No mistake," I was told. Our Tac had allowed the 49th Division to exist until the last all-male class left the Academy, almost as a way of apologizing to them for taking away the Academy that they had come to know as plebes. In fact, if you ask a cadet from one of the classes '77 through '82 about his Academy experience, one of the ways in which he will measure success there is in terms of the women: the class that was the toughest on the women, the company that "ran out" the most women, the class that kept the most women from leadership positions, and the all-male platoons to which these men were assigned. For some continuing reason, if it was all-male or anti-female it was better and something of which to be proud. At the time, though, much of this attitude eluded me; I was still striving to survive a very demanding freshman year.

At 6:05, plebes assigned the duties of minute-callers appear in the hallway. "Sir, there are ten minutes before assembly for breakfast formation," they scream into the halls with a chorus that could wake the dead. They announce, as much in unison as possible, the uniform for the formation and the menu for breakfast. Then they disappear into the safety of their rooms, awaiting the calling of their next minute. At five minutes before the formation, the minute-callers return to the hallway. They call minutes at 6:10, 6:11, 6:12, and 6:13. To this last minute, the caller adds an addendum, shouting, "This is the last minute to be called for this formation. Do not forget your lights. Two minutes, sir!" Then the plebe heads outside to take his place in the formation as the company commander calls "Fall in!" and the company is marched to the mess hall. (At West Point, unlike the other service academies, cadets march to every meal.)

Breakfast lasts until about 6:50. Plebes return to their rooms to sweep, dust, and make their beds before leaving for class at 7:15. Cadet rooms are inspected every day prior to lunch. Classes take up the majority of the day, from 7:30 A.M. to 3:20 P.M. (cadets take twenty to twenty-two credit hours per semester and attend classes on Saturday). They then have twenty minutes to return from class and change into appropriate attire for an afternoon sport or parade practice, both of which are usually completed by 5:45, giving the plebe thirty minutes before the evening dinner formation to deliver upper-class laundry or mail, or, one of the duties I was frequently saddled with, running messages and mail to the regimental commander.

This was a miserable duty, the one that plebes dreaded the most. But many plebes transitioned into yearling year never have to perform the duty of regimental runner. There were only four regiments in the Corps and, unless your company had someone on regimental staff, there was no need for a runner to take him his mail and messages, or pick up any distribution he wanted delivered. For the 4th Regiment, however, the commander himself was from my company.

The staff was located on the seventh floor of the last division of our barracks. The runner had to climb the stairs that passed through a different company on the way up to the staff floor. Because the cadets who lived in that company delighted in standing in the hallways, waiting to play games with the plebes (male or female), it often took plebes a full hour to make it up to the staff area, and they had to face these same cadets on the way back down. This situation did not please anyone, because the plebes were late delivering the correspondence and were often late for formation as well. Rather than ask the cadets to lay-off the plebes while they were trying to complete their task, the first sergeant would simply assign only the best cadets to this chore. As a result, the same few of us ended up pulling this duty week after week. Another of my classmates, Cadet Blackwell, and I had a running bet going as to which one of us would have pulled this duty more by the end of our plebe year. Even though we were considered good cadets, it still took us well over thirty minutes to make it there and back.

I didn't mind the cadets of Company H-4 that hazed the plebes along the way as much as I minded actually getting to the seventh floor. It was an all-male floor (no women in the Class of 1979), and I was received in much the same manner that I had been received by the men who lived in the 49th Division of my company. My only saving grace was that the head guy, the regimental commander, was from my company and had checked out my reputation among his classmates in my company. If someone on his staff would persist in hazing me, he'd intercede by saying to his classmate, "C'mon, I need to get that paperwork to the company in a hurry," or "Let her go, I need to talk to you before formation."

This was Leo Brooks, a handsome black cadet who probably should have been the first black brigade commander at West Point (that notoriety went to his younger brother the very next year). Cadet Brooks was intense, articulate, masculine, and very military. He presented me with my award for best cadet in the company. But what I remember most about him was how, when so many of the cadets around him were so vocal about their feelings toward the females, he remained a gentleman. I'm sure that Leo Brooks, like the majority of the men at West Point, was probably not in support of women at his soon-to-be alma mater, but he never showed it. He was fair; I always got the feeling that he didn't care about the sex of the cadet, only that the cadet be good. He'd tear a kid to pieces if he was a lousy cadet, male or female, but there was no reason to haze a good cadet, and he didn't. Not even when I walked in on him while he was undressed.

As I mentioned, the seventh floor was a male domain and thus

men were frequently unclothed. I would knock loudly, using the required two knocks, on the door to the commander's room, which he
shared with the executive officer. Upon hearing a casual "Come on in,"
I'd open the door and step into the room, finding Cadet Brooks in his
underwear, startled. Without hesitation I'd step back out of the door
and stand, with my nose pressed against the door, in the hallway,
awaiting further instructions. Sometimes the cadets in the hall would
yell at me for just standing there, and other times Leo's roommate
would yell at me for a few minutes to occupy my time until Cadet
Brooks was dressed enough to receive me again. But always, Cadet
Brooks would make it a point to stop by my company formation before
taking his place in front of the regiment and apologize for putting me
in that situation. "Miss Peterson, that was not your fault," he'd say,
even though his classmates tore me apart as if it had been. "It's just
that I'm not accustomed to women showing up on the seventh floor —
you're the first one — and I never consider that it could be a woman
when I hear the knocks. I need to get used to that. I'm sorry for placing you in such an embarrassing situation." He didn't have to offer me
an explanation, or an apology. He'd been through three and a half years
of this place and I was barely getting started, and he owed me nothing.

After the third occurrence of this nature, Cadet Brooks added,
"This won't happen again." And it didn't. It's a good thing too, because one evening when I was making my delivery I saw a female officer, on duty as the officer-in-charge, walking around on the seventh
floor. The embarrassment he felt when he allowed me to walk in on
him would have been nothing compared to the harassment he would
have received had he allowed her to find him less than properly
dressed! I had great respect for Cadet Brooks; I admired the fact that he
could be an outstanding cadet as well as a gentleman.

At 6:15 P.M. the minute-callers began announcing minutes and
menus for the dinner formation and meal. All other plebes had to be at
the formation early to be quizzed on their knowledge by a group of
yearlings known as "plebe chasers." This duty was created as more of
an attempt to get the yearlings involved with the fourth-class system
than to hassle plebes. After all, plebes were hassled and quizzed even
more when they were standing in formation and were fair game for any
upperclassman.

Dinner was usually over for all four classes by 7:00 P.M. Plebes
hurried back to their companies to finish plebe duties before call-to-
quarters, when academic study time would prevail until taps. As soon

as the plebes hit the company, however, the seniors, feeling content after a good dinner, were just waiting for the opportunity to play with plebes before academic limits took effect. We'd be lined up, down the stairs, out the door, and around the corner as a group of cadets, usually seniors, had their fun with us. I worked hard to earn a reputation as a good cadet, not an easy feat as a female being judged primarily by the last all-male class. Unfortunately, the seniors, in an attempt to reward good performance, made some of our classmates mad at us. When the company commander, and president of the Class of 1979, Cadet Jim McGorry, saw me in line at the bottom of the stairs, he'd yell, "Miss Peterson, post!" which meant get up there immediately. I'd step out of line and hop up the stairs until I was standing in front of him on the landing.

"Miss Peterson, are you staying straight?" he'd ask me.

"Yes, sir!" I'd reply.

He'd smile and cock his head in the direction of my room, saying, "Get out of here," allowing me to return to my room and leaving my classmates standing on the stairs. This didn't happen every time, but it happened enough to upset some of my classmates. It never dawned on them that, while they were standing in line on the stairs, I was performing plebe duties which they were unable to assist me with. As the firsties let plebes go, those plebes would begin helping with the plebe duties so that, by the time the plebes at the end of the line were dismissed, the duties were done. It's called "cooperate and graduate," a theme heard repeatedly throughout plebe year.

There was a trick to performing some of these plebe duties. Besides trying to get the duties accomplished, it was also necessary for plebes to be noticed in a positive manner. Though this would not assure good ratings by the upperclassmen, it would guarantee that a plebe would not receive poor ratings from them. The easiest way to be noticed while performing these duties was to look different from your classmates. Most plebes carried one or two bundles of laundry at a time, delivered them, then returned for more. Not only did this create extra effort, running up and down the stairs, but the plebe looked like all the other plebes. I was only 5'4" tall and weighed 115 pounds, but I carried three or four bundles of laundry at a time, and I tried to deliver them to different people each time. Too many plebes were afraid to deliver laundry to upperclassmen in other divisions and, therefore, never became known by any other upperclassmen than by the ones in their own division (only one-third of the company). Of course, you had to be extremely "squared away" if you were going to be noticed like this. Once you were noticed, either for carrying extra laundry or for visiting an unfamiliar division, you opened yourself up for criticism and those guys would rip you apart if you weren't squared away.

Most plebes chose to play it safe by not calling attention to themselves. You could be a mediocre cadet and still graduate, but your chances of participating in the running of the Corps as a senior were slim. As a female, it was pretty difficult at that time *not* to be the focus of some sort of attention, so it may as well have been the positive kind. Besides, I loved West Point and believed that, by being the best I could be, I would never let down the reputation of the Long Gray Line.


I had analyzed West Point at the end of the first day of Beast and determined that it would not be difficult to be a good cadet; I would simply be a good actress. And that's what I did. Throughout junior high and high school I had been extensively involved in fine arts, winning dramatic and UIL awards including Ready Writing, Poetry Interpretation, and One-Act Play honors, and was also a member of the Thespians. I had been performing in plays and dance productions, including community theater, since I was seven years old. I was a good actress and, as such, I knew I could be a good cadet. After all, West Point had given me a detailed outline of exactly what characteristics it required in a cadet and provided me, almost immediately, with a personification of those characteristics in a larger-than-life role model, Tony Cuccolo. All I had to do was follow the script and accept a role that all actresses dream of, a role I strongly believed in.

For me that was the key: I actually believed in what I was doing. No one had to remind me to clean the soap dish during my plebe year, even though most of the inspectors stopped inspecting them after Beast Barracks. I believed that West Point had good reasons for every rule it made, and if I was going to be a good cadet I was going to follow *all* of the rules, not just the ones they checked up on. This is what's referred to by the cadets as "being gray," not always meant to be flattering. It was good to pal around with someone who was "gray" because the association looked good, but having that person as a roommate was not easy. It was difficult to shine in that person's shadow, and difficult to place a hundred percent of your trust in that person. This second difficulty bothered me.

I never even suggested that my roommates or friends adopt as strictly as I had the rules or ideals of West Point. I've always said that I have to be true to myself and do what feels right to me. I respect anyone else's right to do what feels right to them, and I don't criticize; I only ask the right to be allowed to do "my thing" with the same respect. I would never have turned in a friend or roommate for breaking the rules, and anyone who knew me knew that and trusted me with their most intimate secrets. Still, they didn't trust me with *all* of their secrets.

For instance, after a company party during first semester of our plebe year, the male upperclassmen asked my roommates to keep a six-pack of beer from the party in our bathroom. The male officers rarely ever checked the women's latrine, and would certainly never expect plebes to have the guts to sneak alcohol into the barracks. So, when I found the beer and went, shocked, to tell my roommates about it, I was equally shocked to find that they already knew! Why hadn't they told me? They were afraid I'd snitch. Now that would have been interesting. Who would I have snitched to? Our squad leader, of course. And it was his beer! It was convenient having female plebes in his squad.

At first I felt hurt that my roommates didn't seem to believe that I would never betray them. Then my roommate Debbie put me at ease when she said, "It's not trust, Donna. It's just that you really believe in this stuff, and you're going to go places in this man's army. If someone found the beer and asked Karen or I about it, we'd be punished. We'd walk a few hours on the area and we'd still graduate from this place. It wouldn't be a big deal to us. But to you . . . you'd be devastated, seeing the hard work you've done be blemished. This way, what you don't know, you can't be hurt by. You had no idea the beer was there. You're safe." Debbie had more common sense than any other female in the company. So, my roommates sheltered me from possible regs violations, and I cleaned their soap dishes. Cooperate and graduate.

Debbie also had guts. She was only about 5'2" and weighed 105 pounds dripping wet, but she could do more pull-ups (during the weekly pull-up survey for plebes) than any other female I knew in the Corps. And she was not afraid to take chances. I never felt it took an extreme amount of guts to follow the rules, but it did take a great many to break them.

One of the ways in which West Point makes plebes suffer is by depriving them of all music and radio during the first six months and television during the first year. By the time Christmas break rolls around, plebes would pay one hundred dollars to hear just the chorus of a song on the radio. My mother sent me a small battery-operated tape deck and some of my cassettes just a few weeks before the Christmas break, so that I could listen to them on the plane during the trip home. Debbie had a huge portable stereo sent to her early in the semester. She kept it locked in her trunk during the day but listened to it at night, after taps, through headphones. Since no upperclassmen were allowed in a plebe's room after taps — one of the protections of the fourth-class system — there was no danger of her getting caught unless the Tac decided to inspect her footlocker someday. Occasionally, she'd let Karen or I listen to a song or two. In this case, the risk was definitely worth taking. Six months without radio or TV is extremely difficult for young people who are products of the age of technology.

To this day, whenever I hear a song from Billy Joel's *Stranger* album or Meatloaf's *Bat Out of Hell* — two Top 40 albums on the market that Christmas — I'm filled with a strange inner peace, probably because these albums signified my return to a world filled with music.

After Christmas, plebes were allowed to have stereos, one per room, so you had to learn to share. Having done without for so long, sharing was not a problem. Besides, with headphones, one person could be listening to the radio and the other could be plugged directly into the tape deck and be listening to a cassette. The only problem my roommate and I encountered was due to my occasional vociferousness. I'd be singing along with the tape or radio, headphones on my ears and oblivious to the world around me, when my roommate would grab my shoulders from behind to bring me back to reality. There is nothing quite so frightening as the snarling, dripping fangs and flesh-digging claws of a roommate awakened from a precious afternoon nap by off-key singing. Other than that, the system worked pretty well.

The different degrees of compliance with the fourth-class system felt by my roommates and me didn't seem to pose a problem. Generally, cadets only received demerits for their own faults or failings. But that was not the case on the day I was to receive my first company Best Cadet award.

All three of us had a class at 11:00. I was the first to return to our room prior to the lunch formation. When I got to the room on this particular day, it was a shambles! Dresser drawers had been removed from the cabinet, their contents strewn about the floor and left on top of the dresser. I quickly checked the inspection card we kept posted on the wall. Each day when the inspecting cadets came by they would list any deficiencies beside the name of the cadet. I only had time to check beside my own name. My squad leader had written "wrinkle in green girl" (green girl was the endearing nickname for the extra blanket that cadets kept at the foot of their beds). I looked at my blanket. It had a small wrinkle, hardly enough to rip a room apart for. Just then I heard a loud ruckus and my two roommates came scurrying into the room.

"What happened here?" I asked them.

"Hell if I know," Debbie said. "But Belcher [the executive officer] wants us downstairs ASAP!"

Just then I heard the XO yell, "Libbey, Sheets, Peterson get down here, now!"

I quickly changed into my best-shined shoes, we gave each other quick dress-offs, then we headed downstairs, with me in the lead. When we got to his room, which he shared with the company commander, the XO was still screaming. He had us line up against his locker and ordered us to begin reciting knowledge. He kept repeating, "I can't hear you," until we were screaming plebe knowledge at the tops of our lungs. Then he stood nose to nose with each of us while we were still reciting and told us how ugly we were and how he couldn't stand to look at our disgusting faces and ordered us to turn around and face his locker. A crowd was growing outside of the XO's room as well as inside. The place was packed!

In the short time I had been at the Academy I had never seen this type of a display or heard this much commotion. And I wasn't even sure why it was happening. The fourth-class systems officer, who was in charge of seeing that the rights of freshmen according to the system were not violated, saw me standing in the lineup and told me to turn around and stop reciting.

"Cadet Peterson, I'm surprised to see you here. What's this all about?" he asked me calmly.

"Sir, I do not know," I replied. He was visibly surprised.

"Come on, Miss Peterson. Cadet Belcher makes this much of a public spectacle of you and your roommates, and you have absolutely no idea at all?"

"Yes, sir," was the only honest answer.

"Well, just think for a minute. Why do you possibly think you could be here?" He was asking me these things because Cadet Belcher was too busy making himself hoarse to talk to him.

"Sir, the inspection card said I had a wrinkle in my green girl," I told him seriously. I'm sure it sounded funny because he snickered before he regained his composure. Just then the company commander walked in. The fourth-class systems officer went over to talk to him, but he brushed past and moved to stand directly in front of me.

"Miss Peterson, what's going on here?" His voice was filled with confusion as well as concern. Before I had a chance to answer, the fourth-class systems officer took him aside. Then the two of them, accompanied by the XO, stepped into the hallway, where the three of us could not hear their conversation. The CO ordered us to stop reciting on his way out. After about a minute, the CO asked me to step into the hallway with him. As I stood at attention in the hallway, I could hear the minute-callers announcing two minutes before formation. The formation was to be held early today, due to the award ceremony.

"Miss Peterson, I'm sorry you got caught up in this," he began. Then he mentioned something about some messy drawers and a calculator that had been hidden in a drawer rather than locked up. "There is such a thing as guilt-by-association, and that's what you are a victim of. You're only guilty of being the third person in the room, but because of the commotion and the public display that the XO made out of this episode, there is no way that I can let you stand out there and accept your award. There isn't enough time to explain to the upperclassmen that it was a mistake, that you hadn't done anything wrong. I'm sorry. Perhaps you can try for the award again next month."

So, that was the end of it. Guilt-by-association. Those words still ring in my ears. But I was surprised that I wasn't overly upset. I actually felt sorry for the CO, because I didn't think he liked taking the award away from a cadet, but I understood why he had to. In the Cadet Prayer there is a line that states, "Make us to choose the harder right instead of the easier wrong." What Cadet McGorry did that day was the best solution for all concerned, including me, though it took me a few days to forgive my roommates for it.

One of the most interesting things that happened to me during plebe year was being asked to assist with the making of the movie *Women at West Point,* which was filmed that year.

I received a phone call in the company orderly room one morning. It was one of the women in the Class of 1980 whom I'd met on my prospective candidate visit. She asked me to meet her at the front entrance to the gym that afternoon. Linda Purl, the actress starring in the film, and several officers from the Public Affairs Office were with her. The female cadet made the introductions. It seemed that the actress wanted to talk to a plebe, to better understand her role.

"Could we go someplace and talk?" the petite blond asked me. She was a doll. I remembered her from "The Young Pioneers" on television. She had already cut her hair in preparation for her role as a cadet.

We sat on some bleachers in one of the dozen gyms of the gymnasium complex while she asked me how I felt in many of the situations I faced as a new cadet and as a plebe. We spoke for about an hour. As she rose to leave, she smiled and thanked me, her tiny button nose wiggling cutely as she spoke. "Thanks so much. You've really been a great help."

Though I was preoccupied with Linda Purl, most of the other females spent their time stalking Andrew Stevens, who played one of the male leads. The male cadets were enthralled by the visit to the Academy from Stevens' wife Kate Jackson (one of "Charlie's Angels"), who ate dinner with the Corps. They were rumored to be very disappointed, however, by the time she left. Apparently, she stuck to her husband like glue. In order for the cadets to get a glimpse of her, they had to get near him, and she forbade it, to the point of angrily throwing the cadets out of the barber shop when they came to see him get a military haircut. She was only at the Academy for a few days, but during that time I saw eager anticipation turn to bitter disillusionment. This was no angel.

Actually, the movie disrupted very little at the Academy, probably because cadets are used to seeing celebrities and VIPs and having a great deal of media interest focused on them. Even the huge recreational vehicles which served the stars' dressing rooms caused little commotion after the first day.

Before the movie premiered to the public, cadets were offered a private showing in the West Point theater. Most cadets agreed that the movie was disappointing. The cadets were portrayed as silly and eager for a good time, and the entire basis for the movie was the blatant fraternization of a plebe female with an upper-class cadet, to include clandestined meetings in the remote "stacks" of the library, and weekends taken together away from the Academy grounds.

I won't say that those things don't go on, but they are a very small part of cadet life, especially as a plebe — and particularly as one of the first women to attend West Point, which she was supposed to be. That first class was so closely scrutinized that they used to make jokes about the men clocking the amount of time they spent in the bathroom! And plebes are *very* scared young people; they walk around that way, they live that way, they look that way. No one in the movie was really scared. This movie definitely did not enhance the image of West Point the way that *Top Gun* elevated the U.S. Navy. But at least it wasn't another attempt to cast a completely negative light on the Academy, as most media attention about the institution seems to do.


It's impossible to present a picture of life as a plebe without attempting to explain life inside of the cadet mess hall, rarely seen by anyone outside of the cadet corps. On R-Day, parents are treated to a glimpse inside the cavernous six-wing building which sports several wall-sized murals, fraying state and military flags, carved statues, and a two-story stone archway and "poop deck" from which visitors are presented and make their speeches to the Corps. (General MacArthur's famous "Duty, Honor, Country" speech was made to the cadet corps from this perch.) Over the entry doors is a huge stained-glass mural depicting the life of George Washington.

What parents are not treated to is the most remarkable attraction of all: 4,400 cadets being fed, family-style, at one sitting, within forty-five minutes. They are seated at rectangular ten-man tables, each equipped with the same set-up: ten each of dinner plates, bowls or small plates for salad or dessert, tumblers, and silverware; salt, pepper, sugar, ketchup, peanut butter; water pitcher, large beverage pitcher, and ten pint-sized cartons of milk.

After the cadets are ordered to "take seats" by the corps adjutant, all thirty-six company mottos echo through the mess hall, spouted by the three plebes assigned to each table. Then the Corps sits down, in unison, and a contingent of mess hall workers pulls the hot food from heated "waiters' carts," centrally located in each wing, and places it on each of the more than 400 tables. Again commensurate with the purpose of plebe training, the plebes have duties to perform. The "gunner" is responsible for ensuring that the table is properly equipped, as stated above; the "cold beverage corporal" is responsible for memorizing the cold beverage preferences of all of the upperclassmen at the table; and the "hot beverage corporal" is responsible for knowing the hot beverage choices of all of the cadets at the table. The gunner has the most dreaded job: he must cut the dessert into the exact number of pieces desired by the cadets at the table, and each piece must be exactly equal. The dessert, after it is cut, is always sent to the cadet at the head of the table for inspection. Rarely is a dessert perfectly cut. (However, MaryAnn once cut a pie into eleven pieces, though there are never more than ten cadets at a table, and the head cadet never even caught the snafu! "A perfect job, Miss Bates," he decreed, and proceeded to show it off around the mess hall!)

There are elaborate procedures to follow and sayings to memorize to enable plebes to successfully complete their table duties and be allowed to eat, all of which are detailed in the *Fourth Class System Manual*. Throughout the meal each plebe must sit erect with his head up and his chin pulled in, his spine exactly the length of one fist from the back of the straight wooden chairs. The plebe must confine his eyes to the area of the table only, except when addressing another cadet, at which time the plebe must look the cadet directly in the eye. The only hazard about being regulated into this position, however, is that it is often very difficult to see what's happening on your plate. As a result, I never ate peas, at least not after the first time I caused all table activity to cease by dropping peas off my fork and down into the front of my shirt. There is absolutely no dignified way to recover from this situation. All you can do is hope that, since peas don't make any noise when they fall off a fork, none of the upperclassmen notice. It would have worked that way, except, when no one noticed, I got nervous and giggled. Then I had to explain myself, and none of the plebes could eat while I was being yelled at. I never again ate peas while I was a plebe.

Table regulations are numerous and often quite minute in detail. There is no talking, except as regulated by the manual. No more than two or three bites of food may be cut at one time, bites must be kept small, and silverware must be placed on the side of the plate and hands placed in the plebe's lap before he can begin chewing his food. He must wipe his mouth with his napkin before taking a drink from his beverage glass. Drinks must not turn into gulps, though several drinks may be taken if the hands are returned to the lap in between each. And the plebe must not drop his napkin. There is no way to make it through a meal without one, and no way to pick it up without breaking the regulated posture. Therefore, you must ask permission from the senior cadet at the head of the table, the "table commandant," to retrieve your napkin. Usually this cadet will turn the situation into a media event by making the plebe put ketchup bottles on his eyes to "search" for the napkin as if using the periscope on a submarine. When the napkin is located the plebe asks for "permission to dive" and, upon receiving same, makes loud piercing submarine sounds like those in the movies, *Waah, waah, waah, dive, dive, dive,* then picks up his napkin and returns it to his lap. Of course, until this scenario is completed, the plebes must stop eating; either all eat or none eat.

A favorite trick of the upper-class cadets is to prevent plebes from eating by keeping them constantly busy with table duties. Since plebes also have to take all dirty dishes to the waiters' carts, cadets pass their plates to the plebes one at a time, rather than several at once, to keep the plebes busy — and hungry. This situation is usually the exception rather than the rule, with much less of it occurring since women have been in attendance at the Academy. With all of the media attention focused on the Academy with the introduction of women to the Corps, public opinion would not support mass deprivation of meals, which is rumored to have existed at one time, especially among the members of the hockey team. For some reason this group of cadets, who generally hailed from the Boston area, were particularly picked on in an attempt to run them out. "If it wasn't for toothpaste," one hockey recruit told me, "I would've starved during Beast!"

Of course, during the academic year, plebes are free to purchase and eat any amount of food they wish on the weekends, as long as it is gone by academic limits on Sunday. Cadets can purchase food from the post exchange (PX), the deli at the PX, the cadet "Boodlers" located above the barracks area near the cadet radio station, or the on-post pizza parlor located in the basement of the building which houses the cadet bank and the cadet honor boards. Tony's pizza was the finest pizza I had ever eaten, and there was nothing like their calzones, loaf-like hunks of bread filled with cheese, spices, and meats. The Old World Italian family of uncles, cousins, and nephews who owned and operated Tony's were good to the cadets. They had a contract with West Point which ensured that a certain quality, variety, and price would be offered to the cadets. But they offered so much more. If you didn't have the money, "Fat Sal" would hand you the pizza and wave you away, saying, "You pay me next week." He never even recorded the name; he just trusted that we'd do the right thing. If the food was a little too well done, they would give you two of what you ordered, saying, "I didn't like the way the first one looked." And, if a cadet's check bounced, which happened occasionally and carried a huge punishment from the Academy with it, the family would just hold the checks until the cadet came in to pick it up, never notifying anyone or even calling the cadet. As taps approached, Tony's continued to cook food orders. I recall running, pizza in one hand, soft drinks in the other, across the area and through the barber shop tunnel en route to my barracks in North Area while taps was playing over the loudspeaker. At taps, any extra pizzas were given to the cadets who manned the Central Guard Room on twenty-four-hour guard, free of charge.

Unfortunately, Tony's lost its contract during my senior year based on a recommendation from several of my classmates to give someone else a try. It was such a huge mistake. The pizza was not nearly the quality, the selection was poorer, and the price was basically the same. Worst of all, they stopped cooking at a quarter to taps ("You shouldn't be here at this time, anyway," the man behind the counter told me), and gave the cadets one chance to pay before they notified someone in authority about a bad debt ("Cadets aren't supposed to bounce checks," they told a friend of mine when they called him about a check).

When Tony's Pizza lost the contract in 1981, the greatest loss was in the way they had treated the cadets. The family at Tony's had been outside the gate for years, watching generations of West Pointers grow up and graduate, and they had a deep respect for the process.

Once the first semester of plebe year is over there is little need to purchase food elsewhere. By then, plebes are comfortable enough with the mess hall routine that they have ample time to eat, and the food is some of the finest found in any military service. If anything, there is too much of it: three full meals per day with menus that include eggs, waffles, pasta, steaks, seafood, chicken, roast, plenty of carbohydrates and vegetables, breads and rolls, fruit drinks, and desserts specially baked in the ovens below the mess hall. Well over 4,000 calories per day was available to each cadet, every day. This overabundance of delicious food had created a condition, not so prevalent today, known as "Hudson Hip Disease." This term was used to categorize the weight gain of the women in the first several classes, mine included. I would hear the men bragging about their weight gain: "I have to buy pants four inches too large in the waist just so that the legs fit over my thighs." Yet, when females record the same type of weight gain, with thighs in exaggerated proportion to the rest of their body, they have a problem to be ashamed of and ridiculed for. The men were extremely cruel on this score.

In 1980, as problems developed and women began to speak out in their own behalf, meals in the cadet mess hall began to change. Water or unsweetened iced tea was made available at all meals. A tray of salad was pre-set on each table as an alternative to the heavy main menu, with low-calorie salad dressings also being provided. The young, enthusiastic female dietician for the mess hall began growing sprouts to add to the salads. Tables were designated in a separate section of the mess hall to receive half of the standard amount of the average cadet meal, with salad and lo-cal or diet drinks, and fresh fruit rather than dessert to round out the meal. Cadets, male and female, with weight problems were required to sit at these tables; others could request a seat. By the time I graduated in 1982, all tables offered salad, water or tea, and fresh fruit, in an attempt to offer an alternative to the traditional high-calorie meals without having to remove a cadet from his or her company tables. In contrast to attempting to lower the caloric intake of many cadets, several sports teams requested additional food. These included teams such as the football, baseball, and basketball teams and the weight-lifting team.

In addition to these normal menus, several menus during the year — Thanksgiving, pre-Christmas, Thayer Award dinner, dining-ins — are elaborate feasts which feature lobster, shrimp, filet mignon, or crab. Cadets eat well, and the Academy does everything in its power to accommodate all cadets where mealtime requirements are concerned.


The Academy tries to provide the cadets with the very best of everything, from the food in the mess hall, to the quality and extent of the military training, to the opportunities for recreation. Cadets are offered gourmet cooking classes, ballroom dancing lessons, concerts by top pop and rock bands and classical and jazz performers, and road shows of original Broadway productions. When senior cadets order their army uniforms, the Academy brings in Haas uniform service to provide custom-tailored uniforms to those cadets desiring them. "You are the country's brightest and best," we are told. West Point takes these diamonds-in-the-rough and polishes them to exquisite brilliance, at great expense. Given all this, I never thought those at the Academy would let us get hurt. But they do.

So many cadets are hurt, either during summer military training or during athletic participation during the academic year, that the orthopedic surgery clinic at Keller Army Hospital is one of the finest in the military. It is not unusual to see a large number of cadets transporting themselves around the grounds on crutches or walking casts, or wearing special wooden shoes due to injuries. The pink scar created by knee surgery is seen frequently when cadets don athletic shorts.

I suppose that all of the injuries can be attributed to the fact that the military is a rough life, not for the weak of spirit nor weak of form. West Point, in an attempt to prepare officers for this life, does not coddle the cadets. The training is extremely realistic, physically demanding, and dangerous. Though many cadets have been injured by the training, I am aware of only one cadet who died because of it, from an injury sustained after a boxing match (all male cadets are required to take classes in boxing and wrestling, while women take courses in self-defense). Other cadets have died, usually as a result of automobile accidents while they are away from West Point, on passes or on leave, and the effect is as devastating as the loss of a police officer to a community.

The first time I realized that cadets could be seriously hurt was when the Academy towed the smashed skeleton of a firstie's brand new Corvette into the cadet area as a lesson to cadets that "speed kills." The owner of the car had been a cadre member in my Beast company and, miraculously, he lived, though the cadets said prayers for several weeks for him to come out of his coma and return to the Corps. Eventually, he recovered.

Later that year, I attended what most cadets agreed was an overwhelming and unforgettable ceremony. An announcement was made prior to taps one evening that all cadets were invited to a memorial for a cadet who had died in an automobile accident. Interested cadets were to assemble on the apron of the Plain after taps. All lights in the barracks would be turned off until after the ceremony. I didn't know the cadet, but I felt compelled to attend. He was a part of us; the 4,400 of us *were* the Academy.

All of the lights went out across the Corps as my roommates and I walked solemnly out to the Plain. I have never seen anything as hollow and ghostlike as the Corps in complete darkness. The majority of cadets were in attendance, but I wouldn't have resented those who chose not to come. It is an emotionally ripping ceremony. We gathered there, huddling near the great stone statue of George Washington, watching thousands of cadets filter slowly through the gray stone archways toward the edge of the Plain. This was not a parade, no one marched or moved in unison. No one spoke. After a moment a lone bugler played taps to our fallen comrade from a station high above us, at the Cadet Chapel overlooking the barracks. The notes fell around us and there was an eerie sense that all the ghosts who connect the living to the past were standing with us. As the notes faded, we were left standing in a silence more terrifying than the first; it was as if a piece of our souls has been torn from us. Not a word was spoken as the cadets returned to the barracks.

That night my roommate and I went to bed without turning the lights on again, remaining in that darkened state until morning. I remember thinking that, standing on the Plain that evening, I had my first real sense of what being a part of the Long Gray Line was all about. I felt connected to men I'd never known — generations of them.

Unfortunately, I had three more occasions to attend identical ceremonies during my next three years, one of which was a double memorial to two classmates, both of whom I knew well. I hated those vigils, for all the tragedy they represented, but I always attended to say goodbye.

Sometime around the beginning of the year, all plebes had been required to sing a few bars of "My Country 'Tis of Thee" during mandatory choir tryouts. As a result, I was asked to join the Cadet Chapel Choir. I was flattered, but I declined the offer. I had to be realistic. This offer did not signify that I was a good singer; rather, it seemed to indicate that my class had a bad batch of singers in it that year and I was one of the best of the worst. It was through that audition, however, that I was able to try out for a position in a mixed ensemble that performed with the world-renowned Cadet Glee Club. This group was great fun. Basically, the eight of us, four men and four women, sang and danced to selections from the musical production "Grease." We even toured with the Glee Club occasionally.

I can still remember pulling into a college town in upper New York state and waiting at a church for the townspeople, whose homes we would be staying at overnight after the concert, to greet us.

"Oh, I suppose so," I heard one woman comment as the chairman of the event pulled me near her. "My husband and I wanted a real cadet — you know, a boy — but I guess we'll take her," she said as I stood beside her, my arms laden with my luggage and dance outfits. But I was too excited about the performance to let her disappointment at being saddled with me ruin the event. After the performance she and her husband took my roommate and me to her home (she wanted one boy and ended up with two girls). We settled in to the rooms she had prepared for us then headed toward the living room, where she had invited us for tea and cookies. This was Friday night and we were plebes, away from the Academy on a rare excursion. Yet, here we sat, eating three (that's all we were offered) homemade gingersnap cookies, drinking Earl Grey tea, and answering questions about "how it feels to be a woman at West Point." I could just imagine all of the fun the male cadets were having. Leslie and I finally excused ourselves to go to bed around 11:00 P.M.

The next day we didn't have to imagine what the guys' Friday nights had been like. We had to close our ears to keep from hearing the recanted stories.

"We barely got in the door before the husband threw us his car keys, handed us each twenty bucks, his daughter and her girlfriend, and said, 'Have a good time!' It was great!" two of the Glee Club cadets kept repeating.

Then two other cadets who shared the same residence the evening before joined in: "This guy pulled a fifty-dollar bill from his pocket, handed us the keys to his Jaguar, along with written directions to two of the hottest clubs in the area, and told us not to wake him when we got in!" Why didn't these things happen to us?

"Sure," Leslie said. "Some guy is gonna hand us his sports car and his son, right? These guys probably gave their sons the Porsche and twenty bucks and told them to 'get out of the area because two female cadets are coming over.' We're probably lucky to get little old ladies who want us to sip tea with them."

Given the uniqueness of our situation and the images people fabricated in their minds of "any woman who would go to West Point," I was certain that she was right.

The next stop on our tour wasn't any more thrilling than the last, but at least the people I stayed with *wanted* a female cadet. I was told they specifically asked for one. Now I felt like a sideshow attraction at a carnival. Actually, these people were lovely to me. They gave me their daughter's room (she was away at college) and fed me a fabulous meal before they began their questions about the Academy.

I was used to it by now. Even when I walked around the Academy, especially when I wore my skirt on the weekends, tourists would ask me to stop so that they could take pictures of me and, as is usually the case, they would ask if they could take a picture *with* me. I've mugged for the camera with a group of Korean businessmen, elementary school students on a field trip, and each and every member of a retired military organization attending a fall football game (about twenty of them in all). I've been walking down the road and had cars screech to a halt as the passengers literally ran me down to pose with them for pictures. Dave said it was "embarrassing" the number of times tourists stopped me for picture-taking. It was so bad on weekends that he hated to walk anyplace with me. He'd usually ask me to meet him wherever we were going, so that he wouldn't have to put up with the tourists. I usually complied, but I wished he would have handled it better.

On one occasion, my parents were visiting me and as we walked into an academic building one Saturday, a woman walked out, threw her arms around me, and said, "We're so proud of you!" She was smiling at my parents as she did this, so I assumed she knew them. After my folks and I got into the building, my mother said to me, very matter-of-factly, "Who was that woman?"

"I thought you knew her!" I said, astonished. "I've never seen her before in my life." We laughed about this incident the rest of the weekend. I always figured that this "went along with the job," so to speak, as do the myriad questions I'm constantly faced with. And I really don't mind; I enjoy interacting with people.

My most vivid memory of my association with the Glee Club was the trip the plebe group members made en route to our final performance. At the end of every academic year, during graduation week, the Glee Club performs for graduates and their guests one evening in Eisenhower Hall. Also during that week, the plebes are relocated to Camp Buckner, about ten miles from the West Point garrison, to receive initial orientations about the training they will receive during their first summer as upperclassmen. In order for the four or five plebe members of our group to attend the performance, we had to be trucked from Camp Buckner to West Point and back. The trip, in the back of a canvas-covered 2½-ton army truck, was bumpy and cool, but none of us seemed to mind. Graduation was in two days, and for us that meant "recognition," the jump to upper-class status, and going home.

On the return trip someone began singing: "All my bags are packed, I'm ready to go" and we all joined in, harmonizing impromptu to "Leavin' on a Jet Plane," and rewriting many of the lyrics as we sang. "I'm leaving on a jet plane, don't care if I come back again.

Oh, babe, it's great to go!" . . . "When I come back, I'll wear that yearling brass!"

We sang that song every meter of the trip. It was great to think that the year was almost over for us. Soon we would all converge at the New York airports, en route to home.

The next day the plebes returned to West Point to participate in the graduation parade and recognition ceremonies. After the parade, the plebes were lined up near their company areas. The upper-class cadets then filtered through the lines and "recognized" us, usually by extending the traditional handshake. In addition to the handshake, another West Point tradition is the permanent scarring of the highly polished brass breast plate worn with the parade uniform. To accomplish this, the upper-class cadet uses the tip of a bayonet or the endsight of the parade rifle to scratch his name in the brass. The plebe can then save his brass for posterity.

That night the graduating seniors have a dinner and dance; their cars are already positioned in the areas near their companies for rapid exits after graduation the next day. The newly recognized plebes sleep on bare mattresses that night, all their bedding having been sent to Camp Buckner to await their return in three weeks.

The next morning the plebes dress and attend breakfast. For the first time, plebes do not have to operate like mummies or maneuver around like wind-up toys. The formation is relaxed, the meal easy to digest. Then the company, minus the seniors, assembles for the march to the stadium, where they share in the send-off of another graduating class.

As we ascended the hill on the way to the stadium, I felt a strange mixture of emotions. I was overjoyed by the thoughts of becoming an upperclassman and of seeing my first West Point graduation, but I wondered what life would be like at the Academy without the guidance of the Class of 1979. As I thought of the many men and women who had shaped my career thus far, I saw Cadet Cuccolo walk past my company, up the steep hill, en route to his graduation. I was certain that this would be the last time I would ever see him, and I just couldn't let him pass by without saying something to him.

"Run with the Pack, sir!" I shouted nervously. My heart was in my throat. Cadet Cuccolo, who was obviously in a rush, slowed his pace and looked toward my group. He saw me and smiled, but continued to walk on ahead. Suddenly, he turned and walked back to my company, which was still marching toward the stadium, and worked his way through the formation until he was marching beside me in the group. He took the white glove off of his right hand and offered it to me, saying, "Donna, isn't it?"

I shook his hand and nodded affirmatively as he said, "Tony," and I repeated, "Tony."

"Good luck in your future career," he said, while continuing to grip my hand. "I know you'll do great."

I smiled and said, "Thanks, and congratulations . . . Tony." Then he stepped out of the formation and I watched him walk out of my life. If I could have been granted any wish at that moment, I would have wished to make that walk arm-in-arm with him, a man who made my heart skip a beat every time he looked at me.

The graduation ceremony was impressive, just as I imagined it would be. I clapped and yelled loudly for Leo Brooks, Jim McGorry and, of course, Tony Cuccolo, but I don't remember much more than that. My mind was miles away from the stadium that morning. It was on a plane bound for Houston, Texas.

After the graduation, I hurried back down the hill, taking the shortcut through the woods behind the barracks, to my company. I changed into civilian clothes (no blue jeans allowed), added my uniform to my already packed suitcase, and headed for one of the twenty buses parked near the Plain that would transport the Corps to area airports for the long-awaited trip home.

As I settled into a seat on the bus, I put behind me my plebe year, Beast, Tony, and all the associated memories of the past eleven months. I was thinking of only one thing now: summer fun! After all, I think I earned it.

# CHAPTER 4

# Camp Buckner

*"The Long Gray Line has never failed us {the nation}. Were you
to do so, a million ghosts in olive drab, in brown khaki, in blue
and gray, would rise from their white crosses thundering those
magic words — Duty-Honor-Country."*

— Gen. Douglas MacArthur, address
to the Corps of Cadets, 1962

C amp Buckner was the most physically demanding experience of
my life. That summer had been specifically designed by the Academy to incorporate the most extensive array of tactical military training offered in any officer training program with leadership developing
exercises, while building class esprit for the yearlings, who were operating as upperclassmen for the first time.

This "camp" offered more than creature comforts. To begin with,
cadets were housed in metal buildings rather than the pup tents we had
utilized during Beast Barracks field training. For the first time since
women were admitted to the Academy, the women were housed in a
small section of each platoon building, separated from the main section
only by two thin metal walls. The first two classes of women had been
removed completely from their respective platoons, being housed col-
lectively in one separate building, which resulted in significantly re-

95

duced peer ratings when compared to the women's ratings of the academic year. Under this new concept, four women lived in each
"room," which had a single bathroom, including shower stall, attached to the end of it.

I had three terrific roommates that summer, especially Holly, a
pretty blond who was a good runner and the daughter of a high-ranking army officer. She had a sense of humor that kept our room laughing, usually when we needed laughter the most.

As yearlings, we had privileges after training was over, which allowed us to take advantage of the ice cream parlor, movie theater, Coke
machines, and, of course, the beach. The blocklong strip of sand was
bordered on one side by a wooded picnic area and on the other by beautiful Lake Popolopen. It was often extremely difficult to concentrate on
training in the sweltering July temperatures, knowing that the lake
was barely a glance away. On the weekends when the cadets weren't
committed to training, the cadet hostesses sponsored dances in a rustic
western dance hall located near the beach. Yes, this place had everything for a cadet's summer enjoyment — but first you had to earn the
opportunity.

The stress and demands of Buckner were different from those of
Beast, and complex to explain to someone who has not experienced
them. The Department of Physical Education (DPE) at West Point got
very involved with our session of cadet training. Life would have improved 200 percent for the cadets that summer if the DPE officers had
gotten lost on their way to the camp. They showed up in the morning
— every morning — like a recurring bad dream. Officers from the department monitored the morning reveille PT sessions and runs. After a
year at West Point, these officers expected a cadet's physical stamina to
have improved greatly over that required of them as a plebe. Most of
the runs were accomplished over a four- or five-mile distance, travers-
ing hills, in formation, while wearing combat boots. In addition to
these morning eye-openers, DPE conducted the confidence course and
the obstacle course (on which they provided us with several opportunities to rehearse) and conducted PT instructor training in which cadets
learn to lead army soldiers through unit PT, grass and guerrilla drills
(excruciating conditioning drills).

When DPE finished with us, we showered and attended breakfast
in the mess hall, where all meals were characteristically "attend if you
want, eat if you want" since there was no assigned seating. The rest of

the day was filled with whatever phase of military training the company was scheduled to cover.

Cadets were assigned to one of eight cadet companies that summer. Training was rotated among the companies so that no two companies were going through the same phase together. Cadets from the junior and senior class held the highest leadership positions at the camp and assisted us with our training, having already been through it themselves.

Before a cadet graduates he must participate in either the induction of new cadets during Beast or the training of yearlings at Buckner. Many cadets feel that they receive more valuable and realistic leadership training from leading what is essentially a group of their peers, than by harassing unsuspecting new cadets. My friend Dave felt that the leadership experiences he would undergo at Buckner were closer to those of the real army, so he requested a position as a company platoon leader there. His company was just down the hill from mine.

I was eagerly anticipating our open dating at the Academy. Camp Buckner was to be our first opportunity for that. Because of the conflicting training schedules, Dave and I knew that there would be several weeks during the summer when we would not be able to see each other, but we counted on seeing each other when the training did allow.

Initially this worked well. After dinner each evening, Dave and I would sit by the lake and watch the moon on the water, take walks around the camp, or go to a movie. When I had to perform duty as an overnight "fire guard," walking up and down the famous "Second Company Hill" in the middle of the night, I'd frequently stop along the route and try to stay awake by writing notes to him in my green military notepad. After I completed my portion of the watch, I'd wake my replacement then steal down the hill to Dave's company. He slept in the bunk next to the door, which was always propped open for relief from the summer heat. That made it easy to slip the five or so pages of penned emotions under his pillow, kiss him on the cheek, and return to my own barracks undetected. Sometimes he'd wake up when I arrived, and a tender kiss could turn passionate very easily. But the fear of our being detected prevented me from ever staying more than a brief minute or two. On the weekends, he and I would lie next to each other on the beach during the day, then attend the dance that evening. We'd leave the dance early and sit on the steps of the long stairway that joined his company to mine, talking and stealing a few kisses before taps separated us again.

The first time I realized that there might be something wrong between us was when he refused to discuss the day's training with me. The problem escalated from there.

Dave and I had seen each other over the summer, before we returned to New York and Camp Buckner. Though our simultaneous attendance at Buckner had nothing to do with Dave's request for a summer assignment there, he was looking forward to our being together. That changed quickly, however. Soon he was telling me that he didn't know if he could take it.

"When I saw you today in full field gear, jogging along the side of the road with the rest of your platoon, I wanted to cry," he wrote me in a note which he pressed into my hand as taps began to blow. He had seen me returning, muddy and wet, from combat engineers training, one of my favorite phases that summer. We built bridges, learned mine warfare, dug foxholes, and experimented with demolitions. I saw him, leading his own platoon to a training phase that afternoon, and smiled. He just looked away.

"I can't stand to see you going through this!" the letter continued. "It doesn't bother me at all to see the women in my own platoon go through it, but I'm not in love with them."

When Dave and I spoke the next evening, sitting on a rock near the water, Dave elaborated on his letter. He told me that he thought I would realize by now that I didn't belong there and would quit.

"You belong at a regular college where you can wear pretty clothes and run for homecoming queen!" he told me. "You don't have to go through this anymore. You could marry me when I graduate and still be able to experience West Point, as a wife."

I couldn't make him understand why that wouldn't work for me; that was not what I wanted for myself. And though the morning runs were a problem for me, I thoroughly enjoyed the training and I was good at much of it. During "Scopes" training, I low-crawled about 100 meters through the woods without being detected, which took me over fifteen minutes, and maneuvered myself around behind the enemy bunker to single-handedly capture the objective after the rest of my squad had been wiped out in the confrontation with the enemy. Dave wasn't interested.

Fate intervened to provide us with a solution. Dave's company was scheduled to fly to Kentucky for armor training at Fort Knox by the end of the week. He would be gone for about six days, and when he returned, the first detail — and his assignment — would be almost over. Until then, we met in the evenings, I tried to stay out of his vicinity during the day, and we passed notes. The night before Dave left the camp, we took a long walk, barefoot on the beach. He leaned against a tree and kissed me, and promised that our relationship would be better once the academic year began again.

I missed not being able to see Dave, but summer training was becoming increasingly demanding and it was better that my attentions were not distracted. The land navigation training provides cadets with navigation and map-reading skills that have become impressive characteristics of West Point officers. Cadets learn during the two daytime phases, then put that knowledge to practical use during the night phase.

For the night patrolling, the yearlings pray for a bright moon. During my training, there was no moon at all. We shined flashlights on the illumination ("glow-in-the-dark") marks of our compasses before darkness fell. Since no lights, except the red map reading light, could be used, we placed our open compasses around our necks, with the face of the compass to the rear, so that the person behind us in the patrol would have something to follow. I stared so intently on the dimly lit dial in front of me that my shins still bear the scars I earned by walking into the sides of "BFRs" (Big Fat Rocks, or any other word that a cadet might wish to substitute for the word fat). I can still hear the muffled cries from cadets who were stabbed in the face by twigs and tree limbs. Those woods were dark at night — so dark that, if the person in front of you moved more than four feet ahead, there was no way to see him or his compass dial.

One section of the trail was particularly black. I grabbed onto the back of the cadet in front of me; the cadet behind me did likewise. The patrol began moving extremely slowly, then stopped, just as we heard a muffled "Uh" come from one of the cadets. The guy in front of me was gone!

"Let's move it," one of the instructors whispered loudly as he inspected our section of the line.

"I'm not going anywhere!" I told him in my own loud whisper as beads of sweat burst on my forehead. "The cadet who was in front of me isn't there anymore, and I'm not taking one more step until I know what happened to him!" I was scared: one second I was hanging on to him, guiding myself along, and the next second he was gone. And whatever cliff he fell off of I was determined to stay away from! The instructor, using his flashlight, soon located him. He had stepped into a four-foot-deep crevice that ran along a portion of the route.

"Took one step too far to the left," the instructor told him as he offered him an assist. "Gotta stay exactly on the path of the person ahead of you," he warned us. I was glad when that evening was over.

During the infantry phase, cadets learn patrolling, combat readiness, survival techniques, and confidence-building exercises. This was the most difficult of the summer training. The training is conducted primarily by Special Forces "Green Beret" soldiers, who know their subject intimately well. During the patrolling training, each squad spent several days and nights assuming the leadership positions of a patrol. Cadets traveled around the training area, on too little sleep and at the oddest hours, assaulting enemy positions.

At the beginning of each patrol, the instructors called out the names of the cadets who would fill certain positions. They had a list of our last names and first initials, which they used to make their selections. I had just completed my turn in the position of patrol leader. Since the instructors were supposed to change the leadership positions for every patrol, I went to sleep, deservedly so. Soon I felt someone shaking me.

"Wake up," my classmate said. "You're the next patrol leader."

"I was the *last* one!" I yelled at him. "They just picked another one. Talk to him."

"Yeah, well, he was the patrol leader while we were stopped. We're getting ready to move. It's you again," he told me. I didn't know how the instructors' process of elimination was determined, but I knew it wasn't working. And it didn't do any good to argue with these guys. They were hard-asses, and I didn't think those Airborne Infantry Special Forces Rangers liked the idea of women in the service as anything other than nurses. So, I wrote the operations order and woke up the cadet who had just navigated the last patrol to "ask him" to lead this one.

"Sorry," I told him when he protested in the same way I had, "but life's not always fair. I'm tired this time, and I need the best navigator I can get. That's you. I'll buy you a beer this weekend if we live through this," I offered in consolation.

Just when I thought this phase couldn't get any worse, it did.

After two tours as the patrol leader, I was ready for a relaxing patrol as a regular member of the group. The instructors called out the leadership positions for the next patrol, and, just as I took a deep, relaxing breath, I heard, "M60 machine gun, D. Peterson." I couldn't believe my dumb luck. That weapon is heavy! From patrol leader to machine gunner . . . why didn't someone just shoot me and get it over with?

My classmates were looking at me and each other, feeling obligated to relieve me of my burden. "Would you like me to take it for you?" one of my squad-mates asked. That was really nice of him. No one, female or male, ever wants this position.

"No, but thanks for offering," I told my surprised classmate. I hated to accept help of any kind, unless I really needed it. Besides, if I couldn't do the job, or at least try to do it, I didn't deserve to be there. The least I could do was try.

We spent the next two days climbing up and down mountains which were so steep that they had to be climbed by digging into the dirt with your fingers to keep from slipping to the bottom. Laden with the heaviest piece of firepower we carried, I was exhausted. Yet, every time the patrol changed, the machine gunner didn't. I developed sores on my shoulders from the chafing caused by the friction of the M60 over my pack, my uniform shirt, my T-shirt, and my bra strap.

Finally, on the fourth patrol, when a classmate who hadn't received a position for the patrol asked if he could take the machine gun for me, I jumped at the chance.

"I really appreciate this," I told him.

"You should've let someone take it for you sooner. You pulled your weight. Fair is fair," he said as he handed me his rifle and slipped the gun strap over his head. I was surprised. This was the same "tough guy" who had grabbed the back of my neck a week earlier and told the entire squad exactly how "gross" he considers any woman "who shaves the back of her neck." (At that time the female cadets had no choice of hairstyles. Male barbers cut our hair the same way they did the males.)

At the end of the patrols, as our group was taking a break for lunch, our crusty instructor was whittling on a stick instead of eating. "I don't eat C-rats," he told us as we munched on ours. He was certainly an unsociable cuss. This was a rare occasion for him; usually he'd stop the patrol and disappear completely into the woods until our break was over. He never chatted with any of the cadets, and seemed imposed upon when any of the cadets would ask him questions about his military experiences. So, the cadets just sat off by themselves and waited for him to announce the end of the lunch break.

It wasn't long before our instructor folded his pocketknife and told us to get our gear together; we would sleep in our own beds that night. Just before the patrol moved out, he gathered us around him, told us that the patrol back would be "very informal," then he reached into the bottom trouser pocket of his fatigues and pulled out a well-worn green beret. Handing it to me, he said, "I'd like you to have this." Then he told me in a very quick and rational manner that he "didn't much care for" women in the service, especially in combat. "But I really put it to you the last few days. You did okay," was the last thing he said before he turned and stepped into the woods.

I stuffed the cap with the Special Forces brass on the rim into my shirt, threw my pack on my back, and followed obediently, along with the rest of our group. I was honored by his gesture, but the severely unemotional nature of his gift left me confused about it. I was actually more impressed by the realization that this lean combat machine was human after all.

As part of the survival training at Camp Buckner, cadets were given large coffee cans, a small bag of potatoes and carrots, and two live chickens per squad and told to fix dinner. Prior to this, however, cadets had been instructed about the proper techniques for killing wild animals, particularly chickens.

The *New York Times* reported, when told by a dismissed cadet, that women were forced to bite the heads off of chickens at the Academy as an act of hazing. The truth is that the instructors pick the most squeamish-looking cadet to bite the head off. Since women have been in attendance at the Academy, the most frail-looking cadet has usually been female. This selection isn't determined because of sex, it's made based on attitude. When the instructor announced that he would be "selecting a volunteer" to do the honors, I raised my hand to volunteer, as did several male cadets. My strategy was to volunteer, knowing they wouldn't pick me if I appeared to want the assignment. It worked like a charm. They picked my new roommate, however. Tears filled her blue eyes and her bottom lip began quivering uncontrollably as the instructor pushed her head down and forced the neck of the chicken into her mouth, in front of all of our classmates. I felt so sorry for her. She ran behind the bleachers, her blood-soaked blond hair marking her face as she fled. For the instructor, it provided exactly the type of show that he was looking for.

Actually, if my roommate hadn't been frightened of the ordeal, the recipe for biting a chicken's neck is simple. Just part the feathers of the neck with your hands, then tear the exposed skin with your teeth as you tug on the head. The head comes off easily. Of course, you're left with a moving beak in one hand and a wiggling body in the other.

When my squad began the chore of preparing our supper, I offered to make stew out of one chicken and half of the vegetables; the males wanted to cook the other over an open fire. I also offered to kill one of the birds (though it was more for show than out of actual desire to do the deed), but two of the men grabbed the honors first. All was fine until one of the men botched the job and the chicken ran off, screaming, its neck only partially removed and blood spurting rhythmically from its throat. The screaming was horrible, almost like that of a child. No one made a move to stop the sound. The second chicken, petrified by the commotion, was attacking its holder. I ran over to where the first bird was running in circles on the ground. I threw it down, placed my foot on one side of its neck, and pulled the head off with my hand. Silence followed. "Thank God! I can't stand that noise," was all I said as I went back to my stew. With all of the activity surrounding the deaths of our dinner, I knew the chicken would be difficult to eat.

"Are you sure you don't want to put that one in the stew as well?" I asked one last time. The response was negative.

In the end, the stew was at least edible. I had packed salt and pepper packets in the equipment pouches on my ammo belt, which we added to the stew. Both of the chickens had unshelled eggs inside of them, which we added to the stew. They ended up as hard-boiled eggs and never needed to be shelled. In the end, it was a good thing that there was plenty of stew available; the chicken on the spit was too tough to eat, though the pride of one of the chefs wouldn't let him admit it.

My favorite phase of training during the summer was the overwhelming favorite of most of the cadets: the armor training at Fort Knox. We flew to Kentucky on Air Force transports. Once there, we stayed in old wooden army barracks and had to pull fire-guard shifts every night because of the potential for disaster. We ran every morning of our weeklong excursion, but the runs weren't as difficult as the ones at Buckner. The highlight of the training, of course, was actually driving the tanks over the red clay tank trails. For me it was fun, and it never lasted long enough. Each of us also had an opportunity to command a tank, and to load and shoot one as well. Besides this education,

Fort Knox also provided me with the most frightening training of my four years.

During the mechanized infantry training at Fort Knox, a squad of combat-equipped troops was driven by personnel carrier to a simulated battlefield and dropped off. The back of the carrier opened and we descended the ramp amidst sounds of gunfire and explosions. "Follow your squad leader" was the last thing I heard before we exited the vehicle. Once we cleared the vehicle, I hit the dirt and low-crawled to a spot behind a nearby tree. I saw my squad leader motion for us to follow him. We ran in three-second bursts, then fell to the ground and fired our weapons. I buried my face in the dirt as an explosive device went off in a pit several feet from me. My forearms were cut and bleeding from the stickers and wild berry bushes we were maneuvering in, oil from the drums containing the explosive simulators speckled our faces with each blast, and my M16 jammed while I was firing it (unjamming procedures are difficult to perform while you're attempting to stay alive and keep up with the rest of the squad at the same time!). Follow my squad leader? I couldn't even find him, let alone follow him! If an enemy soldier had walked up beside me at that moment he would've had to be wearing a sign that read "I am the enemy" for me to have noticed him.

I felt like such a failure. It was the most confusing and frightening training experience, and it was designed to be. *If it's this scary and disoriented, when we know it's a simulation,* I thought, *imagine what it must be like when we know it's for real.* I gained a great appreciation for a little of what our country's combat veterans must have gone through. I told myself that I'd never take what they did for granted.

Before the battlefield exercise was over, I thought I'd had my first brush with death. After the actual battlefield portion, our squad reassembled and headed into the woods to pursue an unknown enemy. As we ran through the woods, following our squad leader, the two cadets ahead of me suddenly fell over. It looked like they died right in front of me!

As I moved over to one of them to see what had happened, I too fell over. I couldn't breathe! My body was involuntarily collapsing. *This is it,* I thought. *This is realistic training and I'm going to die!* Then I remembered the gas mask I wore on my hip. In practice, I could get it out of the case and onto my face within ten seconds. When I needed it, though, I couldn't pull the snaps apart, and there was a cardboard piece stuck in the face compartment (placed there during storage of the mask). I knew I was going to pass out, or die, before I got the mask on my face. Once I did, however, I yelled, "Gas! Gas!" as I had been trained to do, then moved over to my fallen classmates and helped them with their masks. The whole procedure probably took less than thirty seconds, but time is disoriented during a crisis situation. It was so frightening. I never saw any smoke or gas, never saw anyone who could have "popped" some gas, and never smelled anything. One second I was standing up, running, and the next I was on my knees, gasping for breath.

After the rest of my squad reassembled, we charged ahead to catch up with our squad leader. When we got there, he couldn't have been less concerned about what had just happened to us. Instead, he chewed us out for being a minute behind our other squad-mates! The Academy had promised us realistic training at Camp Buckner. I would never doubt them again.

A much safer aspect of the armor training was the Fort Knox Officer's Club, which we were authorized to visit after our training each day. Since I love to dance, I spent most of my time on the dance floor with my classmates or the local lieutenants. Leslie, however, spent most of her time visiting with classmates and enjoying the opportunity to drink beer on a weeknight.

One night I was ready to catch the bus back to the barracks and went over to the table to ask Les if she was ready to go.

"No," she said. "I've made some friends and they're going to drop me off. Let me introduce you." I didn't like this at all. These guys were warrant officers, and they had to be forty-five years old, at least. I sat down with them for about fifteen minutes, until the last bus back to the quarters drove up. I left the club thinking, *If something happens to Leslie, at least I'll be able to identify these guys to the police.*

Leslie was in her bunk when I awoke the next morning. We went to breakfast in the army mess hall next door to our barracks, then went to separate training areas for the day. After my group drove the personnel carriers which had dropped us at the simulated battlefield the day before, we assembled in the bleachers and received a lecture about the combined arms effect of armor and aviation assets. Two aircraft, an AH-1 Cobra Attack helicopter and an OH-58 Kiowa Scout helicopter, were on display in the open field in front of the bleachers.

After the lecture, one of the pilots, a warrant officer, told us he would give two or three short rides to several cadets. "Who's the youngest person in the group?" he asked. I could see what was coming.

I wasn't the youngest or the oldest, so I didn't stand a chance. "Would you like to examine the OH-58 Scout?" another one of the pilots asked me as I moved away from the main group.

"Sure," I replied, walking toward the second aircraft. Then I heard a voice call my name.

"Cadet Peterson, don't you want to ride in my Cobra?" It was one of the pilots of the Cobra. I had no idea why he was singling me out, and how did he know who I was?

"Of course," I answered, apologizing to the Scout pilot for changing my mind. As I moved near the aircraft, I began to understand how I had received the coveted third ride in the chopper.

"How is Cadet Hyde feeling today? You are her roommate, aren't you?" So! These were the obnoxious warrant officers from the club the night before. Great detective I was. I couldn't even recognize these guys after they had talked to us for an hour!

"She's fine, and yes I am," I responded as I inspected the craft and prepared for my ride, feeling badly about my unfriendliness of the prior evening. When I returned to the barracks that afternoon, I thanked Leslie for her input.

"I just told them that you were interested in an aviation career, and told them your name. They did the rest," she said modestly. They sure did. The ride only lasted about five minutes (and included a modest "gun run"), but I was smitten. That aircraft was exactly what I needed to take the place of the Air Force aircraft I had passed up by turning down the Air Force Academy appointment. I was impressed!

The week was over too quickly. It was a shame that the plane ride back to Camp Buckner wasn't as brief. The way the Air Force cargo planes are configured, there are no bathroom facilities. On some flights, the crew chief will place a rubber tube in a small port hole in the rear of the craft for the men to urinate into (the urine being expelled outside the aircraft). On our plane such a service was available, so all women were told to sit in a section of the plane farthest away from the tube. It was convenient for the men, after consuming their box lunches and fruit drinks. For the women, we had to wait.

By the time the plane landed at the airfield near West Point, the women were beginning to feel uncomfortable. It wouldn't have been too critical if we all hadn't been loaded onto the back of the army's 2½-ton trucks for the twenty-minute ride back to Buckner. Each bump in the rural roads along the route only aggravated the situation. When we finally arrived at the camp, after about five hours, the cadet officers commanded, "Okay, everybody line up in formation before we release you. We have some announcements."

Announcements? As I hopped off of the truck I could see at least a third of the cadets, male and female, dancing, prancing, and even holding themselves to keep from wetting all over their clothes. My roommates and I said, "To heck with formation," and made a mad dash for the nearest latrine. At that point, getting in trouble for missing formation was better than embarrassing yourself in front of your peers.

As it turned out, no one got into trouble for leaving the formation. The cadre knew our bladders would be ready to burst when we got back; they had made the same trip to Fort Knox during their summer at Buckner. Having been through it, though, they were smart enough not to drink the fruit punch until they landed in New York.

After a two-day respite, our company prepared for a traditional slice of Camp Buckner training. It was our turn to tackle the infamous "pits." This was supposed to be punishing self-defense training. The pits were filled with rocks, dirt, and sawdust. We were dropped for push-ups for any and every reason and made to run around the pits as punishment, before we ever even started the training. Finally, the self-defense training began. Men were paired with male partners, and I had a female partner, at least initially. After she got something in her eyes and had to be taken out of the pits, I was left without a partner. The instructor did not relish the idea of partnering with me. Finally, several "throws" had been demonstrated to the other cadets, but I was still standing alone at the side of the pits.

"Okay," he said, offering me his arm. "Why don't you try one on me?"

His tone was less than enthusiastic, and I understood. I was working toward my brown belt in judo before I came to the Academy. I had "played" with several very highly ranked black belts and had never gotten hurt. However, when I was thrown improperly by a novice white belt, I spent three weeks nursing a swollen knee. I couldn't wait to see the look on his face ten seconds from now.

I grabbed his arm with one hand, loaded him on my hip with the other, and deposited him three feet away on the ground with a solid, "*He-yah!*"

"You've had some training!" he exclaimed as he walked back to where I stood. I was glad it showed. He asked one of his assistants to take over the group training for a few minutes while the instructor and

I sparred on the side of the pit. He was really good, of course, and it was fun practicing actual judo throws from standing positions instead of self-defense moves from kneeling positions, as we did in plebe DPE classes.

The last week of training brought the much dreaded "enduro-run," a timed two-mile run with full pack, weapon, and gear. It pushed all of us to our physical limits. I hated running along for twenty minutes with the sound of my stressed breathing echoing in the heavy steel helmet I was wearing. This was the event that sparked the most criticism of the women by the men. It's a tough event, and too many women weren't even completing it at all, let alone passing it. Two-mile runs on the hills at Buckner were difficult enough without being heavily laden. I passed the run with eleven seconds to spare. But as far as the men were concerned, by passing with such a slim margin, I failed. At least after this dreaded obstacle was completed, the rest of the training was supposed to be fun.

During the mountaineering phase we learned to rappel off the side of a cliff. As I stood backwards on the top of the cliff, with the rope around my waist, I looked behind me, over the edge.

"Get off my rock," the instructor shouted gruffly at me. "Push off!"

There was a large piece of granite protruding from the cliff about three feet below me. "But what if I don't clear that protrusion?" I asked him, panicking a little.

"Then you smash your face into the rock. Now get off!" he barked.

I pushed off, clearing the rock and half of the cliff as well. Once I reached the ground, my only thought, like those of most cadets after their first time, was my lament at only being able to do this twice! After the rappeling, cadets had an opportunity to climb back up the cliff, using only their hands and feet. There were no ropes or nets. An instructor stood on the ground below to guide you if you needed help. At one point I clung motionless to the cliff.

"Just put your left hand in that crevice about a foot from your head," the instructor coached me. The "crevice" he was referring to was actually a crack which was barely big enough to fit my fingernails into.

"What happens if a cadet falls?" I inquired down to him.

"That's what the ambulance is here for!" he shouted back to me. Instructors never made the cadets feel overly safe, that's for certain.

After my next move, a small protrusion the instructor told me to rest my boot on gave way beneath me and I slipped several feet back down the rock, skinning my left elbow even through my shirtsleeve.

"That's good," he yelled to me. "Now you're in a better position to put your hand on that good crack near your right hand." This guy had no sympathy. If I hadn't been fortunate enough to catch myself, I would have careened all the way down the cliff to the rocks below, and I doubted the landing would have been a soft one.

The successful completion of summer training was marked by two traditions: the "Slide for Life" and the "Camp Illumination Formal." The Slide for Life is a long wire device that is strung across a small finger of the lake. To mark the completion of the training, cadets climb what resembles a three-story electrical tower (no net) and slide down the length of the wire into the water. On the platform at the top of the tower, an instructor stands waiting to explain the only acceptable way to accomplish this obstacle. "You must let go of the hanger when the person on the other side of the lake waves the flag. Do you understand?" he questions. On the other side of the lake, where the end of the wire is attached, stands a cadre member with a red signal flag. When the flag is waved, the cadet is to drop from the sliding device into the water. Failure to drop at that time could result in serious bodily injury, as the water gets very shallow near the shore. Just in case, tires are placed along the bank at the end of the slide to break the cadet's fall should he or she fail to drop on time.

As I grabbed the hanger with both hands, the instructor said, "Do a pull-up." I started to panic. That was a long way down, and he expected me to hold a pull-up the entire time?

"Do a pull-up!" he repeated. Without thinking any further, I complied. Then he pushed me off the platform as I yelled an extended, "Recondo!" On the way down I watched for the flag to dip, then dropped into the cool water below. Again, just as so many times before during this summer training, I only wished I could have done it again. But this was one to a customer, and it was over too quickly.

As for the formal dance, Dave had left explicit instructions for his best friend Chuck, who was part of the second detail cadre, to accompany me. Many of the cadets invited their girlfriends up for the weekend, which was nice. What was inconsiderate, however, was that many of these cadets took advantage of the fact that the women were now billeted in the same barracks as them.

"Just dress in the female cadets' room," my classmates offered their girlfriends, never bothering to ask any of us. There were already four women dressing in a cubicle that was impossible to maneuver in unless the closet doors were closed and three of the women were sitting on their beds. There was only room for one person to stand in the small aisle, and only one small mirror on the bathroom wall. Each of the four of us had to shower, fix our hair and makeup, and dress in our formal uniforms. Now we also had four civilian women, with their formal gowns, to contend with.

"I'll get dressed early and get out of here to leave more room for the rest of you," Holly volunteered, before we knew about the invitations the male cadets had made. If we had turned the girls away, and put the males in their places, we would have been completely justified, but we couldn't do it to those young girls. So we suffered the overcrowding. What we hadn't counted on was suffering through the naive braggings of the girlfriends.

"Oh, my Lonnie. Isn't he just the sweetest thing?" one of the girls remarked. I wondered if she would have thought him so "sweet" had she heard the way he talked about their relationship to the guys in the barracks at night. Since the walls separating the two sections are just metal strips, it was very easy to hear everything that was said on the other side, especially at night. We repeatedly asked the men to tone down their conversations, given this situation, but they insisted on "speaking their minds." These guys discussed scenes from sexually explicit videos that were particularly graphic and discussed the most intimate details of their relationships with their girlfriends, many of whom weren't yet eighteen years old.

The night when the conversations reached an all-time low was the night that Lonnie was telling the "inquiring minds" on the other side of the wall about his girlfriend, who was sexually innocent before falling for him. He gave explicit details: what he did, what she did, how she reacted, what he said, and so forth.

Finally, it was Holly who spoke up: "All right! That's enough. You guys are pigs. Put it back in your pants and go to bed!" Only Holly could say it like that and get away with it. It shut them up immediately.

"You have to talk to them in a language they understand," she whispered to us. Apparently she was right.

The dance had gone well, and Chuck returned me to my barracks early so that I could finish packing for the return to West Point the next day. Soon we were loading our belongings and ourselves onto the backs of the green army trucks for the bumpy ride back to West Point. Every muscle in my body ached, and I was looking forward to the less strenuous demands of the academic year. My body needed a rest, and a warm hug from Dave.

JOHN TOWER
TEXAS

COMMITTEES:
ARMED SERVICES
BANKING, HOUSING, AND
URBAN AFFAIRS

United States Senate
WASHINGTON, D.C. 20510

STATE OFFICES:
DALLAS 75242
1100 COMMERCE ST

AUSTIN 78701
151 FEDERAL BUILD

16 January 1978

Miss Donna Kay Peterson
1008 South Border Street
Orange, Texas 77630

Dear Donna:

I am pleased to advise you that I have today submitted your name
in nomination for appointment to the United States Military Academy.

I congratulate you on your fine performance in the competition thus
far and am confident that the Academy will share my high appraisal
of your record. I hope that you will soon be offered an appointment
by the West Point Admissions Board, for you have proven yourself to
be the caliber of young woman the Academy needs and wants.

You will soon receive official notification of your nomination from
the Academy, and instructions on any further testing which may be
required. Please know that my best wishes will be with you in the
coming weeks and that I will be following your progress with great
interest.

With warmest regards, I remain

Sincerely yours,

John G. Tower

JGT:aw

*Official notice of West Point nomination by Senator John Tower.*

*New Cadet Peterson in P.T. uniform.*

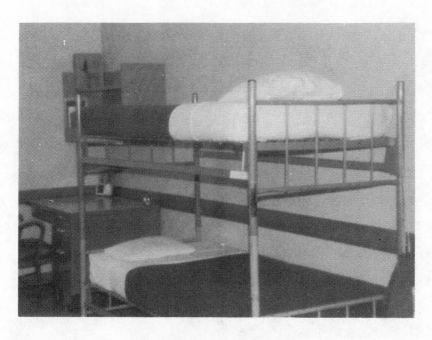

*My room during Beast Barracks.*

*Typical inspection-in-ranks during Beast.*

*New cadets get helicopter tour of West Point.*

*Field exercise during Beast.*

*"Tent City" at Lake Freddrick.*

*Me in fatigues, moving to my new company at the end of Beast.*

*The first time my mother saw her daughter as a cadet.*

*Trophy Point, view of the Hudson River, in the spring.*

(U.S. Army Photo)

*The view in winter.*

(U.S. Army Photo)

*MaryAnn and me, during her parents' visit, Fall '78.*

*During Plebe Parent Weekend, March '79. Jerryl Bennett (football quarterback), me, Randy Odom.*

*My parents at Kissing Rock on Flirtation Walk.*

*The Cadet Chapel, as seen from my barracks window.*

*Statue of Gen. Douglas MacArthur near entrance to the cadet barracks.*

(U.S. Army Photo)

*Christmas vacation yearling year with Dave and my parents.*

*Me at summer flight training, July 1980.*

*Photo taken by my flight instructor after my first solo.*

*Cadet Tony Cuccolo*

AFVN-BBN-CO                                                    9 July 1980

SUBJECT:  Reviewer's Comments - CTLT Counselling on Cadet Donna K.
Peterson

1.  It has been a distinct honor and pleasure to have had Cadet Donna
K. Peterson assigned to this battalion.  During the last five years I
have been associated with this program I have seen some truly outstanding talent evolving through the USMA system but, in this case, I
feel compelled to add to the evaluator's comments.

2.  First of all, there are no apparent weaknesses in her performance
with this unit - experience in the future will more finely hone those
areas in which she has not gained any experience.  The strengths, on
the other hand, are far superior to any of her peers that I have observed.  Her potential as a leader and manager appear infinite.  This
fine young future officer radiates professionalism and epitomizes the
character traits so necessary in our leaders of today.  Perhaps her
singularly outstanding trait, however, is her willingness to get involved in command - she is by no means a "side lines" coach.

3.  Cadet Peterson is now ready to assume any function required of an
officer with three to four years experience.  I highly indorse any
leadership position she may be considered for in the future, with every
confidence that she will excel.

                                  GEORGE A. BOMBEL
                                  LTC, SC
Incl 1                            Commanding


*Performance rating from leadership training at Fort Hood, Texas.*

CHAPTER 5

# Yearling Year

*"No other institution has furnished to the country as great a pro-*
*portion of distinguished citizens as West Point."*
— Gen. John Pershing, 1920

When I got back to my barracks from Camp Buckner, there was a
message waiting for me from Dave. I gave him a quick phone
call to say that I was back, then got down to the business of moving
back into my academic company. My class lived in the same company
for all four years. The Classes of 1978 and 1979 had been rotated after
their yearling year, mostly to guard against the establishment of
"cliques" in the companies affected by the cheating scandal in the Class of
1977. The Class of 1983 would be rotated after their freshman year, to
give those plebes whose cadet careers had not gotten off to exemplary
starts a chance to recover their reputation. So, I was back in G4 with
Leslie Hyde as my roommate, living in the former all-male portion of
the company barracks.

I should have realized that this year was going to be different
from my first when the males of the division refused to give us one of
the five latrines. "Go to the next division and use the women's latrine
over there," they demanded. Finally, after making enough complaints
to our platoon leader, and assuring our male Tac that we did not mind

124

using a latrine that had not been modified for female use, we were assigned a latrine. Leslie and I fashioned a "WOMEN" sign in bold black letters for the latrine door. There were no curtains on the two shower stalls and no doors on the toilet stalls, but we did have our own urinal!

When Congress mandated that women be allowed to attend USMA, cost estimates for facilities reconstruction to modify the Academy to accommodate women was listed as $437,900. This included $126,000 just for latrine modification in the barracks (one commode and one shower per four females!), $4,700 to put shades and full-length mirrors in rooms designated for women, and $100,000 to place laundromats in the basement of all barracks (because, supposedly, women couldn't send their bras and panties to the same laundry that the males used). Reading the Operations Plan (OPLAN 75-1), which outlines the planning for the admission of women cadets, it becomes obvious that the separate departments that provided input to the report were doing all in their power to provide one overwhelming reason for discouraging women's attendance: it was cost prohibitive. One section of the report, dealing with latrine modification, mentioned that the doors, shower curtains, and capping off of the urinals would cost "$2,400 per female cadet." That figure sounded astonishing, but that was only based on the women in the first class. Women would be using these facilities over decades, at least, reducing that cost per cadet figure significantly.

In addition, many of the male officers who reviewed the OPLAN, after requesting advice from their wives, agreed that laundromats were not necessary for women's undergarments since they could easily be washed with those of the males in the cadet laundry. These wives were also instrumental in removing a large cost estimate for sanitary napkin dispensers in each barracks when they explained to their husbands that, in a building where women live, they would purchase their own supplies of this nature, and would not need these machines. Additionally, they reminded their husbands that, though full-length mirrors would be nice to have, if male cadets didn't need them, females wouldn't either, since all cadets wear the same uniforms.

"I thought my wife was absolutely brilliant," one high-ranking officer who reviewed the plan told me. "We [the hierarchy at West Point] created so many obstacles to the admission of women which were solved easily by simple common sense. The hierarchy, supported by the powerful Alumni Association, was doing everything in its power to delay, if not halt altogether, what was happening. You could see our heel-marks across the Plain as we were being dragged into the future against our wills."

It's true. Much of the OPLAN creates that impression. In another section of the plan, women's physical fitness standards are discussed. The Academy conducted surveys of local women's sports teams, women in the army, and women ROTC candidates across the country, and asked them to perform the same events required of women on the physical aptitude exam, the test all prospective West Point candidates take prior to acceptance. For this test the flexed-arm hang is substituted for the pull-ups, which males are required to perform, because "experience has indicated that very few women can do pull-ups" and, therefore, the flexed-arm hang "has been nationally accepted [by the] American Alliance for Health, Physical Education, and Recreation Youth Fitness and should be an adequate indicator of the upper body strength of women USMA candidates." Almost ninety-five percent of the women in each of the three test groups could not perform even one pull-up, and the average for the groups on the flexed-arm hang (the test is measured in seconds) ranged from eight seconds to eighteen seconds. Despite these scores, the Academy created a scoring scale for the female West Point candidates in which it took fifty seconds to achieve the maximum (100 percent) score, and anything less than thirty-three seconds was failing. Then, once the women became cadets, the flexed-arm hang was discontinued and women were required to perform pull-ups, just as the men did. In addition, the scoring scale for the two-mile run for the women differed dramatically for women at West Point than for women in any other branch of the service. For example, women in the army, performing in running shoes, could receive a max score (100 percent) by completing two miles in 17:05. Female cadets, running in combat boots, failed the run at 17:20. It could certainly be construed to look as if the women were meant to fail.

What surprised the Academy personnel was how very well the women performed. So very well, in fact, that after just a few years the standards had to be revised to make them even tougher. When too many female cadets achieved max standards, the max scores were lowered to become closer to the average, and new max scores were created. It should not be surprising, then, that female graduates perform impressively when faced with the physical requirements of the army, as do male graduates. The physical testing standards for both women and men at West Point greatly exceeds those required of officers in the active army.

Another obstacle indicated in the OPLAN was the design of the women's uniform. It was, of course, necessary to keep the design as close to the traditional uniform as possible. To this end, the Academy selected four commercial design consultants to create a uniform for the women: Hart, Schaffner & Marx (a renowned men's clothier), Jonathan Logan, David Crystal Co., and Imagewear by Rollins. Once again, common sense was misplaced during the selection process. Despite the uniform samples presented, the selection committee decided that, due to the shapely nature of women's posteriors, the tuxedo tail of the dress coat should be cut off for the women, "so that they will not stand out." As a result, females in the Class of 1980 were issued dress coats with no tails.

Standing in parade formation beside men, whose uniforms had tails, the women stood out like sore thumbs. It not only looked ridiculous, at an Academy whose hallmark is the identical appearance of its cadets, it was impractical. The women's jacket was so short that it caused them to walk around pulling it down in the back to keep their T-shirts and the waist of their trousers from showing. They were still wearing them like that when I got there, but my class eventually was issued the identical coat to that of the males. Before these females were seniors, they were reissued coats identical to the rest of the corps and turned in their tailless coats. Many of the women bought their initial coats and kept them for historical reasons. This had been the biggest uniform flaw in the Academy's history.

In all fairness to the Academy hierarchy, however, throughout the OPLAN it is evident that many officers who did not necessarily support the influx of women wanted the assimilation of women to occur in the smoothest manner possible, for the sake of the Academy. The public affairs section of the OPLAN attempted to define the problem: "USMA personnel have publicly strongly objected in the past to the admission of women; the U.S. Congress has overwhelmingly approved the admission of women to the Military Academy; admission of women to USMA will arouse extremely high press interest in West Point; many USMA personnel have incomplete knowledge of how the the admission of women as cadets will impact on the institution. Many are also unaware how thoroughly Army women have been integrated into non-traditional military specialties in recent years." Their plan was to provide as much information about the process of admitting women to as many concerned persons as possible while providing a campaign stressing the significant contributions made by military women throughout history.

The superintendent, commandant, and selected Academy personnel met with the USMA staff and faculty, families and civilian employees at West Point, and the Corps of Cadets, by class and as a corps. They also communicated with army personnel, West Point parents' clubs, and alumni groups to foster confidence in the Academy's ability to make this transition while still maintaining "West Point traditions, the unity of the Corps of Cadets, and professional excellence and value to society of the West Point graduate." In addition, the Academy found that too few army officers were sufficiently aware of the contributions made by women in the defense of our nation. To counter this, they conducted a symposium on "Women in the Army" and "Women at West Point" to educate the officers and cadets, and provide them with an opportunity to "voice their attitudes and ideas on women cadets." I can just imagine what those sessions must have been like. One cadet from the Class of 1978 told me that the most frequently asked question was "What if they cry?" The answer, of course, was to do the same thing you do when males cry.

"Male cadets don't cry!" came the enthusiastic response.

"Bullshit! They cry and you know it. You don't let them get away with it, so don't let the women," the officer countered. This same former cadet told me that the superintendent, LTG Berry, had been very vocal about his negative feelings toward the admission of women (his comments are a matter of public record) and had told the cadets to continue to oppose the admission of women because "we can still beat this thing." He was replaced by LTG Goodpaster, who helped to ease the transition by telling the cadets that there was nothing they could do to change the admission of women, but their continued resistance could tear the Academy apart. Goodpaster also told an assembly of alumni that the Academy supported the decision of the Congress and that anyone feeling strongly otherwise was free to leave the Academy grounds because "you're not wanted here."

Actually, the normally dutiful cadets accepted the decisions of their commanders with little public dissension. "After all," a cadet from the Class of 1977 told me, "there was nothing we could do to change things, and the official Academy position was made clear. Cadets don't argue with the Academy hierarchy. Once back in our rooms, however, we let rip with our feelings about [women] becoming cadets, and it wasn't pretty."

The cadets' support for public policy didn't surprise me. One of the best attributes of the members of the Corps of Cadets is an extremely high sense of "duty" and supreme loyalty to the institution of West Point. There isn't much they wouldn't do to preserve its dignity and reputation. Most cadets believe that placing their own personal considerations behind those of duty to their country is the highest honor. They suppress their personal feelings when in public, but sound off vehemently in private situations. When the superintendent appealed to cadets to help the Academy through the transition with as few scars as possible, they did, because they could relate to the ultimate goal of his request — the Academy's preservation. Cadets take this sense of loyalty to the institution with them into the army as well.

One rather famous example of the graduates' fierce loyalty occurred when Academy Superintendent General Samual Koster became the object of a great deal of media attention because of his role two years earlier as the commander of the American Division in Vietnam and speculation about his possible participation in the My Lai incident of 1968. When it became clear that the Peers Committee would require him to testify before them, he resigned the superintendency, saying, "I have therefore requested reassignment in order to separate the Military Academy and you of the Corps from the continuing flow of public announcements or any other connection with the alleged events which took place in Vietnam involving elements of my former command." Most cadets, and much of history, believed that Koster was a sacrificial lamb who accepted responsibility to appease the media and the bureaucrats who were hungry for a high-ranking execution. He separated himself from West Point, was demoted, and retired as a brigadier general, leaving the Academy unscathed.

I joined the Cadet Public Relations Council during my yearling year and began volunteering as a public relations representative for West Point. Up to this time, when people would ask me if West Point was tough for the women, I would reply that "West Point is tough for the women, and men. It's just plain tough!" I always tried to be fair with my responses. But, as the year progressed, and as I survived the next two years, my answers got less "fair," and more truthful. West Point is tough for everyone, but there is an additional stress placed on the women, who are required to perform equally alongside men while enduring ridicule from them. The humor I had witnessed as a plebe was vanishing. The jokes were old and degrading and had gotten more vulgar with every passing day.

Most of the harassment during my yearling year was sexual in nature. I returned to my room after classes one morning to find a condom filled with hand lotion in the middle of my desk. The accompanying note read: "You are the object of my wettest dreams!" Sometimes the condom was filled with something other than lotion. Often, notes would be left on a female cadet's desk, threatening retaliation if she failed to follow the party line (as determined by the male cadets, of course). The males had even created a new type of joke. In addition to Aggie (Texas A&M) jokes and Polish jokes, there were now Female Cadet jokes: "Why don't female cadets wear odor-eaters? They can't keep them from crawling up their legs." Or, two males would jump on each other and roll around as if having sex and say "Gotta be better with a man than with a female cadet." Then they would add, "Come to think of it, there's not much difference." There were so many others: "What do you call female intramural swimming? The Bay of Pigs." And "What do you call a female cadet standing beside two plebes? Pork and Beans." One company even published a pamphlet of these jokes and provided them to the female cadets.

The language turned particularly vulgar when a woman walked into the room, despite regulations prohibiting this type of behavior. There was little point in reporting these guys. It was difficult to prove that it was occurring maliciously, and you always came out looking like you were the one who had no sense of humor. Of course, a cadet could not get away with making jokes about *racial* minorities. This was strictly a conflict of men versus women; even men of racial minorities told female cadet jokes.

Harassment generally went far beyond a few distasteful jokes. While women were away from their rooms on the weekend, males would (it appeared) ejaculate sperm onto the sheets and pillowcases of the females, then remake the bed so that the female would find the semen only after she lay in it, or do the same to the clothing folded neatly in the bureau drawer, prepared for inspection. Sometimes the males would leave pornographic pictures lying around for us to find, or create drawings of females in unflattering or homosexual positions and post them on the company banisters or bulletin boards for all to see. And whenever a male cadet could find nothing derogatory enough to say to a female cadet, he would grab his crotch and make filthy suggestions about what the female could do with that part of his body.

This harassment was fairly continuous, and it was difficult to escape.

"A female has got to accept that some of that will go on in the work place," one female executive told me at an organization meeting. But this wasn't the work place; we *lived* there. We couldn't "go home" at night to get away from it. It was occurring in our home! And because it was happening in the one place we should have felt safe enough to relax, we could never completely let our guard down. It's extremely stressful to never be able to relax for four years.

In all fairness, however, not all male cadets participated in the harassment of the females. I established some deep friendships with many marvelous male cadets who were very secure in their masculinity and never felt threatened by the presence of the females. Many of these men were vocally supportive of the women; some of them weren't, but neither were they openly condemning. I could respect that.

For me, the highlight of yearling year was being selected to serve on an Academy Honor Board. It was my chance to participate in the very process that had drawn me to the Academy in the first place. West Point realizes that, because their time is limited, due to the tremendous demands placed upon them, cadets frequently don't get 100 percent out of everything that is thrown at them. And, if they don't absorb all of their academic training, they'll make up for it at graduate school. If they don't absorb all of their military training, they'll be able to pick it up in the officer basic course or specialty training in the army. But if a cadet does not leave the Academy with a highly ingrained sense of honor, it's doubtful he'll pick it up somewhere in society. It's the code that sets West Point apart from other civilian and military schools. No matter what else a cadet may have to compromise in his life, honor is not to be forsaken.

It sounds self-righteous, but the bottom line is that it's important to cadet life. After all, the Honor Code was developed and initiated by the cadets themselves, and enforced casually until after World War I, when Douglas MacArthur assisted the cadets in developing the tenets of the code and officially incorporating it into Academy life.

Today the Honor Code remains as it was developed: "A cadet will not lie, cheat, steal, nor tolerate those who do." It is the only aspect of West Point that has no rank structure; all cadets are equal under the system. The code works because the cadets believe in it. General Feir, a former superintendent of West Point, said of the Honor Code, "It's their system, that [is] its great strength." The *Honor Instruction Booklet* (which each cadet receives) states that "the Honor Code and System belong entirely to the Corps of Cadets."

The theory behind the Honor Code can be explained simply. Cadets often break regulations. That's expected. Oftentimes these violations are not detected, and the cadet escapes without punishment. When the cadet is caught violating the regulations, however, he should accept his punishment like an adult and own up to it. Breaking regulations can result in a cadet walking punishment tours on the area; lying about it will result in a cadet's dismissal from the Academy.

Explaining the Honor *System* is much more complicated. Basically, each cadet company has two honor representatives who belong to the Honor Committee. The chain-of-command for the system moves from the company reps to the regimental honor rep, to the vice-chairman for investigations, the chairman, the commandant of cadets, and ultimately, the superintendent. When a violation is reported, a preliminary investigation is conducted at the company level, and findings are sent up the chain. En route, a decision can be made to dismiss the charge, conduct further investigations, or send the case to a full honor investigative hearing. The process to this point is quite extensive and time-consuming, but it's done to provide the accused cadet every opportunity for acquittal before a full board is convened.

A "board" consists of four cadets from the Honor Committee and eight cadets from the Corps at large. A representative from the Judge Advocate General's Office (an attorney) is also present to protect the rights of the accused. Both sides present arguments, and the accused cadet may also present character witnesses in his or her behalf. A vote of 10 to 2 is required to find a cadet guilty, though most votes are unanimous. After serious and lengthy deliberations, a paper vote is taken, and the results sent to the superintendent. If a cadet is "found" (guilty) the Supe has several options: separate (expel) the cadet, overturn the findings, or agree with the findings but elect to retain the cadet (which usually carries with it an award of punishment tours). This is known as discretion, and the Supe will take into consideration whether the violation was self-reported (which occurs often), whether the cadet was under extreme duress at the time of the violation, how long the cadet has lived under the code (plebe versus firstie), and whether the cadet exhibits a sincere desire to live honorably in the future. It's a very involved process, but one that cadets believe in very seriously.

A report of the honor process published in 1973 attested to the emotionalism of the process by describing the scene in the courtroom: "Friends of the accused cadet frequently stack the gallery and shout advice or even attempt to intimidate certain members of the Honor Committee. As a result, the Academy has been forced to install a heavy curtain between the gallery and the committee; it is drawn when the gallery becomes too vociferous. All votes are taken in the open . . . Only one vote for the accused is required for a finding of innocent." I was shocked when I read that description of the honor process, because that is not at all the way the system worked in 1979.

Hearings are held in a building known as Division 1, the old First Division barracks where Douglas MacArthur lived as a cadet. The basement of the building houses the pizza parlor, the first floor is where the cadet bank operates, and on the second floor, in a large open room with a long wooden table, is where the honor boards are convened. Any member of the Corps may sit in on the hearing, provided the accused has no objection. No one is permitted to be raucous in any way. There is no heavy curtain to separate the gallery from the board. Votes are taken by secret ballot; 10 to 2 is the voting margin. Every consideration is given to the accused cadet, and much leniency is allowed during trial proceedings.

During the first of the two boards in which I participated, we deliberated less than an hour when reviewing the evidence that indicated a cadet was guilty; then we spent four hours reviewing the evidence which could possibly provide him with a vote of innocent. Yet, this was a fairly obvious case, with the cadet (a plebe) admitting his guilt. We nevertheless deliberated for five hours after the end of the trial, which took an entire day in itself. The beauty of the system is that the Honor Board members do not *want* fellow cadets to be guilty and will go out of their way to try to prove that. The system is jeopardized only when outside forces act upon it, as was the case with a member of the Class of 1981 who fraternized with one of my female classmates (a violation of regulations).

Though the cadet was observed by the cadet-in-charge-of-quarters, when the cadet was questioned about the offense, he lied. Both the CQ and the female plebe testified against him at his hearing. It was one of the most open and shut cases the Honor Committee has ever brought to a hearing. But the entire investigating process took a little over ninety days to complete. Keep in mind that the cadets run the system while they are trying to keep up with all of their other Academy requirements, and they conduct other potential honor violations investigations at the same time. Cadets are busy people who *volunteer* to be members of the Honor Committee. Unfortunately, the civilian concept of "due process" would like to see the honor process improved to provide a finding in less than ninety days, which is almost impossible given the structure of the cadet environment and the desire to give the cadet every opportunity to be determined innocent. In the case of the fraternization, however, the system was tampered with.

The "found" cadet wrote to the congressman who had originally appointed him to the Academy, Senator Sam Nunn of Georgia. Many congressional egos are on the line where their West Point appointments are concerned, and Nunn was no exception. As a member of the Senate Armed Services Committee, Nunn spoke to the secretary of the army (then Clifford Alexander) and convinced him that due process was not observed, which subjected the cadet to mental cruelty (having to wait so long for a decision on his status). Alexander ordered our superintendent, LTG Goodpaster, to reinstate him in the Corps. At an assembly of the entire Corps one evening in the theater of Ike, the Supe relayed these events and told us that he refused to malign the system in such a manner, but that he would reinstate the cadet if specifically ordered to do so by his superior, Alexander. Alexander made it an order, and the cadet was reinstated. However, knowing the Corps would be up in arms at what we saw as a travesty of justice, General Goodpaster suspended the cadet for two years, with full pay and allowances, and gave him the option to return at the end of that time to finish his cadet career.

"Additionally," Goodpaster said to the outraged group seated noisily before him, "the secretary of the army anticipated some outrage from the Corps, so I had to give him my word that the cadet corps would comply with his order. There will be no letter-writing campaigns to the President or to your own congressmen. Events in life are often not fair. I believe the cadet was guilty, as all of you do. I fought this decision in every way that I could. In the end, our boss, yours and mine, has ordered us to accept this situation, and that is what we must now do. You present your arguments in every way you can, but ultimately the decision belongs to your commander. Whatever he decides, you abide by. This is a good lesson for your army careers. Please don't let this destroy your faith in the Honor Code and System; it still works, and works well."

I don't recall a day at the Academy when I felt more empty. I blame this failing of the system on the ego of a man who had no concept of what the West Point experience really encompasses: how you believe it with your mind, nurture it in your heart, and adopt it with your soul. The only fear I have in revealing this incident (which respected sources have asked me not to do) is knowing what men like that can do if left unaccountable for their actions.

The Long Gray Line is not a list of 30,000 dead men. It's a spiritual bond to generations of men who kept the tenets of Duty, Honor, Country alive and inspired them in others — men who proved that choosing "the harder right" over the "easier wrong" is a successful way to live. It is possible to be a member of the Senate Armed Services Committee or even to be the secretary of the army and not understand how the system at West Point, or any service academy, works. This is not a normal college experience. And if it seems "tough" in a modern age, well, it has to be if society wants today's graduates to live up to the history that West Point graduates have forged over the past almost 200 years.

It is difficult to understand West Point, no matter how many books are written or movies made about it, unless you have lived through it. Before my younger brother attended West Point, he'd listen to the often tearful phone calls I'd make to my parents and remark to my mother, "It can't be *that* bad. Besides she's so little, and she's a girl. No place could be that terrible." After three days at the Academy, he called home (he slipped into the golf clubhouse while trying out for West Point's golf team to make the call).

"Remember how tough Donna said this place was? It's ten times worse!" he screamed into the phone. "How did she ever do it?!"

When he left the Academy two years later, he told my parents: "I have the greatest respect for Donna! You just don't know what it's like unless you've been through it."

Does this mean that nongraduates aren't entitled to know what goes on at West Point? Certainly it does not. That's one of the reasons I became involved in the Public Relations Council. I always tell my audiences that, as the taxpayers who support the institution, they should feel free to ask me anything about West Point, no matter how sensitive they may think the subject is. In these times of huge national debt and overstuffed military budgets, I don't want Americans to feel that one dime of their tax money is misspent on the education and training of young people at U.S. service academies. But, just as a man who'd never driven a car would probably not be the best choice for CEO of

Chrysler, someone who does not have a West Point background is not a good candidate to make decisions about West Point. Similarly, it makes no sense that the secretary of the army is a civilian position which requires little or no prior military experience.

Despite the reinstatement of several "found" cadets by higher powers and several "scandals" associated with the system since the code was established, I can say without reservation that the Honor Code works. In the classrooms, cadets sit at adjoining desks and take tests, often (though not always) unsupervised by instructors. The instructor hands out the tests, face down, tells the cadets the start and stop times for the exam, then goes into the hallway, where he can be found seated if a cadet has a question. The cadets turn the paper over and begin the exam at the correct time, and the cadet at the head of the section announces "cease work" when the time is up.

I can remember feeling so good inside the first time I took a test without the instructor in the room. It was a relatively simple calculus test, so I spent most of my time looking around, wanting to see for myself if the system really did work. I don't remember the test grade, but I'll never forget how proud I was to be a part of such an unbelievable system.

When the system fails, it is an individual who fails, unable to adapt to the higher moral-ethical code required by the system. In the much publicized "silencing" of Cadet Pelosi, Pelosi was reinstated to the Corps based on a technicality that was found when he enlisted the help of an attorney to fight his dismissal (outside influence again). He was found guilty of changing wrong answers to correct ones on a self-graded quiz. There were several witnesses. The Corps, who owned the code, voted on the silence and enforced it, until the media misrepresented the case against Pelosi and generated public sympathy for him, which had the potential to hurt the Academy. Before the Corps would allow this to happen, they voted to end the nineteen-month silence. Silence or no silence, Pelosi was guilty, and cadets won't tolerate it — and shouldn't. The American public shouldn't want them to, either. It's a serious system: No one dons white robes and runs around the Academy grounds late at night. It may not be perfect, but it's the best system available at any academic institution today.

Stealing is also a violation of the code. There are no locks on any cadet doors at West Point. Cadets have thousands of dollars' worth of stereo equipment in their rooms, not to mention record albums, calculators, and personal computers. There isn't any stealing. It's a marvelous feeling to live in such a trusting environment. Of course, we leave our trusting attitudes behind when we enter the world outside the gates at the end of four years. But the system works at the Academy because everyone *wants* it to work.

Dating at the Academy is done from a unique perspective. Since there is no public display of affection (PDA) at the Academy, cadets have to be very careful. Hence, the famous "Flirtation Walk" was created. This area was supposed to provide cadets with some privacy for romantic moments.

When I first visited the Academy, I heard many stories of passionate moments and even sexual conquests occurring along the walk. As a cadet, I couldn't wait to finally see this anomaly. It wasn't until September of my plebe year that I first accepted an invitation to "Flirty." Randy and I decided to visit it one Saturday night. I was so nervous. Given all I'd heard about Flirtation Walk, I wondered if it was a place for "nice girls." And, for the first time, I questioned Randy's motives: Did he really want to see Flirty or take advantage of the privacy?

My heart was pounding wildly inside my chest as we found the well-hidden entrance to the walk. An overhead archway announces "Flirtation Walk" and a smaller sign cautions "Cadets and their Guests Only." Even officers are supposed to leave this area to the cadets.

We weren't inside the walk for more than two minutes before fear and anticipation gave way to ridiculous humor. This wasn't a place for a young lady, or any lady, especially not one wearing heels. It was better suited for billy goats! A cadet would have to be desperate to bring his date here. And as for all the things cadets boast of doing along the walk . . . well, I suppose anything is possible, but it's just not as probable as I had come to believe. Randy was surprised as well. As we walked the rest of the way we made jokes about the stories we'd heard.

I went back there only once more during my plebe year, to show my parents when they visited for Plebe Parent Weekend (when all of the upper-class cadets leave for spring break, but the freshmen remain and run the Corps). I guess I wasn't ever desperate enough to go back. But, if it's daytime (and you're wearing the proper shoes), Flirtation Walk is well worth the visit.

Along the often narrow and generally rocky path is located the ever-popular "Kissing Rock." It is alleged that, if a young man and woman pass this spot without kissing, the huge overhanging boulder will fall upon them. More traditionally inclined cadets tell that West Point will lose the Army–Navy football game if they're not kissed at this spot. The rock is very hard to miss: painted on the ground underneath it is a huge set of red lips.

If you survive this first test, you can go farther down the path, where the thick woods part at a small cove in the river, and find pieces of the great chain wall which was built across the Hudson during the American Revolution to keep the British armada from journeying any farther up the river. George Washington credited the construction of this chain as a key element in defeating the British and winning the Revolutionary War. On down the walk, at the edge of a clearing on top of one of the many cliffs, are several park benches from which can be seen some of the most breathtaking views of the Hudson River Valley. In the summertime, cadets often sit secluded there, reading and watching the *Dayliner Ferry* carry sightseers up and down the Hudson, to and from New York City, or they spread a picnic lunch on the ground before the bench and share the scenery with a friend. But at night, the walk is very definitely dangerous.

For the most part, dating at West Point provides emotional support rather than physical favor. We would meet each other at the pizza parlor in Central Area, go running together at night through the housing area and talk about the problems of academics or the unfair demerits we'd gotten that day, or not talk at all. Often it was nice to just share the silence with someone who cared. And on Saturday nights there was always a dance. Whether the dance was held at Ike or at Cullum Hall, both buildings, located along the river, provide the cadets with romantic balconies for strolling with a date and admiring the moon on the water and twinkling lights of the towns across the river. At an institution where, for 200 years, the presence of the most masculine of males has spawned three private girls' colleges within a very short cab or bus ride, the opportunity for romance thrives! Finding the time to enjoy it is the difficulty. A Naval Academy midshipman on loan for one semester during the Service Academy Exchange Program told me that, compared to the Naval Academy, West Point was a "prison."

"Then it's the most romantic prison in the world," I added as we watched a shooting star fall into one of the many mountains skirting the riverbank.

Of course, in an environment where time is of the essence and there is always too much to occupy one's mind, dating is often more humorous than it would be in a "normal" world. Most "dates" take place on Saturday evenings (Friday nights are out due to Saturday morning classes), and by the time a cadet is an upperclassman, he or she is comfortable enough with the Academy's regulations that, if two cadets are dating each other, they can return to the barracks to "be alone."

In the case of my roommate and myself, we both had cadet boyfriends during our yearling year and often brought them back to our room on Saturday nights. Whoever arrived first would see to it that the lights were on and the door was open — a strict Academy policy. We usually placed the metal trash can in the doorway to ensure that the door stayed open. This also served as a signal to the second roommate to arrive that there was already a male visitor in the room. Of course, that meant it was a signal to any cadet walking by that our room had company. (This was often a sore point with male cadets, whose girlfriends were not allowed to return to the barracks, legally, after a Saturday night date. Female cadets did not like having everyone in the company know their personal business. But living in a goldfish bowl was part of being a woman at West Point.) The second roommate arriving would then make some sort of noise, like moving the trash can, to let the first one know that she was entering.

In our barracks, each room was divided into two alcoves by an eight-foot-tall center wall. Leslie and I would sit on our beds with our dates in the semiprivacy of our alcoves and talk and kiss, but the door always remained open and the lights always remained on — and I mean bright overhead lights. The bright lights bothered me at first, so Dave and I would go for walks and sneak a kiss behind a tree when no car headlights could be seen coming down the road. It wasn't very long, however, especially as winter approached and the nights got much colder, that an opportunity to be held and kissed by Dave was more important than the inconvenience of an overhead light.

Most cadets respected your privacy when they saw a trash can holding the door open. Of course, on a Saturday night, most cadets were anywhere but in the barracks. So, returning to your room with a cadet date was standard practice in cadet-cadet relationships. Usually the couple returned to the female cadet's room, and several females learned to share the limited privacy. This was because many male cadets' roommates were dating civilian women, who were not allowed in the barracks, and therefore these roommates were often not as generous about sharing their room on a Saturday night. In our room, however, Leslie and I felt comfortable with our arrangement, and it continued until her boyfriend, who was two years older than she, graduated.

It was great to be in love with a cadet. The relationship provided me with a deep friendship and someone close to care about me. Though Dave said that he too felt our relationship had helped him through some tough times, he still had a problem with my staying at West Point after the end of my yearling year. He did not want me to commit to the Academy by attending classes the next year. (Cadets still hang around outside the classroom before their first class of cow year, debating the sanity of attending class, and, therefore, committing themselves to two more years at USMA and five years of service in the army.)

"No other woman could ever understand as well as I do what you went through here, and what you'll be experiencing as an army officer," I told Dave, pleading my case in front of MacArthur's statue one evening. "Sure, she could be sympathetic, because she sees you hurting, or excited, because of your enthusiasm, but she can't really *know* what you feel, nor understand why. I can."

Dave didn't want to be alone after graduation, like so many other cadets who get married immediately afterwards. It was really tearing him up inside. As a result, our relationship was sometimes strained, but we remained together. We often took weekends together: we'd go out to a nice restaurant and dance until dawn, then we'd return to my sponsor's house on post to sleep.

Each cadet is offered a sponsor, who acts like a family away from home. Dave's cousin Imy was married to an officer stationed at the Academy, Mike Jones, so that was David's sponsor. I grew very close to them. They were wonderful to me, even including me in all of their holiday celebrations. They offered to be my sponsors, but another friend of David's family, a cadet hostess named Mrs. Barbara Brown, widow of Col. George Brown, became my sponsor.

Mrs. Brown grew to be one of the most giving, caring women I have ever had the great fortune to know, let alone to love. She taught the cadet cooking classes for firsties and the etiquette classes during Beast that most new cadets slept through, but she understood about things like that. She had been the wife of a West Pointer, and was loved by a great many cadets before I even thought of attending West Point. I remember that I used to hug her a lot; I think that caught her a little off-guard at first, but she adapted to it easily.

She set up a room for me in her lovely old four-bedroom house and decorated it femininely. She was always opening her home to guests of cadets and former cadets.

"That's Donna's room," she'd tell guests when they stayed over. Her three children and four grandchildren seemed willing to accept me as a part of the family. They were scattered around the country, in service to their country, either directly or by marriage, and visited frequently during the ensuing years.

Initially, my friends and roommates were hesitant to visit my sponsor. "She'll make us use the proper fork or something," my roommates would say with fear.

"You don't understand her at all," I'd tell them. "That's not what Mrs. Brown is all about." When I finally got them over there, they couldn't wait to go back. We held birthday parties there, and surprise wedding showers during our senior year. Between my mother's training and Mrs. Brown's, I became a gourmet cook. Mrs. Brown was always there for the cadets, and provided my parents with a lovely place to stay when they came up to visit.

Though "Mrs. B" had originally planned to retire from her post, after many years of service to the Academy, at the end of my cow year she postponed her retirement.

"There's no way I can leave before Donna graduates," she told everyone about her modified plans. My second mom was there with me all the way.

As yearlings, cadets had two basic duties: performing as the cadet-in-charge-of-quarters (CQ) and serving as a "plebe chaser." The biggest differences between each of the classes at West Point were the type and scope of the duties they were required to perform. Each year the responsibilities undergo a transition, from tasks of servitude as a plebe to administration of the Corps of Cadets as firsties. As yearlings, third-class cadets get their first taste of real responsibility, no longer protected by the innocence of the fourth-class system.

Each company has a yearling CQ who "guards" the company. He is the first cadet awake in the morning and the last cadet to go to bed at night. He answers the phone, delivers all messages, delivers all packages from Central Guard Room, and basically ensures that the company is manned at all times. One of the most important CQ duties is to monitor the whereabouts of cadets, by checking each cadet's absence card (an accountability system which monitors the privileges of each class of cadet) and checking accountability at call-to-quarters and taps. The CQ also checks the rooms during the day for security violations and accompanies any officers visiting or inspecting the company through the quarters. Because of the scope of the responsibilities of the CQ, the person performing this duty can assist or hinder his or her cadet career.

If the CQ chooses to be a hard case, he can write up the cadets in the company for having untidy rooms during the day, lying in their beds before noon (cadets must remain off their beds until afternoon) or having items out that are supposed to be secured or stowed out of plain sight. This is not the best attitude for a CQ to adopt, especially since part of a cadet's evaluations include peer ratings.

A much better attitude would be to leave a note suggesting the cadet tidy up the room, waking up a cadet who is sleeping and warning him to try to stay awake, and putting out of sight any minor security violations. When I was CQ, for example, I would put away someone's watch if I saw it lying out, then leave a short note to explain what I'd done. If the security violation was a calculator, which was required to be kept locked up, I would keep the calculator at my desk downstairs and leave a note telling the cadet where it was. Cadets appreciate a little kindness, and there are many occasions when a favor done without asking can be returned the same way. It's the "cooperate and graduate" idea all over again.

To check accountability, the CQ has to go to every room in the company, open the door, and ask, "All right?" If the cadets are in the room, they answer, "All right." If they are not, the CQ checks the accountability card to see where they are (library, academic limits, outside limits) and be certain that their class privileges allow them to be there. Often, when I would be taking "all rights," I'd knock on the door of the cadets' rooms, be told to enter, and find a cadet completely nude on the other side. Sometimes it was just a mistake and I would simply close the door and say, "Excuse me." Other times it was obvious that I had been set up. The cadets knew what times the CQ was required to make his rounds, and some would lie in wait for me to find them exposed on the other side of the door. After three of these coincidences with the same pair of roommates, I wrote them up for indecent exposure. The Tac officer threw it out without awarding any punishment, which was fine with me; I just wanted to scare those guys. It must have worked, because it never happened again — from those two, anyway. I spoke to women in several companies that year who said that they had similar problems while taking "all rights." At least I wasn't alone.

The second major responsibility of a yearling is to assist with the administration of the fourth-class system. Many plebes are hesitant to get involved with the system, which is responsible for the military socialization of the plebes and provides leadership opportunities gained from senior/subordinate relationships to the yearlings. If yearlings do not participate in the process, the system breaks down, and neither the plebe nor the upper-class cadet develops properly as a cadet. Cadets who refuse to participate in the system often portray themselves as martyrs: "West Point rated me poorly because I refused to haze plebes," these cadets utter. But hazing has nothing to do with the system. Developing as a leader and maintaining a nonfraternizing relationship with plebes, while demanding high standards of discipline and responsibility from them, characterizes the fourth-class system. It is possible for a cadet to be determined "deficient in leadership" because he does not participate in the system, regardless of his physical or academic prowess. West Point develops a well-rounded military leader; failure in any one area could — and does — result in dismissal from the Academy.

(Such was the case in 1987 with a male cadet from Texas. Though he was easily a Dean's List student, he was dismissed from the Academy for failing to participate in the fourth-class system. He and his congressman and attorney created quite a stir, causing an ensuing investigation into the system. Despite the accusations of the cadet, the system stands and the cadet was not reinstated. USMA makes very clear to cadets exactly what it expects of them. If a cadet is unable to meet these requirements or disagrees with them, he or she is free to leave.)

To help get yearlings to participate in the fourth-class system, they perform duties as plebe chasers. They line up before the lunch and dinner formations to quiz plebes on their knowledge requirements and inspect their uniforms, haircuts, spit-shines, and military bearing. Leslie and I, as new yearlings, got involved with enforcement of the system sooner than most of our classmates, but events forced us into it.

After the plebes attended the parade ceremony marking their transition from new cadets to plebes, the two of us were standing in our doorway preparing to confuse the plebes by using the old "New Cadet, halt!" game which had been used on us. The first cadet up the stairs was a dark-haired male plebe of medium build. As he approached the top of the staircase leading to our floor, he tripped over the lip of the top step and went sprawling onto the landing in front of our door, his hat flying across the floor. Then this fresh cadet picked himself up, placed his hat on his head, smiled and winked, and went on his way, saying, "Good afternoon, ma'am." Leslie and I just stood there, speechless. We'd never seen a plebe do anything as bold as that. After he disappeared from sight, Les and I talked about the incident and decided that these plebes must be pretty bold (known as "BJ"), and we weren't going to let them get away with it.

Neither Leslie nor I believed in raising our voices to plebes or correcting them unnecessarily, but we were firm with them. We used positive reinforcement when the situation dictated, and never let them get away with anything. Two things happened as a result. First, cadets in the junior and senior classes used the examples she and I set to inspire our classmates to participate in the system. "You guys need to start participating like your classmates Peterson and Hyde do. They're really showing you up," the cows would tell our male classmates. That didn't please our classmates. Instead of taking an active interest in the system, three of my male classmates approached me one afternoon and asked me to "back off" my involvement because "you're making us look bad." I explained to them that I believed in what the system accomplishes, and I would be letting the Academy down if I "backed off," which I never did.

Of course, these cadets were participating in the system by the end of the first month, some of them with a vengeance! This is an opportunity for each cadet to develop a leadership style and technique that suits them. These guys started out by yelling at the plebes, as they had seen many cadets before them do. But few cadets ever carry that technique through all four years. By the time a cadet graduates he has to be able to lead his peers, and that is only done by earning their respect, not by keeping them in a state of fear. Everything seems to stabilize by the end of yearling year.

I was the manager of the men's varsity squash team that year and, as one of the plebes from my company was on the junior varsity team, I took the opportunity to ask him who the plebes considered the "biggest haze" in the company. He didn't want to answer at first, but I finally talked him into it.

"Well, there are two . . ." he began. "You and Cadet Hyde."

I was shocked. "Me? I've never even raised my voice to a plebe.

I've never talked bad about anyone's mother or called a plebe disgusting or gross . . . What do you mean *me?* Even worse than the firsties?" I finally let him get a word in edgewise.

"No, ma'am, you're never rude, that's true. But no one can ever get away with anything with you. You catch everything!"

I didn't feel quite as bad after he explained what he meant. And he was right. After our experience with that "BJ" plebe the first day of yearling year, Leslie and I were exacting in our standards, just as the Class of '79 had been with us. For that I have no regrets.

One of the problems with the peer pressure at West Point was letting it influence you to do dumb things to save face with your classmates. Before the Christmas break of my yearling year, I developed an upper respiratory infection, probably as a result of having to take the mandatory flu shot. I had gone on sick call and been diagnosed with the infection, I had a 102-degree fever, and the doctor gave me antibiotics and aspirin for the pain in my bronchial tubes. I was given two days of bedrest to stay indoors (breathing the cold air aggravated the bronchial tubes). But cadets did not look kindly on bedrest. I was determined not to take the bedrest, especially since that meant missing classes, and it was only several weeks from the start of final exams.

For four days I would return from class, change my sweat-soaked T-shirt and bra, wipe myself down with a cool washrag to drop my body temperature, and take an extra-strength aspirin to help me with the pain and reduce the fever. Then I'd head to my next class. There were times when I would cough so violently that my roommate thought I was going to die before I would be able to take a breath! The pain in my chest was unbearable at times, but I was determined to be tough.

What I had been was stupid: just a nineteen-year-old kid who had never succumbed to peer pressure in her life, but was doing a darn good imitation of it now. Finally, after the fourth day, my military history professor, who was older and wiser than I, made me promise that I would return to sick call. I did, ended up taking my two days of bedrest anyway, and eventually got well. This is one example of the reason why Tac officers are assigned to monitor each company and guide the cadets. Cadets, though they often appear mature and capable, are still young kids who often need the wisdom an adult can provide.

Most cadets have more to worry about during their first two years than what they want to be when they grow up. I was no exception, for the most part. I really had no idea what branch of the army I wanted to enter, or how many years I would serve and where. During an academic evaluation one day, my professor told me, "Miss Peterson, if you keep going the way you've been going, you'll be the first female chief of staff of the army." Even Dave would jokingly say, "I don't know if I could get used to being married to a general." It all sounded wonderful, but I only knew that, whatever my future decisions would be, I wanted to return to West Point. I had a burning desire to serve the Academy in a capacity that West Point desperately needed — as a female tactical officer. It was the only career "plan" I had.

The tactical officer, or "Tac," is the commissioned officer placed in charge of a cadet company to oversee, evaluate, and advise cadets. He, or she, acts much like a parent, including prescribing punishments when cadets get too far out of line. The Tac officer is also supposed to be a role model, offering career advice and guidance. Many of these officers were perfectly selected for their roles by the Academy headquarters. Others, however, fell far short.

My desire to return to West Point as a tactical officer probably extended from two basic beliefs: that officers who have not been through the West Point experience are not competent enough to stand in judgment of that system, and that there is a crucial need for good role models for female cadets.

It is impossible for a nongraduate to understand the impact of *one* unfair demerit, of being denied access to a trip section (an Academy-organized trip away from the school on a weekend, usually to support an athletic event), or of being allowed late lights (keeping your desk light on after taps) to study for a test or complete a paper. And how could nongraduates offer advice to cadets in emotional turmoil due to the stress of the complex West Point lifestyle, or provide support to confused cadets trying desperately to reconcile the love-hate relationship that most cadets grapple with when considering resignation? The answer is, they cannot.

And they don't. Cadets generally find some other officer, frequently a professor or a sponsor with a USMA diploma, or even other cadets. And never forget that cadets are sly. The most beloved (notice I did not say respected) Tac officers were Air Force officers. Reason? They seemed the easiest to manipulate. Their careers had been less strenuous, less demanding; they had little knowledge of the army or

West Point; and they took on the role of interservice educator ("Let me tell you how great the Air Force is") rather than leader or role model. How the leadership at the Academy lets this slip by them amazes me. They take the finest young people in the country who enter the Academy with high levels of self-respect, turn them into fine young leaders who now show increased levels of self-respect, and believe that these leaders could respect an officer of *any* service who has not been through even half of what they've been through. That's hardly realistic. And yet the surveys that the Academy asks the cadets to fill out show a great deal of satisfaction with Tac officers from other services. Certainly! It is much easier to have a malleable "buddy" handing out privileges and punishments than a respected leader. That's like asking a young child to choose Mommy over Grandma. Cadets aren't dumb.

The second problem is one that hits even closer to home: the lack of adequate female role models for the female cadets. This idea expands on the problem stated above. Since there were no female Academy graduates when I attended West Point, there was no possible way in which the Academy could have provided female Tac officers who could earn places as role models. To begin, no other female on active duty in any service has been exposed to the training and experiences that female West Pointers can attest to. There is a good reason for this: there are numerous specialties and occupations in all services which are not available for women to work in. In the army, these include the branches of infantry and armor, specialties in field artillery and aviation, and specialty schools such as Ranger and Special Forces. So most women are never exposed to any of these military elements. At West Point, however, every cadet is exposed to all aspects of army service, in order to assist them when they make their career occupation selection and to give them an understanding of the entire realm of a military they may someday command (thirty-four of the thirty-eight corps and division commanders in World War I were West Point graduates). If the men have to go through it, so do the women. I thoroughly loved driving tanks during summer training. In fact, if they had allowed me to choose armor as a branch I probably would not have made my career in aviation. I have never met a non-West Point female who has ever driven a tank.

So, the Academy brought in female officers to "help the females adjust to military life and act as role models." Military life has nothing to do with adjusting to life at West Point, and if you as a female cadet have been better trained than your female Tac, there certainly exists no relationship as a role model.

There were three female Tacs while I was at West Point. It's a sad fact that their primary contribution was to provide credibility to those males who already harbored resentment and exhibited a lack of respect toward females in the military. One of these army captains went by the name of "Bunny" and was rarely seen without her bright pink lipstick (though she was extremely kind and always seemed to be smiling); one was very athletic and masculine in appearance; and the third, unfortunately my Tac during my last two years, was known as "Aunt Mary." The male cadets in my company still keep in contact with her. They enjoyed their power over "Aunt Mary" even to the point of subtly threatening her to win their way of management of the company. She was unmarried and unstriking in face and figure. Her branch was combat service support (as far from meat-and-potatoes combat experiences and training as one could get), and physically and scholastically she probably never would have received an appointment to West Point. The worst thing about having Mary as a Tac was that she seemed to be jealous of the successful female cadets, and she easily succumbed to the false flattering attentions of the handsome male cadets. In an environment where it's particularly difficult to be a female, we certainly did not need additional inequities heaped upon us by another female — an outsider at that, and especially one in a position to enhance or hinder the cadet career that females had struggled every single day to earn.

There exists very little that I would like to see changed about West Point, but in this case I think change is essential. Most women cadets agree that it is better to have no female Tac officers at West Point than to have poorly qualified, non-West Point female Tac officers making life even more difficult for the female cadets.

Since there were no quality role models for women in this male-dominated world, what did the women do without someone to mold themselves after? This was one of the most discouraging observations I made while at the Academy. The truth was, most women floundered, becoming confused about who and what they were and how to act. The women in the Class of 1980 seemed to try to be better men than the men who were already at the Academy. I don't fault them for that; given the tremendous odds they faced as the first women to infiltrate this prestigious center of macho-dom, I'm certain they felt that this was the best way to survive. For their survival I will always be grateful. But, having survived, they became cruel to the women who followed.

There was at least a slight kinship between the females in the Classes of 1980 and 1981, but by the time the Class of 1982 entered, many of the females in the Class of 1980 were unkind and cruel. They all but tortured the younger females.

My class was told that we brought into the Academy the highest quality (statistically) of females that the Academy had seen. And we were young and enthusiastic. By this time, the women in the Class of 1980 were bitter about their experiences, confused about their roles as women and military officers, and many were overweight (due mostly to the extremely heavy feeding regimen the cadets were exposed to at the time). They had been through a great deal, without the benefit of adequate female role models and only themselves for support. I'm certain that they did not want the younger women to take their sacrifices for granted. But I'm also certain that, for many of those women, jealousy clouded their professionalism. I have to admit that, as a senior, seeing the young and enthusiastic female new cadets running about and hearing the resultant comments from male cadets, I, too, felt a twinge of jealousy. I understood how the first females at the Academy might have felt upon the arrival of a new crop of females. However, no excuse was sufficient for the extreme poor treatment that these women heaped on the younger female cadets.

When my class entered the Academy as plebes, these women were juniors (cows) and had accepted their first leadership roles. Many of them went out of their way to degrade and hassle my classmates. Of course, all plebes are hassled at the Academy; that's part of what being a plebe is all about. But the women could take liberties with their harassment that male cadets would find hard to comprehend, let alone copy. I remember vividly the nightly visits of one particularly rude and unfeminine woman who would enter my room in the barracks, without knocking, then stand my roommates and me at attention while she referred to us as "sluts," "whores," and "bitches." She'd back us up against our lockers and accuse us of "batting eyes" and "swinging hips" to get attention. She didn't even know us; we'd only been in the company for three weeks. Though we were threatened severely to keep quiet about these "visits," after the second one I told my squad leader, who assured us that her behavior was in direct violation of the fourth-class system. The next time she entered our room and let loose with her guttural imagery, I mustered every ounce of courage within me and informed her that I had more morals in my little finger than she had in her entire body. I then asked her to "please leave," telling her that I would inform our squad leader of her visit.

Before I got to West Point, I couldn't wait to meet the women in the first class, to thank them for the hell I know they must have gone through. At that moment, however, I was sorely disappointed. I wanted to like them, to emulate and respect them, but I just couldn't. Not as a group, anyway. The female cadet left the door open as she exited.

The females in my company had no further problems with that particular female cadet, but there were others to take her place. At the end of the plebe year, each freshman had an appointment with the Tac officer to discuss the cadet's performance during that difficult first year. Of all the ratings I had received, only one had any negative comments. In fact, both my roommate and I received the same poor comment: "She must learn to be more professional. She cannot use her femininity to achieve leniency from the males." I was shocked! I had won the company's Best Cadet award and received surprisingly outstanding ratings from the male cadets in the Class of 1979. When my Tac asked what I thought of that evaluation, I told him (I had a strict male Tac then) that I was shocked and I was certain the evaluation had been written by one of the 1980 females. He couldn't believe I had guessed correctly, and I was certain he could see how very obvious this was. He eventually dismissed the comment, telling me that I was one of the highest-rated cadets in my class. And he reminded me that I had learned a valuable lesson about cadet life (and life in general) that day. He was strict and very tough and I liked him because of it. Before I left his office, I asked him to tell me the name of the person who supplied the negative rating, so I could face my accuser. Ratings, however, were confidential, and I was left to guess the name of the guilty party. Leslie and I were certain it was the work of the female who had made the repeated visits to our room, but I had to be certain. We were well into the football season of our yearling year before I had the chance to find out.

I was assigned duty as the CQ, and the Tac asked me to pick up several cadet files for review. I took the opportunity to add my own name to the list and went up to the fourth floor of Washington Hall, where the records were kept, to get the files. Once I had them, I stopped at the female latrine, went into one of the stalls, and looked through my file. I couldn't believe my eyes: My roommate and I were wrong! Of the four 1980 women in our company, it was the one we suspected as least likely to write such unfounded negative comments.

This cadet was tall, rather slender, and blond. She was a pretty girl, though probably the least military of the four women. She was much more involved with the men she was dating and keeping up with current fads and styles as revealed in *Glamour* magazine. She never even paid any attention to us, positively or negatively. Yet, she had her say — anonymously, of course.

I closed the file and returned it to the records office, taking the rest of the files, and my newfound knowledge, back to my company. Years later I ran into this cadet while we were both lieutenants in the army. She wanted to be friends, but she hadn't changed. Her military reputation was less than successful, and she spent five minutes explaining how crowded her dating schedule was. I could not forget how unkind and cowardly she had been.

Although the women in the first class were now seniors, they were still unable to dismiss their bitterness toward the younger females. On one occasion, while walking through the mess hall, I heard, "Miss!" I looked around and saw an upper-class female looking at me. I didn't say a word. "Yeah, you!" she continued, moving closer to me. "I think your hair is a bit long. See to it that you get to the barber shop today." I knew her. This was Joy, another female from the Class of 1980. "Do you understand me?" she prodded.

Now, some of the privileges of being an upperclassman included being able to walk slowly to classes, hang around in the hallway for no reason, and being able to refer to the cadets in the upper classes by first names rather than by "Sir" or "Ma'am," while they no longer referred to you as "Mister" or "Miss." Not the greatest privileges, but hard-earned ones nonetheless. So her attitude, even if she had been correct, was unacceptable.

"First of all, my name is Donna, not 'Miss.' Secondly, I have a chain-of-command who inspects my haircut on a daily and weekly basis, and therefore your opinion means nothing to me. If you have a problem, take it up with my company commander." As I turned to leave I thought of one last comment. "By the way," I mentioned, "you have a real attitude problem," and I went about my business. I can relate a dozen more stories of the same nature that I witnessed before the class with the first West Point females graduated. I used to say that if I had a choice when walking across the area to pass nearer to and be hazed by a senior cadet from the "last all-male class" or a female cadet from the class of 1980, I'd choose the male. The male class disliked the women being at the Academy, but at least there was a chance that they would be fair with you.

Overall, the attitude of the women in the Class of 1980 disappointed me and every one of my female classmates I have ever spoken to about it. Individually, however, I knew several women from that class who did not contribute to that evaluation. These included a cadet who managed to transform her bitterness into humorous anecdotes in an attempt to bolster morale for both women and men; Patty Walker, a fellow gymnast and one of the few black female cadets at the Academy; and Becky. I noticed Becky from across the area one day while I was still a freshman, and I thought she was the most beautiful woman ever to set foot at the Academy. She was a tall, slender brunette, soft-spoken and kind, and very unaffected by her beauty. The perseverance of these, and all of the women in the Class of 1980, during that first difficult year was recognized and admired throughout the world. Now, however, it seemed best for the Academy that these women graduate and leave, taking with them the scars I know it took years to heal, and finally allow the U.S. Military Academy to move into the future.

The day the first woman graduated from West Point started out the same as the first graduation I had witnessed: with the pomp and pageantry, hustle and bustle of 4,000 cadets. At about 10:00 A.M., the 900 graduating cadets marched onto the football field from opposite ends of the stadium under a sky of blue and golden sunlight. The academic board and USMA dignitaries were introduced and the guest speaker took his place at the podium.

That year the speaker was the secretary of defense, the Honorable Harold Brown. He spoke of the Middle East and problems of foreign policy and matters of State. It probably was a very good speech, but, although the 4,000 minds he addressed in the ninety-degree heat were in distant lands, the Middle East was not one of them. Each of those cadets was anticipating some form of a new life to begin this day. The firsties received their army commissions, the cows pinned on the long-awaited black brass of a firstie, the yearlings were about to embark on a summer as leaders in the real army, and the plebes became upper-class cadets as soon as the sea of white caps filled the sky. And summer leave would begin for all in three short hours. As he finished speaking, I could almost feel all of those minds funneling back into the stadium and focusing on the astroturf between the two forty-yard lines.

The superintendent rose to graduate and commission 900 cadets. The brigade staff made its salute to the distinguished guests and the crowd. As the brigade commander ascended the ramp to the platform, the corps of cadets and the graduating class rose and applauded, not in tribute to their leader, but in tribute to the class which he led. He received his diploma and returned to join his class on the field. Then the class valedictorian received his diploma, and again the stadium was filled with applause for this outstanding cadet and academician. The honor graduates would be next to receive their diplomas and then the rest of the Class of 1980, in alphabetical order. (The traditional Order of Merit had been abolished several years earlier when it was decided that the honor of graduating from the Academy was more than sufficient in itself and that the order in which a cadet graduates only demeans the honor.)

The first several cadets graduated rather routinely, parents and friends applauding for their favorite cadets, the Corps applauding for all of their former members. Suddenly, it seemed everyone in the stands was reminded of why this graduation day would be remembered differently in the history books. As Andrea Lee Hollen stepped forward to receive her diploma, a resounding roar filled the stadium; it was a combination of proud clapping and scattered grumbling. Among the thousands of people in attendance, very few made an effort to clap harder or cheer louder; almost no one rose to applaude. The response did not seem remarkable enough to befit this momentous occasion. I was upset with myself for being surprised at the lack of enthusiasm; I should've known that the crowd would not consider this a great day. But *I* did, and so did the media.

As flashbulbs popped and cameras whirred and clicked, the first woman in the history of the United States of America was graduating from the U.S. Military Academy. Not only was she West Point's first female graduate, she was also a Rhodes Scholar. A tingle started in my toes and danced its way up my spine. I shuddered and clapped harder. Tears rolled effortlessly from my eyes. I stood up a little bit taller, held my head a little bit higher, and felt more than a little bit prouder to be wearing the same uniform as the first woman graduate from West Point. I knew how much she and the other female graduates had endured to be seated on that field, and what they'd given up as women.

The rest of the graduation went on as planned. The "goat," the cadet with the lowest grade point average to be allowed to graduate, also received an ovation from his classmates on the field and Corps mates in the stands. Parents and friends looked toward the Corps in bewilderment, not understanding our display. The Academy had outlawed any distinction of a last graduate; but then, there were always a few traditions the Corps refused to let die. This was our way of honoring him. He took a bow as he accepted his diploma, with a grin from ear to ear. As the last row of cadets rose to receive their diplomas, they removed their hats, faced the audience in the stands, and bowed to salute and thank the parents and friends who'd helped them to this station in life and who came to share in their joy. No one seems to know where this tradition started, but it's a very important part of a cadet's final moments at West Point.

The superintendent pronounced the class "graduated," then the cadets raised their right hands and spoke their commissioning oaths as officers in the regular army. This completed, the cadet first captain announced, "Class dismissed," and the white hats flew.

On the way out of the stadium, one last tradition must be carried out: the presentation of a single silver dollar to the first person who salutes the new officer. Usually this is a cadet, and very few graduates get out of the stadium area without giving up their silver dollar. Some cadets have a particular friend or relative they choose to share this experience with so they completely ignore any and all salutes until they can find the designated person. I witnessed several fathers who were career noncommissioned officers saluting their sons for the first time and receiving the silver heirloom in a marvelous display of family warmth and patriotism. Even a sister duo made the same exchange.

Once back in the barracks area, there was little left to do but change clothes and mutter any last goodbyes. Cadet cars, fully packed the night before, lined the area between the barracks. Cadet uniforms lay in piles around the outside of the barracks and protruded from overstuffed dumpsters. Most of the uniforms would be resold to other military schools such as the Virginia Military Institute (VMI) and the Citadel. However, many cadets would keep their uniforms for the sake of nostalgia, pulling them out years later to remember with confused emotions the love-hate relationship they endured here. With graduation over, the Long Gray Line welcomed its newest members — and its first females.

# CHAPTER 6

# "Best Summer of My Life"

*"I am not worthy of the position. It would take one much greater than I to lead West Point."*

> — Gen. Robert E. Lee, upon being asked
> to become superintendent of USMA

A fter a brief summer leave, I began what I could not possibly have known would be the best summer of my life. This was the summer when cadets are given the opportunity to serve as junior officers with an active army unit in a program known as Cadet Troop Leader Training (CTLT). It is nicknamed the "Best Summer of Your Life." In addition to CTLT, or the Drill Cadet Program if the cadet prefers, cadets are afforded the opportunity to attend one of several Cadet Military Specialty Training (CMST) programs including airborne, air assault, northern warfare, jungle operations, survival, evasion, resistance and escape, and flight training. With the myriad options available to cadets it promised to be an exciting summer for each of us, but I could never have predicted just how exciting.

I selected the CTLT option at Fort Hood, Texas, only five hours from my parents' home, followed by flight training at Fort Rucker, Alabama. I settled into the Bachelor Officer's Quarters (BOQ) at Fort Hood, then donned my khaki uniform to make the trip to my CTLT

155

company. I was assigned to a Signal Corps company about a half mile from the quarters. The lieutenant who was "sponsoring" me picked me up in her car. Even in the evening the Central Texas heat was oppressively hot; the radio weather report said it was ninety-seven degrees at 7:00 P.M.

Once we arrived at the company, I was mobbed. Every female soldier who saw me, dressed in my khaki uniform, was overly excited because she thought the army might be issuing the much sought-after uniform to women. Not so. Only the West Point females of the first few classes had been issued these uniforms. Normally, only males were issued this uniform. Since men and women at the Academy had to dress as identically as possible, West Point women were issued the popular tan uniform. I spent the next several days explaining this to every female I met, then I changed into my green fatigues and was no longer besieged with questions.

I spent most of the next day getting in-processed, with the aid of my sponsor, and didn't meet my company commander until late in the afternoon. We talked for about forty-five minutes, then he said, "How about I show you the Officer's Club? I have to meet my girlfriend there later this evening anyway." I accepted, went to my room, and changed from my sweat-soaked uniform into a sundress.

We were seated at the bar of the area of the club known as the "pub." After about thirty minutes, the captain excused himself to make a phone call. As he did, I wheeled around on the stool and saw a group of CTLT cadets and what appeared to be lieutenants talking about five feet behind me. I surveyed the group to see if there was anyone I knew, and saw several of my classmates. I walked over to the group to ask them what units they were assigned to for the summer. As I approached, a lieutenant standing near the head of the group turned toward me. I stopped and smiled.

"Hello," I said calmly to the enigma standing before me, though inside my body I was anything but calm. *I'm not a plebe anymore*, I thought, *and I'm not going to act scared like one!*

"You look very familiar to me," the officer said. "Do I know you?" I was disappointed. He didn't even recognize me. I nodded that he did know me, but didn't offer any clues to our association. Just then one of the cadets I didn't know asked if I was a cadet. I said that I was. The lieutenant looked as if the lights of the Empire State Building had just turned on in his head.

"Donna, isn't it?" he said as he offered me his hand. Déjà vu.

Same words, same gesture, same dark eyes, same fluttering heart, same Tony Cuccolo! "You look different. I didn't even recognize you!" he continued. His comment made me feel better about his not recognizing me.

"Correct," I replied, trying to sound like an adult. "How are you, Tony? It's been a long time." It had been more than a year since I'd last seen him en route to his graduation, but he was still just the same as I remembered him: outrageously charming and gallantly desirable.

We talked for about five minutes, until I saw my company commander returning to his seat. I made some polite comment about how good it was to see him, and said goodbye, returning to my place at the bar. The captain couldn't get in touch with his girlfriend, but he was going to try her again in fifteen minutes. I'm sorry to say that I don't remember a word that passed between us during those next fifteen minutes. The presence of Cadet — now Lieutenant — Cuccolo was having its old familiar effect on me. Just after the captain left his chair a second time, I noticed the air fill with a wonderful aroma. Tony peered over my shoulder.

"Who is your friend?" he asked. I grabbed my drink with both hands so that he wouldn't see them shaking. I explained the situation to him. "Good," he said. "If you're not doing anything tomorrow, would you like me to show you the area? It's not much, but it's home, and I'd love to."

*There is no way that this is happening to me,* I thought, *so wake me up and stop tormenting me.* "Great!" I heard myself reply. "What should I wear?" I always ask this question when I accept a date; it must be something inborn.

"Casual. Shorts or jeans. I'll pick you up at nine. We'll go to breakfast first, OK? What's your BOQ number?" I told him and we said goodnight.

I asked my commander to take me back to my room, and he complied (his girlfriend had been detained and would meet him later). I couldn't wait to call my mother. I relayed the conversation to her verbatim, several times.

"I've never seen you like this over a guy!" she said with a hint of confusion. Mom was great to share these things with because she always kept the enthusiasm alive; she never rained on my parade.

I think I was still in shock when he showed up at my door the next morning. We got into his white Corvette and headed toward Temple, Texas, for a day of mall-walking. We had a great time, laughing until we were almost in pain. I found that I could sit for hours and listen to his stories about his experiences as an infantry platoon leader. We grabbed a bite to eat and returned to Tony's house. While sitting on the couch and listening to "Casey Kasem's Countdown" on the radio, I heard a long-distance dedication from a female service academy graduate to all the women who had graduated from U.S. service academies several weeks earlier. The song was "I Am Woman."

I lost track of time after that. I remember sitting on the couch as the lights of the stereo grew brighter, enjoying the smell of aftershave in the room and the curves of the shoulders and arms of the man wearing it. The next thing I remember was the explosion of fireworks and skyrockets as our lips slowly met in a soft and gentle fantasy kiss. I had heard people tell tales of magnificent light shows produced by a single kiss, but I was a nonbeliever until this night. The heavens collided when our lips met. This feeling was new to me, and I was enjoying it thoroughly.

I don't know how long we touched, kissed, and embraced in the amber light of the stereo that night. Whether it was two hours or ten, I was unaware. I only know I never wanted it to end. Neither did Tony. "I don't want you to leave," he said softly as he broke the silence of the past few hours.

"Say that again," I pleaded. I couldn't believe how much better this dream continued to get. His lips were smooth and soft, his manner caressing and deliberate. It's a good thing that Tony didn't ask me to marry him that evening because I honestly believe that the answer to the question I have almost made a career of responding "no" to would have been "yes."

I took a deep breath and sighed as a stranger's voice filled the air. "Will you take me back to my room?" It was a female voice, therefore it must have been mine. "Tomorrow is another day," I added, trying to reassure him that my mind, body, and soul wanted to remain there with him, but some part of me knew I had to leave. If I'd stayed any longer, I doubt I would have had the willpower to leave until morning. Despite all my marvelous fantasies, I wasn't ready for that kind of reality.

The rest of my stay at Fort Hood was heavenly. I saw Tony at every opportunity. I was slimmer than I'd ever been, tanned, and in love. I thoroughly enjoyed being a platoon leader and, with Tony's guidance, was a success at it. "Just remember, you have the right to demand any standard of these troops you want. Just don't be too disappointed if you don't get it," was Tony's guidance to me.


The first morning I took over as the platoon leader I held an inspection-in-ranks and gave every soldier an opportunity to make cor-
rections on his appearance before the last formation of the day. To my
delight, the soldiers conformed, and I earned instant recognition from
the battalion commander who had witnessed these events, Lt. Col.
George Bombel (now Brigadier General Bombel). Before he pinned on
his star and departed Fort Hood, he told me an interesting bit of news:
Before he accepted me into his unit as part of CTLT, he was unsure
about the program. Afterward, he made a nuisance of himself, complaining to the commanding general at Fort Hood that he never got
enough West Point cadets sent to his unit as a part of the program. In
an optional evaluation of my summer performance he wrote: ". . .
There are *no* apparent weaknesses in her performance . . . Cadet Peterson is now ready to assume any function required of an officer with
three to four years experience." He also told me that he had never written so glowing a report on any female officer. "Perhaps I'd better take
a closer look at some of the female officers in my command," he said. I
was very fortunate to have served under George Bombel. I probably
learned more about "people management" from him that summer than
at any other time in my career.

When I was preparing to leave the unit, he asked me what I felt
was the secret to my success. I tried to illustrate my answer: My prede-
cessor spent a great deal of time screaming at her soldiers. When I first
took over the platoon, after I finished the two inspections, I sat the soldiers down in the shade of one of the few trees at Fort Hood. There I
was, a small, blonde female West Pointer, looking at my totally black,
Hispanic, and Puerto Rican platoon. The platoon sergeant I was supposed to look to for guidance was in the process of divorcing his wife,
was living out of his car, and was an alcoholic. But he could speak
Spanish, and I needed him because some of my troops could speak very
little English.

This was not working out the way I was told it was supposed to.
West Pointers were characterized as lieutenants who failed to go to
their sergeants for guidance often enough. But I was willing to be
"molded" by a fabulous platoon sergeant, and he was nowhere to be
found. As I looked into the soldiers' faces, I could tell that they were
unsure about me. So I tried to ease some of their fears.

"Let's keep things simple," I told them at the start. "Don't yell at me. I won't yell at you. Don't cuss anywhere within earshot of me. You'll never hear me cuss. Most importantly, don't lie to me. I can solve anything, if I know it's coming. But I can't help you if I get blind-sided. And if I catch you in a lie, I don't care if it's whether you're chewing gum or not, I'll nail you to the wall. Any questions?" Now they certainly didn't know what to make of me. Don't cuss? This was the army. The "LT" must have taken a wrong turn somewhere!

"It'll never work," the commander said after hearing my demands. But it did. If you can inspire respect in your subordinates, you can achieve success. I made the same three demands of the personnel in the two aviation platoons I commanded years later, and they worked there too. I never believed that being a successful officer meant completely following a male role model. I did what felt comfortable to me, and it worked well. In different platoons I may have fallen on my face, but in these three situations I had no problems. My success as a platoon leader that summer gave me confidence in my ability to perform a job at which I was previously very uncertain about being successful, and it also enabled me to spend more time with Tony.

Tony and I spent some time talking about women at West Point. "The one phone call every father of a West Pointer dreaded getting was 'Dad, I'm in love with a cadet,' because it meant you were gay. When I called home to tell my parents about you, it was a phone call I never thought I'd make, but it wasn't difficult at all," he told me. Then he continued about female cadets in general.

"I remember sitting at the table with my dad and talking to him about my position as a company commander in Beast. He asked me what I would do if one of the women fell out of a run. I made a gunlike motion with my hand and pretended to blow the cadet away in much the same way you'd shoot a horse when it's down. But once I became the commander and saw the effort those women put out — and how they had to work so much harder to stay up — I almost felt protective of them.

"When one of your female classmates was hurt when she fell off of an obstacle, they didn't tell me right away. When I found out they had allowed male soldiers from the 101st Division to take her away without out a cadet there to watch out for her, I suddenly felt like a father who had to protect a daughter. I ran out to the road, flagged down a jeep, threw the driver out and said, 'It's an emergency. I'll bring it back later.' Then I drove like a maniac to get to the aid station, burst through the door, almost ripping it off the hinges, and shouted '*Where is she?!*' She was sitting calmly on the table with her leg in ice, waiting to be transported to the hospital. I felt foolish, but the thought of something happening to one of my females was overwhelming."

So, what's not to love about this man? The more I knew of him, the more I liked. I even got the chance to meet his parents that summer (no wonder Tony is the man that he is).

Meanwhile, Dave was on CTLT in Fort Lewis, Washington, where the weather was so cold that his unit had to wear their uniform sleeves down. He was miserable up there — a San Antonio boy who craved the summer sun and tanned like a native. Although our relationship was deteriorating with each phone call, we agreed to meet for the Fourth of July to celebrate my birthday and attend a family picnic at his grandmother's house in Brackettville, Texas. It was great to see Dave and the picnic was fabulous, but Tony Cuccolo was a hard act to follow, especially given the way Dave felt about my remaining at West Point until graduation.

Dave dropped me off again at Fort Hood. He had a long summer leave facing him, and I had my flight training in Alabama. We agreed to write while I was at flight training, but our relationship was never the same after that.


As far as flight school was concerned, suffice it to say that I would rather fly than breathe, if I did not have to perform the latter to stay alive! Helicopters are absolutely the closest thing you can get to actually being a bird. There is nothing else like them. Not even the navy's high-performance aircraft can give you the seat-of-the-pants feeling that these little birds do.

I had seen a television special about a test pilot who had flown most of the world's high-performance aircraft before he tackled helicopter flying — on a dare from a buddy. I couldn't believe it when he said that if he were limited to only one aircraft for the rest of his life, it would be a helicopter. I understand now. It takes a great deal more concentration and manual dexterity to fly a helicopter. There is no auto-pilot and you are "working" the entire time you are flying. Your head is on a swivel, combing the sky for obstacles (power lines, antennas, flocks of birds), and your hands and feet are continually moving to affect or correct the flight of the helicopter. But that's part of the excitement. Aviators say that, when you really get a feel for the helicopter and become an aviator and not just a pilot, you won't be strapping yourself into the aircraft, you'll be strapping the aircraft onto you. I couldn't wait for that feeling.

We had been in Alabama only about four days (I still wasn't able to keep the helicopter within a grid square on a map when I hovered) when a cadet friend of mine offered to take me to the O'Club for dinner to celebrate my birthday. I remember that it was taco night, and that I met a very special man.

He was a lieutenant, Class of 1979, West Point. He was seated at the table across from my friend and me. He heard us talking about the Academy and, since I was a cadet, he thought he'd ask me about some of the female cadets he had in his squad when he was a cadre member during Beast. He was an aviator who was going through flight training in the UH-1 Huey helicopter at the time I met him. We talked for a very few minutes, and I forgot all about him. Two mornings later, he showed up at my BOQ room.

"Since tomorrow is Saturday, I thought you might like to borrow my car to go shopping or something," he said as he handed me keys to a car I'd never seen.

"What will you drive?" I asked him, trying desperately to remember his name.

"Oh, I had a friend drive my motorcycle in. I'll ride it to work and back," he said casually, as if none of this was any inconvenience. Now I had to know his name. I apologized for not remembering it from our first meeting.

"Dave Parker," he said. "David Keith Parker. I see the two of us have the same initials," he informed me, pointing at the nametag on my door, which read "Peterson D. K."

I remember my mother telling me that there were wonderful men in the world (as a reason for not marrying too young). And it seemed that, when I least expected it, I met another one. Another Dave.

David and I went to the beach that weekend, then to a movie. The next night he cooked dinner. Good looks, charm, and handy in the kitchen too! And this man *knew* aviation. We spent hours discussing aviation and flight dynamics while Barbra Streisand record albums played in the background. I had never dated anyone who intrigued me more intellectually. When this man said he was headed for the Naval Experimental Test Pilot school someday, I believed him.

After he brought me home that second night, I invited him into my room. I'd never had a man return me after a date to a place where we would be alone. In high school my parents were at my house and at West Point there were a hundred other cadets in my company. But at the BOQ, I had no roommate and I was apprehensive about inviting a man who had a home of his own into my room. Since it felt like the "grown-up" thing to do, though, I did. After about five minutes of obviously nervous chatter, Dave smiled and said, "Donna, you're not at West Point. You don't have to leave the door open when you have a man in your room."

He was right. I had left the door open at a forty-five-degree angle, just like at West Point. I suddenly felt silly. This was a ground floor room and opened onto the street. Every stranger going by could see right in. David walked to the door and closed it.

"You don't have to be nervous," he said, leaning against the closed door. But I was. Very. I had never had a bad experience on a date; never once had to ask a date to take me home early or (God forbid!) had to use the quarter-to-call-home that my father always reminded me to carry on dates. And I was quite uncertain about this young man's intentions at the moment.

"I'm not going to stay," he continued. "I wasn't even going to ask to come in until you invited me." Suddenly, I felt very foolish. I started to apologize for my inexperienced behavior, but he cut me short.

"I just thought you should know something about me before this relationship goes any further." His manner was very matter-of-fact. "You won't be able to get rid of me very easily. I fully intend to marry you. I love you, Donna." Then he turned to leave. I thought his gesture was sweet, though not very rational. What could I say? I muttered something silly about the fact that we hadn't even kissed.

"Donna, I don't have to kiss you to know I love you," he said, smiling. "I'll see you tomorrow." He closed the door behind him, leaving me stunned. I wasn't certain what my feelings were for this very unique man, but I was looking forward to finding out.

David and I dated for the next three weeks. I didn't tell him about Tony and Dave, though I wrote to and received letters from both of them during the training. He never talked about any of his girl-friends, though I was sure there were some. We water-skied and went to parties at his friends' homes. Imagine the look on Cadet Forrester's face when David showed up at one of those parties with me on his arm!

"Do you two know each other, Pat?" he asked a speechless Forrester, who had also chosen aviation as his career field. MaryAnn would be disappointed, I thought. Forrester was married.

My feelings for David grew as the summer progressed. We had some wonderfully spirited discussions about aviation and some sweetly romantic evenings when I forced him to read to me some of the wonderful poetry he'd written for me. He was tender and gentle, and I enjoyed seeing his hand on my skin. He made me feel so safe. The night before I left, I asked him about his marriage comment. He hadn't mentioned it since, except in some of his poetry. Yes, he fully had every intention of marrying me. He knew it was the right thing to do. He just had to convince me of it. I didn't know about our marrying, but I did know that his kisses were the gentlest I'd ever experienced, and he helped to make this a marvelous summer for me. I would miss him when I returned to the Academy.

Of course, the *best* part of the summer training was "soloing." I raced to the stagefield in my tiny two-seater TH-55 trainer, with my instructor in tow, to be the first to solo on the first solo day. My instructor (who had never trained a female student before but handled the challenge admirably) had said I was ready two days earlier. However, no one was allowed to solo until solo day.

That morning I knew I was ready. But when my instructor stepped out of the aircraft and buckled his seatbelt to the empty seat beside me, I suddenly had this overwhelming urge to go to the bathroom.

"Me too," he said. "I'll go now, and you can go when you get back." Then he walked away from the aircraft, and I was on my own.

"That's why they call it soloing," I said to myself.

Each cadet had to make three complete traffic patterns and landings. During the entire first pattern I was too afraid to look at the empty seat beside me, as if something bad would happen if I did. The instructors had stressed upon the cadets that the weight difference caused by the empty left seat (where the instructor normally sat) could easily cause a student to "overcontrol" the tiny craft, and I was uncertain as to what to expect. On the second pattern, however, I was feeling confident and was not having any control problems. So I not only looked at the empty seat beside me for the first time, but surveyed the countryside, looked at the tower below me, and began singing to myself. Who was going to hear me? I was having a great time!

Once I set the aircraft on the ground after the third pattern, my instructor came out to greet me. He was smiling, and I felt great. "What were you doing up there?" he asked. I couldn't figure out what he was talking about. Then he told me that the instructors watch the soloing students through binoculars from the air traffic control tower.

"Just singing and enjoying the day," I replied honestly. "It was fabulous!"

"We could see your lips moving but we couldn't hear you over the radio," he continued. "At first we thought your helmet microphone was broken. By the third pass, we realized what was going on."

Soloing is actually a very dangerous event, one that makes the instructors very nervous, especially when they see something out-of-the-ordinary happening. The aviation community has mourned the death of more than one student who lost control of his aircraft during soloing. (A fellow aviator gave me a plaque that depicts a crashed helicopter with an aviator standing beside it. The caption reads: "A successful landing is any landing that you can walk away from!")

Back in the field house afterward, the ceremonies began. As each cadet soloed, his T-shirt was ripped from his body and the date and place of the soloing written upon the torn fabric. Tradition also dictated that the first instructor to solo a student be doused with beer (we had to use plain water, but the effect was the same).

After my experience at Camp Buckner with the Cobra, and my enjoyment of the hands-on flight training that summer, I knew that I would choose aviation as my army career branch near the end of my firstie year. I enjoyed flying helicopters far more than I had ever enjoyed flying the single-engine fixed-wing aircraft I flew in high school. I originally thought that by giving up the Air Force Academy I had given up all hope of ever flying. At the end of the "Best Summer of My Life," I felt very lucky, and I couldn't wait to return to West Point to make my commitment to the Academy and to army aviation.

# CHAPTER 7

# Cow Year

*"I have a secret and dangerous mission. Send me a West Point foot-ball player!"*

— Gen. George Marshall

My cow year was a sweet/sour year for me. My entire perspective about the Academy changed that year. On one hand it was the year I looked forward to experiencing the most; on the other, it was the year that shaped my disappointment with the Academy and sparked my bitterness.

The year began early for me. As a newly selected cheerleader, I had to return to the Academy one week before the rest of the Corps. There was much to do, organizing a cheerleading dance team, and I was eager to begin — even if it meant giving up a precious week of my summer leave.

The girls on the squad decided to fashion our new troupe after the famed University of Southern California Dance Team. One of our "coaches" was a bubbly, leggy blond who had been an alternate on the USC squad and was an excellent choreographer. She was the wife of one of the assistant football coaches. I helped her in the choreography of some of the routines. All of the routines had to be performed for the wife of the commandant of cadets, who was personally sponsoring our attempt to refashion the squad. She was the reviewing authority, and she frequently nixed dance sequences that she felt were "too provocative" for West Point cadets to perform. She wanted us to be feminine and sexy while we were performing our routines at the games, but "sweet" at the same time. After all, this was a new venture for the Academy. It would be the first time cadets and graduates saw cadet women in a feminine role; the first attempt to show the world that, contrary to the more popular belief, female cadets were not ugly, masculine, knuckle-draggers. We were normal, healthy females who were average cadets during the week, but who, when the football players donned their gear on the gridiron, donned our short pleated skirts and sweaters with "Army" scripted across the front and headed for the sidelines. We wore makeup and curled our short hair for our performances at the games, and we *did not* do push-ups under the goalposts as the male cheerleaders did (and the female cheerleaders of the previous two years). We did sexy but sweet dances to the latest Top 40 hits, played by the army or the cadet bands, as well as to the traditional West Point fight songs. The females performed with black and gold pompoms, the male yell-leaders toted megaphones.

Changing the cheerleaders this drastically was a large undertaking. The entire operation was run like a secret military exercise. No one knew of these drastic changes unless they were somehow involved with the project.

When I would tell people I was trying out for cheerleader (known as "rabble rousers" at the Academy) they would sneer and look disappointed. "Oh, I think you might be surprised when football season rolls around," was all I could say. The former squad had less than a feminine reputation. The Academy sponsors of the team felt that the women on that squad should portray the ultimate standards of cadet life, in an attempt to show the Corps that they, as women, were equally as qualified as the men to be in attendance. Therefore, the female cheerleaders' haircuts were the shortest in the Corps; they rarely, if ever, wore any makeup; and they joined the male rabble rousers under the goalposts for push-ups whenever our team scored. Their uniforms were severe black and gold vests and skirts with unflattering stripes, which incited the Corps to refer to them as "bumblebees." The cadet radio station, WKDT, ran a very ridiculing commercial about the first cheerleaders, which only fueled the flames of discontent. The spot would start off with small buzzing noises which would increase in intensity until the noise almost overwhelmed the listener. Then some-

one would scream: *"Ahh! Ahh!"* as if being attacked. The radio person-
ality would come on next and say, "The Swarm. Coming soon to a
football stadium near you." The commercial would close with one single buzzing noise and the sound of a swat.

When I was approached by the commandant's wife about the
prospect of trying out for the rabble rousers, I explained to her that I
would need assurances that the squad would be refashioned, because I
had no desire to become a part of the type of cheerleading squad that
already existed. Four years after the Academy made what it believed
would be a good decision, allowing women to become cheerleaders, it
was painfully obvious that the image of women at West Point was suffering as a result. And it was not the fault of the young women who
had the courage to say yes to that idea and place themselves in judgment before the entire Corps of Cadets. They were pretty girls, many
of whom had been cheerleaders in high school, but who were poorly
guided by the officer representative for the group. Had it not been for
the insight of Connie Franklin, the lively young wife of our commandant, the USMA Dance Team, which still exists today and, flatter-
ingly, has changed very little from our original concept, would never
have been created. The women at West Point had been obviously successful militarily, academically and physically, yet the public image of
females at West Point needed strengthening. I agreed to help assist
with that change.

Returning to the Academy also meant seeing Dave (the first
Dave) again. We hadn't seen each other since the Fourth of July weekend I spent in San Antonio with his family, so we agreed to meet at the
Academy a few days before classes began. I was at my sponsor's house,
having just returned from a morning cheerleading practice, when he
called to say he was on his way over.

"How long have you been in town?" I asked, expecting the answer to be given in hours.

"Two days," he said coolly. "I had some thinking to do."

This didn't sound good to me. I ran upstairs to change before I
saw him. I don't know what I was thinking; I suppose I wanted them
both — Dave and Tony. Why not? Sailors do that sort of thing all the
time. Dave was here, Tony was there. I could handle them both. But
Dave never gave me the chance.

He walked in the door sporting the mustache he'd grown during
his long summer vacation. (This was common for cadets to attempt
over the summer break, since cadets are not allowed to wear mustaches

at West Point.) Dave knew I preferred clean-cut men, but he wanted me to see how well he could grow one, and how he looked. He was correct; it made him look even more like Burt Reynolds than before. I ran up to him and gave him a big hug and lingering kiss. "It looks good," I said with mild enthusiasm. "But I still prefer you without it." I didn't mean for it to sound so unkind, but it did, and the conversation didn't get any better.

"Listen," he began, "I know how you feel about Tony. You never made a secret of it. The whole world knows your feelings toward him. I know you love me, but I also know that I don't stand a chance against him, not if you have a choice. And as deeply as I have loved you, I refuse to compete for you. I don't think I deserve that."

Suddenly, I was scared to death. I wasn't ready to be married, but Dave was the first man I had truly loved, the first man I thought I might someday marry. We had spoken about the number of children we would have, and how, at Dave's request, I would convert to the Catholic religion so that our union would be blessed by the church and our children would be raised Catholic. We loved each other's families and our families loved each other. How could this be happening?

"I want to graduate and reserve time at the Cadet Chapel like so many other graduates have done over the years." His eyes were misting as he spoke of his future desires. "You know how very proud I am of you, Donna, but you also know I need a traditional wife, one who'll always be there when I get home at night, not be stationed God-knows-where flying helicopters and calling me on the phone. And I realize now, that can never be you." He was so serious, almost apologetic.

I remembered the tearful talk we had had before the summer began. Dave had asked me to quit the Academy after my yearling year, before I incurred my military obligation, and marry him the day after his graduation from West Point. "Make me the happiest man in the world," I can still hear him saying. But I couldn't. I told him then that, had I quit the Academy without graduating, I would never have known if I could've made it all the way, and, though not intentionally, I might have resented him for that for the rest of our lives.

"I can't take the chance I might hurt you like that," I had told him. "I love you too much. Please try to understand, Dave. I have got to be *me* before I can be Mrs. Anybody."

It had broken my heart to see Dave cry; he was always so strong, almost arrogant. But I knew a very sensitive, very romantic side of Dave that the world was not fortunate enough to know. Today, how-

ever, there were no tears. It was obvious that Dave had done a lot of
serious thinking about the feelings he was putting into words. I had
never been so silent.

"Why are you doing this now, David?" I asked, thinking about
all of the plans the two of us had made for the upcoming year, Dave's
senior year. "What about Ring Weekend?" That was, to both Dave
and me, the most important weekend of a cadet's career. The cadets invite dates or family to fly in from all over the country to mark the special evening. The actual Ring Ceremony is held in the mess hall and is
attended by the cadets only. The Ring Formal is held in the ballroom
of Ike and is attended by officers, cadets, and guests. The ring, more
so than the diploma, is the symbol of four years of hard work and of
dedication to a lifetime of service. Dave and I had counted on sharing
this most special event with each other.

Then there was the Anne Murray concert during the first football
weekend. Anne Murray was the artist who sang our favorite love songs.
And what about my debut as a cheerleader? It was Dave who, knowing
my background as a baton twirler and dance choreographer, actually
convinced me to try out for the squad. He turned away from me when
he heard my question, and we sat in silence while he pondered an answer.

"I, uh, met someone," he said. "She agreed to fly up for Ring
Weekend. Anything after that I'll have to play by ear."

*Met someone?* Those two words were echoing in my brain. Before I
let them take control of me, however, I reminded myself that I too had
"met someone" during the summer. Besides, this conversation wasn't
really about meeting someone new; it was about coming to the realization that, together, Dave and I did not have a future.

"She's not you," Dave said as he slipped his hand over mine. "No
one is! You will always be my greatest love, babe." He turned quickly
and rose to leave.

"Dave," I said, still clutching his hand, "thank you for being
there for me over the last two years."

We shared a tear-stained kiss and exchanged "I love yous" before
I watched the first man I had ever loved walk away from me. I knew
we'd see each other again — the Corps was too small for us not to —
but I also knew that this was for the best.


Keeping busy with the cheerleading squad, at the start of one of the toughest academic years at the Academy, becoming a squad leader and taking command of my own squad, and moving back into the barracks helped me keep my mind off of my terminated love affair.

I detested the incessant moving that cadets had to do. We moved *to* the Academy from home, then *from* our Beast company to our plebe company. To prepare for our Christmas break, we moved all of our belongings down to lockers in a "trunk room." After the holidays we moved all of our belongings back into our company rooms for about three weeks, until new room assignments were made. We then moved all of our belongings into a new room and set it up according to Academy SOP. The week before the end of plebe year, we moved most of our belongings out to Camp Buckner for summer training; the remainder we moved back to our trunk rooms. This went on every semester for four years. This seems like a great deal of extra work, but the Academy tries to explain its reasoning very simply: (1) it is important for cadets to become oriented with one of the main hardships of army life, frequent uprooting; (2) it is important that cadets get used to living with, and adjusting to, different people (our Tac officer would give us "roommate request" forms to fill out, which meant that whatever person you requested to live with would be the very last one assigned to you); and (3) there are times when the Corps is away from the Academy and, during those periods, cadets' belongings must be safely secured. There are no locks on any of the doors. Also, West Point lends itself during the summer months to summer school students, symposiums for exceptionally bright young people and, of course, the newest arrivals at Beast Barracks, all of whom must be housed in concentrated areas of the barracks rather than scattered throughout the Corps.

As soon as I entered the active army I bought a mobile home.

"Why?" my parents asked me.

"Because I'm tired of moving all my belongings. This way I can just move the whole house!" I replied.

I had three male plebes in my squad. Two of them I perceived would be able to make it through the year with little trouble; the third one reminded me of Claire. I would spend hours with him, quizzing him on his plebe knowledge, instructing him on better shoe-shining techniques, and even recommending a better barber for him. Still, he would show up at formation with shoes that looked as if he'd wiped them with a chocolate bar, spouting the wrong number of "days until graduation," and looking as if a drunken barber with a huge pair of shears had cut his straw-colored hair. Oh, Lord. Why me, again? His name sounded like "Buckwheat," which was what the upper-class cadets delighted in calling him. At the squad leader meetings I would vent my anger. "I'm trying desperately to give this kid a sense of self-worth as a West Point cadet, and you people insist on making fun of him. I don't think it's funny, and I don't think it's acceptable behavior under the fourth-class system!" The company fourth-class systems officer agreed and the behavior ceased, but just until the plebe moved to someone else's squad during the next semester. I only cared that he made it to the next semester.

Each squad leader is assigned a yearling assistant to help with the squad. My assistant was a sharp, rather small, blond cadet who came to speak with me after the first week, requesting that I rely on him more and increase the scope of his duties. This was music to my ears. Certainly, he was capable of handling more responsibility, and I was already spread very thinly during this semester. So we worked out a system that gave him greater input with the plebes, per his request. That compliance would later come back to haunt me.

For now, though, the squad was running smoothly and I was eagerly anticipating the debut of the new dance team. On Thursday night before the first game of the season a rally was scheduled. This is the only time when plebes can dress up in outrageous costumes and run around the barracks area yelling and screaming to their hearts' content, all in the name of football spirit. They do not have to wear a complete uniform, they do not have to walk against the walls or square corners, but they still have to respect the senior/subordinate relationships mandated for the freshmen. I asked my assistant to keep an eye on the three plebes for me during the rally.

"Where will you be?" he asked.

"On the ledge," I replied with a wink, pointing to the overhanging roof accessible only from a second-story window.

The operation that night was fairly simple. A theater spotlight had been set up on the sixth floor of one of the buildings on the far side of the area in which the rally was to be held. After the "rally committee" made the rounds through all four regiments of the Corps, inciting cadets to begin the rally, the committee members, using bullhorns and a specially painted "rally jeep," would move the rally into the north area. The normal area lighting system would then be turned off. The dance team would take advantage of the blackness to step out onto the ledge and position ourselves for the first dance number. The cue for the spotlight to light up the ledge would be the first note of the dance number, played by the cadet band, already positioned in the area. Because our new cheerleading uniforms were being saved for unveiling during our debut on Saturday just before the game, we fashioned outfits for ourselves out of the black and gold vests worn by the cheerleaders in past years, with the black cadet-issued running shorts and black high-heeled boots. Our appearance at this rally was designed only to whet the Corps' appetite for Saturday, not to introduce us to the Corps.

Everything was going according to the plan. The rally began about an hour prior to taps. Because of my estrangement from Dave, my mother had flown up to share in the excitement of my debut, and to attend the Anne Murray concert that weekend. The lights went out and the six female cheerleaders slipped out onto the ledge and posed with our backs to the confused audience standing in the darkness. The note played, the spotlight lit up the ledge, and we wheeled about. The all-but-silent crowd gathered in the area began to scream as we performed a hip-swaying, shoulder-shaking precision routine to one of the most popular tunes of the summer, "Freak-out."

After observing about thirty seconds of the routine, my mother, who was positioned front and center, said she began to hear the male cadets remark, "Are those *our* girls?" Then they would answer their own questions, saying, "Nah, those can't be our girls," and after reflecting further saying, "You know, I think those *are* our girls." My mother couldn't keep from laughing as she heard the realization overtake the crowd.

"Those are *our* girls!" I heard a male voice exclaim. The six of us were grinning from ear to ear, pleased with the audience's reaction. We struck our final pose on the last note of the music. Four seconds later the spotlight went off and the area was immersed again in total darkness. When the area lighting system came on again, the girls on the ledge had disappeared as mysteriously as they had arrived. We were a hit!

One or two years earlier I would have interpreted the cadets' response as just that, nothing more. I was less naive now and I could not help but wonder if we would be equally as well received when the men knew for certain that we were "their girls." Dave called me the next day to offer his congratulations. He had been in the audience the night before. He too thought we were "a hit" and couldn't wait to see us on Saturday.

There are no academic classes on a football Saturday due to the

10:00 A.M. parade before the game, which the football players and cheerleaders are exempt from participating in. My sponsor, Mrs. Brown, was the cadet hostess for West Point and loved to entertain. She always hosted the most elaborate "tailgate parties" before the games, attended by thirty to forty people, at her home near the stadium. The army mules, Spartacus, Buckshot, and Ranger (Buckshot is "retired" at this writing and has been replaced by Hannibal II), were always in attendance as well. Shortly before the end of the party and the beginning of the walk to the stadium, Mrs. Brown could be seen carrying out her weekly ritual: feeding M&Ms to the army mascots! This week she also invited the new army cheerleaders.

After the party, we rushed to the stadium where we donned our new uniforms and stuffed ourselves into and onto a Volkswagen that was covered by a huge box wrapped to look like a present. This "gift" to the Corps was pulled by a large motor home decorated to look like a tank. Just after the "game ball" was parachuted into the stadium by members of the cadet parachute team, our group drove onto the field. The stadium announcer read a prepared dialogue to further enhance the illusion, and the cadet band was "at the ready." At the sound of the cannon, we burst from our box and occupied the center of the football field. The band struck up the tune "Celebration," and six enthusiastic cadets performed before the home crowd. Even the football players who stood in the tunnels, waiting to take their places on the field, were watching. Immediately after the performance the six of us ran to the sideline, where the male yell-leader, Bucky, was waiting, microphone-in-hand, to introduce us. The thunderous applause dwindled quickly on the cadet side of the stands when Bucky announced, "Cadet Cindy O'Neill from Company F4!," then proceeded to announce the rest of the group in the same fashion.

In part, the dwindling clapping from the cadet area occurred because the illusion had been too good: "Look, they're bringing in civilian cheerleaders to perform for us." Before women entered the Academy, girls from other colleges would perform cheers on the Army side of the field during the game. Now these cadets were disappointed. And, as always, a faction of the cadets felt that we were just another group of females grabbing the limelight, batting our made-up eyes at our professors to get easy grades. No matter what we did we were not going to satisfy that group. But overall, though the rampant enthusiasm we experienced that first week never returned, we were well-received by not only the Corps of Cadets and officers stationed at the

Academy, but by graduates across the world who tuned into the always televised Army–Navy game and often cable-televised weekly games. Connie Franklin's idea had been a successful one, the result of which had a positive effect on the image of women at West Point.

I thoroughly enjoyed being a cheerleader. Having been accustomed to participating in the football spirit in junior high and high school back in Texas, I missed not being able to participate during my first two years at the Academy. It felt great to be along the sidelines again. The best part of being a cheerleader, though, was meeting so many new people, especially Billy.


Billy Hubbard should have been the brigade commander for the Class of 1981. He was handsome: 6'3" tall and very blond with pale blue eyes. He carried himself with the dignity of Spartacus. He was the perfect model for the picture America desired to paint of a West Point cadet. And we fell deeply in love.

We first met after a football rally. Since the first rally in the north area had been such a success, the rally committee decided to try it once more. Again the ralliers were funneled into the area from all over the Corps. The dance team, in our new uniforms, performed standard cheers from the ledge above the barracks. There was no need this week for the strict secrecy that controlled the last rally, or a special lighting system, since the cadet areas are lit up like daytime until taps sounds. Once the crowd was assembled, we performed routines to the much rehearsed sounds of the cadet band, the yell-leaders performed, and even the mysterious and muscular "A-Man," a phantom in black wrestler's tights and gray cape, was on hand to assist with the spirit of the "12th Man."

As the rally ended, about fifteen minutes before taps, Cindy, the senior girl who led our group, grabbed me by the hand and pulled me from the ledge. "There's someone who wants to meet you!" she said excitedly.

"Who is it?" I kept asking as I was pulled down the stairs and into the area in front the barracks. Along the way her roommate, Donna, also a cheerleader, joined us. "Act cool," they said as they almost ran me into a tall, blond cadet with a woman hanging on each arm. The three of them were dressed in civilian clothing — dresses and coat and tie — having just returned from the First Class Club, a private club for senior cadets and their guests only.

"Hi!" he said, his blue eyes twinkling in the glare of the bright lights. "You really looked great up there," referring to my performance on the ledge.

"Thank you. I'm Donna. Who are you?" I asked. West Point taught us not to skirt an issue but to attack it directly, and I had no idea who this person was.

"Billy," he said as a smile grew slowly from his lips. We chatted for a minute or two, until one of the women attaching herself to his arm reminded him that it was close to taps, so they would have to be returning to their rooms. At that he reached out, and with the last two fingers of his right hand he grabbed the little finger of my left hand and asked, "Would you go out with me sometime?"

Go out? That sort of question sounded strange at this institution. Cadets don't *go out*: they go to, or go with, or meet at, but *go out*? There weren't enough privileges to go *out*. It didn't matter; I knew what he meant. I was prepared to respond with a quick, "No, I don't think so," but I found it hard to speak with both Cindy and Donna's fingernails pinching the flesh on my back and arms.

"She'd love to," Cindy responded for me.

"Let me think about it," I quickly responded for myself. "Call me tomorrow at my company." Billy smiled and winked, and walked away, with a female classmate on each arm. As I turned to go back to my own company, Cindy and Donna pulled me aside.

"So, what did you think? Are you going to do it? I can't believe you didn't say yes! Don't you realize who that *was*?" They fired questions at me without giving me any opportunity to respond. Then I sat through a dissertation on who Billy Dean Hubbard was: He was the cadet that many cadets in the Class of 1981 felt should be the brigade commander (the head of the Corps of Cadets). Suddenly, I recalled hearing Dave talk about a classmate he referred to as "Billy D." Apparently, according to Dave, this cadet should have been the brigade commander but the selection board decided that, in order to recruit better football players to the Academy (we had lost to Navy two years in a row) they would appoint the captain of the football team to the position. The Academy had done the same thing decades earlier, during the days when Army football players were both Heisman Trophy candidates and Rhodes Scholars. They offered Billy the position of his deputy. He refused, requesting and receiving command of the regiment he lived in instead, the 3d Regiment.

So this was Billy. One of only six permanent cadet captains in the

Corps and, obviously, very sought after by his female classmates. Cindy and Donna did everything they could to talk me into dating him. Finally, taps began to blow across the Corps and I left for my room. "Listen," I shouted to them as I walked backwards toward my company, "I think he had a lot to drink at the club tonight and I bet he won't even remember meeting me in the morning!"

The next day I realized, happily, that I had been wrong. Not only did Cadet Captain Billy Hubbard remember our meeting, he came over to see me in the 4th Regiment's wing of the mess hall at lunchtime. It was obvious that his ability to make friends easily had given him a great deal of self-confidence. I had never heard of a cadet captain openly dating one of his own classmates, let alone an underclassman. There were no regulations against it, but the Academy seemed to choose for these positions male cadets who were not completely happy with the idea of women at West Point, and probably would have preferred death to the idea of dating one. Billy was not hung up with the macho stereotypes normally inherited with his rank. In fact, of all the cadets in positions of authority that I ever knew at the Academy, Billy had a reputation for treating cadets, male or female, the most fairly. He was probably the most respected cadet I ever knew, even over Tony Cuccolo, probably because he had fought such adversity to get to this station in life.

He was the product of a broken home, a poor family from Tennessee. He enlisted in the army to get away from his life there, but continually got into trouble for pranks and petty infractions. Finally, he met a colonel who told him to straighten up or there would be "no decent place in life where [he] would ever be welcome." Billy did straighten up, "because this man cared about me and believed in me," he told me. After observing the changes in Billy, this colonel recommended him to the USMA prep school. Billy never thought he could be good enough for West Point. He was wrong. Billy not only entered West Point in 1977, he excelled there. Outgoing and self-confident, he had conquered the shyness and feelings of inadequacy which stemmed from his childhood. He had overcome a great deal to get to where he was today. Why would he lay it on the line to date a female cadet?

"I wanted to date you before this," Billy said confidently, "but you weren't available. And, as for my classmates, I guarantee you, not one of them will say anything unkind about it." Again, he was right.

Billy and I dated throughout most of the year. He liked me to

visit him in the regimental staff area. He liked for us to be seen together. I think one of the reasons that Billy was so secure about dating
a female cadet was that he was older than most cadets; he was almost
twenty-one when he entered the Academy, which made him three
years older — and more mature — than most of his classmates. I got
along well with his classmates and the other members of the staff,
which was good because Billy took me with him to all of his class functions, and, of course, he went to all of mine.

The best part of dating Billy was watching him fall in love. He
made me laugh. This larger-than-life West Pointer was getting the
biggest kick out of being in love and being loved. For the first forty-
two days we knew each other, Billy could not get through the day if he
didn't speak to me or see me. Since he and I were both extremely busy
cadets, the time he made for me in his life was even more special. If he
had a busy day and knew he would probably not be able to see me that
evening, he'd find my table in the mess hall and come by to say hello.
It was funny to see the leadership of my company react to him as he approached my table.

"Hey, Billy. Is everything okay? What can I do for you?"

"Hey, Bud, how ya doing?" he'd say, shaking my company commander's hand. "I just came to see Donna." Then he'd walk over to my
table, touch me on the arm and say "I love you" with his eyes while
telling me about his day or his busy night yet to come, and walk away
smiling at his classmates. He was a confident young man.

His room was conveniently located just off of the apron of the
Plain, the main thoroughfare of cadet travel. About once a day I'd try
to slip by his room and leave him a short note or a card I'd picked up
in the cadet bookstore over in the Academic Building. He loved that!
If I walked past while he was in his room, he'd open his window and
shout, "Hey, beautiful." I had to stop in every time I was in the area
just so he wouldn't embarrass me. Loving Billy was fun, and innocent,
despite the reputation that so many "well-meaning" cadets volunteered to tell me Billy carried: "Love-'em-and-leave-'em Billy." And
Billy didn't deny that he had dated — and slept with — quite a few
women. But Billy had never been "in love." I think he was afraid to
get too close, and to see him in our relationship, it was obvious. The
friends who knew him best delighted in telling me of their observations: "I've never seen him like this!" I had no doubt that what they
were saying was true — his actions told me that.

Since he was one of the six cadets in the Corps who could move about after taps (due to the responsibilities of his position) he frequently showed up at my room just before, during, or just after taps. Leslie and I would hear a mild knock on the door and she'd say, "It's for you," without ever looking. I'd open the door and there would be smiling Billy. At the very least, if he couldn't make it to see me, he'd call just before or after taps to say goodnight. I recall one night when the phone lines to the company were busy and Billy couldn't get through: he left a midnight staff meeting, saying he'd be back in ten minutes, and came running over to my company. It was well after taps, my roommate and I were in bed, all the lights in the company were turned out, and I heard the door hinges squeak.

"Donna, it's me," I heard the familiar voice whisper. I sat up in bed.

"Billy what are you doing here?"

"I tried to call, but the phone lines have been busy since midnight," he told me.

"Well, what's wrong?" I asked, thinking the need to reach me was important.

"Nothing's wrong. I just had to hear your voice. Is that okay?"

I explained to him that in my room there existed a policy whereby, if a handsome man enters the room more than thirty minutes after midnight, he has to kiss the first female he sees. Billy leaned over and gave me a kiss.

"How about the roommate of the first female he sees?" I heard Leslie ask jokingly from the other side of the alcove.

"Sorry," I replied. "One kiss per room. Don't you have a meeting to get back to?" I reminded him. After he left, Leslie and I settled back in bed.

"Donna, is he going to make a habit of this?" she asked me.

"I have no idea," was the truest response I could think of, as I rolled over, smiling contentedly.

After being together for forty-two days, Billy and I were about to spend our first weekend apart: I had to cheer at the Notre Dame football game, and Billy had Academy commitments that prevented him from attending the game. I purchased a stuffed Army mule and left it on his desk with a note that read, "This little guy will keep you company while I'm away, and keep an eye on you for me."

When I returned on Sunday evening I found Billy waiting in the area for the cadet bus and a huge bouquet of roses and wildflowers sitting on my desk in my room. From that night on, whenever possible,

Billy and I studied every night in the library. Anyone who needed to find either one of us knew where we would be. We always sat in the military reading room at a large oval table, Billy on one side ("so I can watch you"), me on the other.

Though Billy had many more weekend passes (being a senior) than I did, he preferred not to use them unless I could get away as well. Sometimes we'd walk to my sponsor's house on a Saturday night, instead of going to a dance or a concert, and just watch TV until it got close to taps. Then we'd walk back to the barracks area, admiring the night sky as we walked along. Some other times, we'd go running on Sunday afternoons. It was Billy who took the time to make me into the type of runner I am today. He'd critique my running, and then run with me, pacing me. When he first asked me to go running with him, I took one look at the length of his legs and said, "You've got to be kidding!" He wasn't. Actually, what Billy did for my running is simple to recognize: He made running enjoyable for me. I had not been a runner before I came to West Point, and running at West Point was anything but fun, even for people who liked to run before they got to the Academy. After Billy changed my attitude about running, my roommate and I would run together five, eight, even ten miles a day.

Billy was very supportive of my career and enjoyed seeing the attention I received as a cheerleader. And I greatly admired Billy and his successes, and understood when his duty commitments took him away from me, except on one occasion . . .

General of the Army Omar Bradley was visiting the Academy one weekend, reviewing the parade and attending a football game. He brought with him his most recent (younger) wife, and her daughter (or perhaps it was her niece or granddaughter). The important fact is that she was "dating age," and Billy was assigned to be her escort and "show her around" during her stay. The colonel that made the assignment asked Billy if he thought I would mind. Billy told him confidently that I would understand, then came straight over to my room to ask me about it.

I had "shared" Billy on many occasions, but this situation seemed like a lot to ask of a girlfriend. General Bradley's wife had a reputation for being very protective of her family members, and I think Billy was assigned the job as escort because people knew that his presence would not only please the young lady but please both General Bradley and his wife as well. The reason I felt I could voice no objection was that he had a rare opportunity to converse, one-on-one, with a part of Americana; to sit down with Omar Bradley. It was like having a date with history, one that, given Bradley's age and failing health, would probably not be offered again. Billy couldn't give up an opportunity like this, and I didn't want him to, even if it meant the plans Billy and I had made for that weekend were now canceled.

Just after he returned the young lady to her quarters on Saturday evening, an elated Billy appeared at my room. He gave me an enthusiastic kiss and a verbatim replay of his conversation with the general.

"It was great!" he began, his eyes dancing with every excited word. "We talked about the military decisions he made, and some of the orders he issued. His mind is so sharp! God, Donna, it was great. You would've loved it! I only wish you could've been there." Billy and I were both ardent history buffs, and, yes, I would have loved to have been able to sit in on that conversation. General Bradley never showed up again at West Point, but the Academy sent a contingent of cadets to his funeral, to represent his alma mater, less than six months later.

As if I hadn't enough to occupy my time that semester, I began working with the USMA Treasurer's Office as the women's representative on the Cadet Store Council. My purpose was to evaluate and recommend changes, with specific applications toward women's products and clothing, in the Cadet Store (a store catering only to cadets, with limited stock and very low prices). I requested, and was given, a list of all women of the Corps to use in dissemination of a survey to garner cadet attitudes about the sizes, type, quality, cost, styles, and availability of women's clothing in the store, and recommend to the council appropriate changes. There was very little that was remarkable about this survey or my position on the council, though quite a few changes were made as a result. What was exciting to me was that I became familiar with the names of the women in the Corps from all four classes, and they became familiar with my name (those who did not throw the survey away). I felt as though I held in my hands the ability to create the first support network for women at the Academy. Looking back on it now, I could have done so much with the aid of that list, despite the opposition I'm certain I would have met with. But this was a very busy semester for me, and already I was spread as thinly as I dared to get. So I did little more than I had originally signed on to do, until the day I received a phone call.

There was a very timid voice on the other end of the phone. She wouldn't give me her name at first, but she'd been told I might help her. She thought she might be pregnant. My mind raced: This was what "they" had been waiting for — counting on — those who fought the hardest to keep women from entering this institution. They fought their battles with frenzied cries of "We'll have rampant sex going on in the barracks. And what are we going to do when the little dolls get pregnant? We'll be paying for abortions for the women of the Corps!" At least that's how it was relayed to me by a retired army general. But this type of thinking was doing the young woman on the other end of the phone no good at all.

I suggested she see a particular Academy gynecologist to confirm her suspicions. This doctor had a marvelous bedside manner but a lame sense of humor. He was particularly interested in helping young women "stay out of trouble." He once told me during a visit to his office, "Young men can make all the babies they want and it doesn't affect them a bit — physically. No one could ever tell. But if a girl creates a life, the result is very unfair. She can't hide it, or pretend it isn't her problem." He went on to explain that he had a teenage daughter, and how that had greatly influenced his feelings about women. It was obvious. On my last visit, just before the Christmas holidays of my yearling year, he did everything short of getting down on his knees and begging me to take some sort of birth control home with me.

"But I don't need any birth control," I told him.

"You might not now," he insisted, "but the Christmas holidays are coming. Are you going to be seeing your boyfriend?" he asked.

"Yes, of course, but I still won't need any birth control."

"Well, take some just in case. These young boys can get pretty convincing during a romantic holiday like Christmas." I was certain that he was correct, in most cases, but he didn't know me, and he didn't know Dave, either. Both of us really *wanted* to make love to each other, but neither of us believed it was the right thing — not at that time. Besides the obvious detriment to my career if I should become pregnant (Dave would've quit the Academy too, not wanting to be an absentee father), there was hesitation about "the first time." Not that I was saving myself for a specific date or a wedding night, but that I was hoping there would only be one person — ever. If I had believed that Dave and I would eventually marry and be together for the rest of our lives, then I would have been voracious in my desire for him. Somehow, when the "forever" feeling came, it just never stayed long enough to make me believe it. For Dave, who was very religious, lovemaking was the ultimate expression of a love between two people; an expression reserved only for a man and wife.

So, though the doctor's heart was in the right place, my answer was still, "No!" But I knew this man would help the cadet who called me.

The doctor had agreed to see her on Friday. She asked me to go with her, but there was no way that I could; my class schedule was too tight and, at West Point, cadets cannot miss class without expressed permission from the Tac officer (or illness). There is no such thing as "cutting class" here. She called me Friday, just after lunch, and her suspicions had been confirmed. Now she had only two choices: leave the Academy and have the child, or remain at the Academy and terminate the pregnancy. She selected the latter of the two after talking to her boyfriend (also a cadet, in a different company than she) and her minister. "Whether the Academy will let me come back or not, I'm not ready to have a child. And I could never live with giving a child of mine away," she told me. The gynecologist had examined her in his office and had not recorded the visit in any way, so there would be no record of her pregnancy. He had also given her the name of two clinics in cities near the Academy area "which had been used by other female cadets" in the years previous. Since it was nearing the Christmas break, however, she elected to wait until she went home for the holidays and, with the support of her family, visit a local clinic. She called me in January to let me know that she had returned to the Academy and that everything was "fine."

At the last Army–Navy football game that I attended, several retired army officers brought this subject up over dinner. "You don't know how many female cadets become pregnant," a retired army colonel told me, with an inflection that insinuated the number was high. He was right, I *didn't* know how many women had become pregnant while they were cadets, and I was willing to bet that *he* didn't either. Attaining the rank of colonel affords an officer a great many privileges, but digging into private medical records is not one of them.

The gynecologist I had referred the young female cadet to left the Academy to be stationed elsewhere during my senior year. Before he left, I asked him how extensive his knowledge of this subject was. At that time, 1981, women had been in attendance at the Academy for five years. To his knowledge, five women had become pregnant (two of whom came to the Academy that way from home). Two of the women left the Academy (whether for that reason or whether they had been planning to leave for other reasons, he did not know), and three of the women terminated their pregnancies and remained at the Academy.

I lived at the Academy while women were there, and I never saw sex in the hallways or heard of any rampant sexual behavior going on. I did hear of two cadets receiving a huge "slug" (having to walk punishment tours) after being caught in bed together (the young man tried to hide the girl in the closet, but the officer opened the closet to make a casual inspection, and found the girl — stark naked — staring back at him). Another incident I know of occurred with a female in my company who, as a senior, slept with her fiancé one Saturday evening while his roommate was on a trip away from the Academy. Luckily, they were found by my roommate, asleep, the next morning, so nothing happened to them.

Though I never saw any sexual behavior going on while I was a cadet, I'm sure it did occur. After all, seniors (all-male class of 1979) were still sneaking civilian women into the barracks on Saturday nights while I was a plebe, just as they had witnessed the Class of 1976 doing when the cadets of '79 were plebes! I don't think things changed that dramatically because of women being allowed in the Corps. When it did occur, it was the exception, rather than the norm. Most cadets were too afraid of the price if they were caught to try behavior that bold. Besides, it's very difficult to find any sort of privacy in a cadet barracks, let alone enough to afford someone the time for that type of activity.

The rest of the semester went by quickly. I loved being a part of the dance team, one of my plebes was awarded Best Cadet in the company, I had been named to an international "who's who" of International Youth in Achievement, and I even "aced" my "drugs" mid-term (got an "A" on my philosophy exam). The semester seemed to be flowing smoothly along, until one day in late October.

I had just returned from a dance team practice that had run late. I was really going to have to shower in a hurry if I was going to get a shower at all before dinner formation. I walked into my room, said "Hi" to my roommate, grabbed my bathrobe and a towel, and headed for the bathroom (which was just outside our door that semester). I heard the shower water running as I approached the door but, thinking that a female from another platoon may have needed to use our shower, I entered anyway. I took no more than two steps into the shower before

I backed out and looked at the sign on the door: WOMEN. Instinctively, I had the solution. I walked back into my room, dropped my robe on the bed, took my extra bottle of shampoo from my toilet article drawer, turned on the water in the sink, and stuck my head under it while requesting, quite matter-of-factly to my roommate, "Leslie, will you go next door and ask the plebes to get their classmate out of our shower?" Leslie's mouth dropped open as she watched me washing my hair.

"I thought you wanted a shower . . ." she said, confusion in her voice.

"I did, but there happens to be a man in our shower, and I don't have time to wait for him to finish so that I can jump in."

"Are you sure? And how do you know it's a plebe?" Leslie asked. She still had not made a move to get him out of there.

"Because when I stepped into the shower I saw an extremely hairy butt bending over, washing some very large feet. I didn't see the face, but I felt confident in assuming it was a man. And if it's a man in a latrine marked WOMEN, it had better be a very confused plebe!"

I wrapped my head in a towel and walked to the doorway. Leslie had spoken to the plebes next door, who were snickering at the thought. One look from me and they decided it wasn't so funny. I shook my head with disappointment as my best plebe stepped out of the women's latrine. I pretended to be too furious to even look at him.

Back in our room, with the door shut, Leslie and I laughed hysterically as we dressed for dinner. Actually, I felt sorry for the poor guy. He'd gotten beaten up pretty badly at football practice that day and had "forgotten" that he had to travel down one flight of stairs to get to the latrine marked MEN. He had no idea what, or how much, I had seen of him, and he was too embarrassed to face me. I walked directly over to him at the dinner formation, but it was I who refused to look at him.

"Did you get a nice shower, Geraldi? Wasn't that a nice clean bathroom?" Out of the corner of my eyes I could see his wide eyes staring at me. He didn't know whether to answer me, or cry. I walked away. By now the news had been passed through the company like rice at a wedding.

Leslie took the opportunity to have a few words with him, as well as several of the seniors in the company. "Mister, I thought I'd seen it all in my four years," said one of the scholarly, normally mild-mannered firsties, "but this has got to be the most appalling screw-up

I've ever even heard of!" I let this continue for about five minutes before I interrupted again. After all, this type of reaction was expected by the plebe and therefore was of no real value. It was the reaction from me that had the young man shaking in his boots, because he didn't know what to expect.

I looked down at my watch, then looked away and said, "Report to my room at exactly seven minutes after the Fourth Class light." That meant that he had to show up at my room seven minutes after the end of dinner. Giving plebes odd reporting times increased the stress load. If I had said to report at 1900 hours (7:00), he would have checked the clock in the company orderly room and reported promptly, escaping a potentially dangerous situation. Since I left the time with room for interpretation (thirty seconds one way or the other), the plebe had the stress of worrying whether or not I would take advantage of the opportunity. It's the uncertainty that causes the most stress and, therefore, builds the most character.

The poor guy couldn't eat at all at dinner. When he returned to the company, all of his classmates were on hand to help him look his best before reporting to my door. I believe that stress builds character, to a point. I never believed in yelling or screaming at people, and I never did it. What that kid had been through in the hour and a half since I first saw him in my shower was punishment enough. When he got to my room, I motioned for him to come inside, and closed the door behind him.

"What happened?" I asked calmly as he stood at a rigid position of attention against my closet door. He relayed the story about football practice and about how badly he felt over what he'd done to me. He was certain he was going to be kicked out of the Academy. I never said a word. Finally, he asked me if he could ask a question. I nodded in the affirmative.

"I know you're upset with me. Are you ever going to speak to me again?" I could see the tears filling his eyes, and I'd decided he'd had enough.

"First of all, that was a statement *and* a question," I said, keeping him on his toes. "I am upset: upset that I didn't get a shower I was very much looking forward to; upset that my best plebe and one of the best in this company not only embarrassed himself, but the entire squad as well; and upset that your actions have forced me to punish one of the plebes I have a great deal of respect for." I handed him a handkerchief and told him to wipe his eyes before he walked out the door into the hallway. "Don't ever let your roommates see you cry," I reminded him. "It can always be used against you."

After he left my room, I closed the door and sat down on the bed. "I was fair," I said to myself. "Tony would've been fair."

I got several letters and pictures from Tony during the semester, including one of him rappelling off of the CAV Tower with his leg in a camouflage-painted cast! Tony wore the crescent-shaped patch of a Ranger School graduate on the sleeve of his uniform, and he refused to let anything stop him, even a broken leg. He had a great sense of humor, and I usually laughed out loud when reading his letters. We called each other several times during the course of the semester. One of the nicest phone calls was the one I got from him just after the Corps returned home from the Army–Navy game. Apparently, Tony and a group of his friends had gotten together to watch the football game on TV, and they saw me in my role as a cheerleader.

"There you were, Donna! They must have held the camera on you for at least twenty seconds! It was great!" Tony's enthusiasm always sounded genuine. "They showed you several other times, too, along with the entire group." Then he mentioned that several of his friends had seen my picture in the November issue of *Soldiers* magazine, and had given him positive feedback.

"You're right, the cheerleaders really have changed," he continued. "All my friends want you to know they approve of the changes!" Hearing that meant a lot (though I doubted they "all" approved). If members of the "last all-male class" approved, perhaps the dance team really was a change for the better.

Christmas vacation was fabulous! Billy flew to my home in Texas at the beginning of the holidays and stayed for four days. Before he left, we attended a dinner in honor of the brigade commander (and captain of the football team), who was from the Houston area. My parents loved having him. The day after he left, Tony drove in from Ft. Hood and parked his white Corvette in front of my house for the next three days. I'm sure my parents wanted me to marry him. As Tony's car was driving away from my house, David, the aviator whom I had met during the summer at Flight School, arrived from his parents' home in Florida to be my date for New Year's Eve. My parents wanted to adopt him.

My adaptation to an orderly and organized West Point lifestyle (and a very cooperative and patient family) enabled me to keep the three separated from each other. I considered myself very fortunate: I had three of West Point's finest, and each one was saying "I love you." For the first time I understood how sailors could have a "girl in every port" and love each one of them.

"They're all so serious about you, Donna," my mother commented. "How are you going to choose between them?"

Choose? Just one? Like Scarlett O'Hara, I did not want to think about that today; I would think about that tomorrow (maybe). Actually, there was no real choice to be made. I wasn't ready for the type of commitment these men seemed to need. Besides, they were ready *now*, and I still had another year at West Point before I could even consider a more permanent arrangement. Tony and David had been out of the Academy for several years and were tired of coming home to lonely houses; Billy tried desperately to believe that he could keep himself busy for a year until I graduated and our careers converged at the Army Aviation Center. Billy had visions of us as the first West Point aviation couple, flying through the skies all over the world. The reality was that Billy had enjoyed being in love, and now he was petrified by the thought of being alone after graduation, even for just a year.

I had grown up believing that it was impossible to genuinely love more than one man at a time, but at this point I was very much in love with all three. Of course, West Point men, in spite of their often infuriating egos, are the most masculine and virile men I have ever encountered. Falling in love with three West Pointers at one time suddenly seemed feasible.

For now, I had the world in the palm of my hand: the love of the kinds of men I had only dreamed about as a girl, my aviation career, a successful and enjoyable military career, and a supportive family. But my parents always told me that nothing in life was free. The last nine months had been the best of my life, and I was about to be presented with the bill.

# CHAPTER 8

# The Betrayal

*"Your youth, your optimism — they give me strength . . . I feel in my heart a great confidence in the future of our country."*
— President Ronald Reagan, address to the Corps of Cadets, 1987

I was actually thrilled to be returning to West Point. This place had been the source of my life's greatest pleasures, and my great personal happiness. I had learned a great deal about life and people, I had met some of the most remarkable and caring people, I had received the type of training that few women in the world ever experience, and was receiving an outstanding academic education in the process. My life seemed enviable.

This semester I would have more time to "smell the roses." There would be very little cheerleading now that football was over (only a small amount of cheering at basketball games) and I was no longer a squad leader. Besides being able to spend more time with Billy, I would be taking some elective academic courses which very much interested me. Up to that point, most of the "core courses" were mandatory courses for an engineering major. Now I would also be able to take an advanced political science (American Institutions) course, a special Civil War colloquium which required a special recommendation for acceptance, and other courses particular to my U.S. history area of concentration.

I had become an avid letter writer, responding to Tony and David's cards and letters. And Billy and I were spending more time together. The end was approaching for him, and he talked often about the future.

My immediate future held a surprise for me after I visited the dentist to get my teeth cleaned, as I did every semester.

"Is that a baby tooth still in your mouth after twenty years?" he asked, fully aware that it was. "Let's take it out, and pull into the space the adult tooth hiding behind it. Most military bases don't have the facilities for this procedure, you know. They'd just cap the tooth or pull it and put in a bridge."

So far it all sounded okay to me. The baby tooth had been fine all of these years, but now there was a small cavity in it and, rather than fill it, this procedure was suggested.

"Of course, we'll have to brace four of your front teeth to pull the adult tooth into place," he continued casually.

Wait a minute. Braces? I was a cheerleader; I *had* to smile. The dentist was an experienced old soldier who was able to cut to the chase: "Is your vanity worth the loss of a tooth you can never get back? The choice is yours."

So, braces it was. But, not before he removed all four of my wisdom teeth — at once. I was less worried about the procedure than I was about how Billy would react when I told him and when he saw me. I shouldn't have been.

Whenever a female was put under the influence of nitrous oxide (laughing gas) another female had to be present at all times during the four-hour operation. Billy offered to be the witness for my operation, but the surgeon told Billy it had to be a female — for my own safety. Billy responded, "No one can look out for my girlfriend's safety better than me." To no avail. So Leslie graciously stood in as a witness, despite the fact that she couldn't stand the sight of blood, during a grueling extraction operation. Billy visited me in the hospital that night (I was kept for observation) and repeatedly told me how beautiful I was.

"Only if you're into chipmunks," I kept telling him. He'd gotten his assistant to take over the regimental duties so that he could stay with me as long as possible. He brought a portable cassette player and played some of our "special" tapes while he sat with me on the hospital bed and brushed and stroked my hair. And, of course, when visiting hours were over, he charmed the female nurses into letting him stay longer. He even brought along the donkey I had given him, to watch over me until the next day.

About an hour after he left the hospital (2200 hours), the phone rang.

"You can't imagine how lousy it is for me tonight, knowing that you're not actually here with the Corps." It was my goodnight call from Billy.

"I love you, too, Billy."

Between the surgery and the braces, I had not had a very good week. Billy was determined to make up for that fact and planned a wonderful getaway weekend to a little cottage in the woods about forty miles from West Point. Mrs. Brown had packed us a delicious picnic lunch, but Billy had other plans. He had been to the cottage earlier that Saturday morning and had set the scene with champagne, Danish cheeses, fresh-baked bread, and chilled wet strawberries on a checkered blanket beside a still smoldering fire in the one-room cabin. At the sight, I gave Billy the kind of kiss that I knew would make up for the last week, and then settled down on the blanket to enjoy the spoiling.

We ate, talked, and kissed, and then walked in the woods until dusk returned us to the still warm cabin. Tonight would be our first opportunity to hold each other until morning.

"You aren't nervous are you?" he asked me, very concerned about the reply.

"No," I responded softly. "I love you, Billy, and I feel safe with you." Billy and I had talked about making love very early in our relationship. I thought he had gotten a little out of line on our second date, and I told him so. We took time out to have a very personal talk. Though Billy had been used to a more physical relationship, he gave up on the idea once he began to fall in love, and we hadn't really discussed it since.

"Maybe you shouldn't feel so safe," he responded. Billy told me that my love meant everything to him, and that he didn't want to lose it. But thoughts of our lovemaking were beginning to consume him. "You can't imagine the situations I'll be in when I think about it: serious meetings, parade practice in front of the entire regiment. I think we need to talk about it," he said.

We did, but I still wasn't ready. I respected his feelings — I wanted him too — but I wouldn't have respected myself any other way. We held each other that night, talking and laughing until sleep began to overtake us. He put his strong, warm arms around me and whispered in my ear, "Goodnight, Angel," and the two of us drifted off to sleep.

Except for Billy's preoccupation with being hurt after we parted at graduation, the semester was one of the most enjoyable I could remember. By mid-semester the U.S. hostages held in Iran had been released, and it was determined that they should first set foot on American soil at none other than West Point.

It was quite an event to witness. As the hostages disembarked from the aircraft, some kneeled, some fell prostrate kissing the ground, some cried. The road from the airfield into the gates of West Point had been lined with thousands of yellow ribbons — welcome home greetings from a tremendous community effort sponsored by the Officers' Wives Club. During their two days at the Academy, the hostages were treated to historical tours, cadet parades, and an evening meal in the cadet mess hall. That dinner meal gave me an urge to kiss the soil at West Point.

The former hostages were seated throughout the mess hall at tables along with the Corps of Cadets. The Glee Club had been stationed on the balcony above the entrance to provide musical entertainment during dinner. Several short speeches were made from the "Poop Deck," and the Corps began to eat. About twenty minutes into the meal the Glee Club began to sing "God Bless America." Instantly, the hostages began to stand and to sing loudly. The Corps, being inspired, stood also and sang along. When the song ended, the Corps, still standing, broke out in thunderous applause for the brave Americans who had joined us that evening. There was a warm exchange of handshakes and hugs throughout the great hall before all took their seats once again. *Yes,* I thought, *God does bless America.*

The most remarkable thing I remember about the visit of the hostages, however, was the way they watched the cadets. The former hostages were free to stroll the West Point grounds, visit the museum, and make purchases from the gift shop. In order to do so, they would pass directly in front of several academic buildings. As the cadets were walking to class, these people would stare at the cadets with wonder and awe. No smile, no questions. One man finally asked me to take a picture with him and several of his friends. Afterward, I asked him about the strange stares. He told me that very few, if any, of their group had ever visited West Point, but they had always known about it, and it was "such an honor" to these men and women that it was "almost unbelievable." I'm glad I asked.

At the end of March came the almost unfathomable news that President Reagan and Press Secretary James Brady had been shot. News updates were posted at every entrance and exit of the academy buildings throughout the day. I cannot recall the number of prayers we said during the next several days while those two lives hung in the balance. Finally, the joyous news was reported to the Corps: "Attention all cadets. The president is out of danger." Then one more prayer . . . of thanks.


It was shortly after this that life, for me, began to turn sour. Tony wasn't at all thrilled with our extended, long-distance relationship. And his former girlfriend showing up unexpectedly and frequently at his home in Texas wasn't helping matters any. David was pushing me for more frequent visits to Alabama and for a greater commitment in our relationship, and Billy's insecurity was surprising to me, but a major concern nonetheless.

Billy and I decided to get away from the Academy one Saturday night to talk about our future. It was a "real date." We dressed to the nines (Billy looked like such a mature adult in his suit and tie) and dined at a wonderful Oriental steakhouse about twenty minutes from the lodge — the Gasho — where native chefs prepare the food at the table. We ate lobster and drank plum wine, then spent several hours holding and spinning each other on the dance floor of a nearby club before returning to my sponsor's house. I loved Billy, differently from the way I loved the others. It was a deep love, the way it had been with Dave, and exciting, the way Tony made me feel, yet intellectual and friendly, like David Parker and I had shared. Billy and I fell in love, then became friends. But we had not been lovers . . .

That night I was prepared to make almost any concession to save our love. I was patient and kind and understanding. But, for Billy, it wasn't enough. As we sat on the small sofa in my sponsor's living room that night, Billy told me that he needed the one thing in our relationship that I was not prepared to give him. I still believe that he was just afraid of graduating and of being alone, a feeling that was foreign to him after the events of the past eight months. Perhaps he was afraid that, once we were no longer together on a daily basis, he would lose me. (This was the man who once told me: "I've never loved anyone enough to have a broken heart. The thought of it petrifies me!") Whatever the real reason was, Billy would never open up to me completely that night. For him, it was too frustrating to stay in this relationship any longer without a physical expression of our love. So, the man who was afraid of losing the relationship is the one who made the decision that changed our futures.

"I've never felt so loved in all of my life, Donna, as I have the past eight months," he began. "I love you, and I'm so damn proud of you! If I had to pick just one person I'd want fighting beside me in combat, or one person to share my deepest thoughts with, or one person to completely trust raising my children, every one of those people would be you. But I can't continue like this. I think we need to be apart for a while."

I was not surprised that Billy was letting go without a trace of tears, but I *was* surprised that I was too. I suppose I was in a state of disbelief. How could our relationship be over? We still loved each other. We'd never even had a fight. We were a near-perfect match. In fact, I never remember crying about my loss. I do remember feeling like I grew up in an instant, though — the instant I saw Billy and his date on their way to his graduation dance just a few months later.

My strained relationship with Billy didn't get much better during the next few weeks, and my military career was about to take a tumble as well.

The senior class would be graduating in less than two months. That meant that my classmates were waiting anxiously to find out what positions we would hold during the summer training, and forward into our own senior year. I had requested a position as a Cadet Basic Training Company commander (following in Tony's footsteps) and felt certain I would attain the position, though there were only sixteen such slots available. Things seemed to be flowing smoothly until I noticed my classmates acting peculiarly one afternoon during class. After class, I spoke to a friend of mine.

"Do our classmates seem to be acting strange to you?" I asked.

"If they are, I hadn't noticed," she replied. "But I'll keep an eye out and let you know."

I supposed that it was just my imagination, and I put it out of my mind. I rushed home after class to join the rest of the cows in my company who were gathering for saber practice in the afternoon. This is a ritual all cows eagerly anticipate. Finally, after three years of parade drill and manual of arms with M14 rifles, we were putting away our weapons and picking up sabers — well, almost. Every other afternoon my classmates and I would borrow a first classman's saber and be instructed by a member of the first class on saber manual (learning to salute, report, and march with long steel sabers at our sides). All of this was done in preparation for our roles as leaders during this summer's Beast and as firsties the next year.

The next day, when walking around the hallways of the Academic buildings, I was certain that my classmates were looking strangely at me, whispering about me. I hurried down to a friend's classroom and caught him just as he was going in. I asked him if he knew, or had heard, anything.

"Of course," he said, as if I knew he did. I must have given him a very confused look because his expression got very serious. "You mean you *don't* know?"

"Know what? This is driving me crazy!" I responded loudly. He leaned over and whispered in my ear.

"Donna, the rumor is that you are being considered as the first 'Queen of Beast.' "

Now, I didn't any more believe this than I believed that fish really could live in the polluted Hudson River. Queen of Beast? I knew that the Academy had come a long way since 1976, but this type of acceptance was too much to hope for. You see, traditionally, there are two "Kings of Beast," the commanders for each detail of Beast. These positions, and the two commanders at Camp Buckner (a position that Billy held), were the most prestigious positions of the summer, one of which would probably produce the brigade commander for the upcoming year. A female had never held any of these positions. The Academy and its graduates around the world certainly weren't ready for it. I sat in class disbelieving what I had heard. When I returned to the company, I asked my roommate if she had heard anything.

"No, nothing," she replied coolly, then made a quick exit.

I didn't give the rumor another thought. Several days later, my roommate and I were sweeping and cleaning our room at about 2100 hours (I hadn't been pulling my fair share of the workload during the last weeks due to the problems Billy and I were having, and I was trying to make up for it), when one of my male classmates, Rocky, came by asking to talk to me.

"Sure, whatcha need?" I asked naively, willing to help out. My willingness to accommodate him scared him away.

"I see you're busy," he replied nervously. "I'll come back tomorrow." Then he turned and left, closing the door behind him. The same scene was replayed the next day just after lunch, but no amount of cajoling on my part could get him to open up to me. It was obvious that something was on his mind, but the more concern I showed toward what I thought was his need to reach out, the more he wanted to forget he'd stopped by. Leslie witnessed both of these scenes.

"Do you know what's bothering him?" I asked her.

"No, I don't have any idea," she said convincingly.

The next morning Rocky stopped by our room again. "Do you have a class first hour?" he asked.

"Yes, unfortunately, but if you want to talk I'll be back about ten o'clock."

"No, that'll be too late," Rocky said. "Never mind." Again, he turned and left. I was concerned about Rocky, but I had done all I could to offer him a shoulder to lean on. I witnessed a crisis he had gone through during yearling year, in which he covered himself with his blanket and rolled around on his bed, probably crying, all evening while people came and left his room and his roommate sat at the desk studying. I thought this might be something similar. I found out who really had the crisis when I got back to my room after my morning class.

Sitting on my desk was a message: "See the Tac, ASAP." Next to that was a copy of a three-page letter. A note was attached to the letter: "Sorry I didn't get a chance to talk to you about this. This letter was taken to the TAC this morning. Rocky." I couldn't believe my eyes! Here was a letter to the company Tac citing the reasons why the male cadets in the company did not feel that I should be given a top position during the summer or the ensuing academic year. They went on to threaten that, if I received a top position despite their protests, these cadets, "feeling as [we] do," could not be responsible for problems with the operation of the company during the ensuing year. It then gave a numerical listing of my sins and was completed by a numerical listing of cadet signatures.

Of twenty-six classmates in my company, seventeen had signed the letter. None of the women had signed it, though I found out later that one wanted to but was threatened by the other three women not to. That left only three men who hadn't signed, and I had a fairly good idea who they were. Because I hadn't seen any signatures from the women in my company, however, I foolishly assumed that none of them knew about this coup.

Leslie walked in as I was reading the paperwork. The look on her face told me she knew about it.

"Have you seen this letter?" I asked her.

"Yes," she said, beginning to feel her guilt. "I thought I had them talked out of using it."

"Leslie, I read the list of their grievances," I began, trying to control my anger. "There is no way they could've known some of those things unless you told them. How could you? What were you hoping to gain? Why?" Her eyes were beginning to fill with tears. "Save it," I snapped as I stepped out of the shoes I wore to class and into my most highly polished ones. "I have to see the Tac. I wonder why?" I questioned sarcastically.

As I walked to the Tac's office, I was not too concerned. I had an exemplary military record. I had proven myself capable and deserving of a top position and had confidence that the Tac would see this display for the temper tantrum that it was. What I heard when I got to her office, however, shocked me.

"Why can't you get along with your classmates?" the captain asked me.

*Me?* I had never even said an unkind word to one of them. What was going on here?

"I understand you've seen this letter?" she asked, obviously misinformed.

"Oh, yes. Five minutes before I walked in here," I replied.

"They told me you were aware of it," she said, seeming confused.

"Then perhaps we'd better call the honor rep right now, ma'am, because the chickens left it sitting on my desk for me to find when I returned from class. I think you've been lied to." She dismissed that idea, saying that whether I knew about it or not was really immaterial. It was the content of the letter "we should be concerned with," she believed.

"Is it true that you asked a plebe to return a library book for you?" she asked, reading the sins that seemed to her the most grievous.

"Yes," I said flatly. "Last semester one of my plebes was going to the library. I asked him if he'd shove my book into the return slot and he said he would. So what?"

"Do you think that was appropriate?" she asked.

"Appropriate?" I repeated. "The kid did not have to go out of his way at all, the book wasn't heavy, and I certainly wasn't yelling at him or telling him I couldn't stand his face or forcing him to do push-ups with his face in a pile of broom fuzz the way other cadets get their kicks with plebes! There wasn't a thing inappropriate about it," I demanded.

"Perhaps you should get a haircut," she said moving down the list. "It doesn't appear to be out of the regulations, but they feel it should be shorter. They say you 'curl the ends' to make it look shorter for inspections."

"Ma'am, the senior cadets check everyone's hair each Thursday, and I have never gotten a single demerit for having my hair too long for regulations. Yes, I curl the ends. So does every woman in this company, and probably fifty percent of the women in the Corps. It makes the hair look neater." I was losing my patience.

"I'm a bit concerned about the comment that indicates you used your assistant squad leader to run your squad because you were hardly ever there," she said, looking at me the entire time as if she had that accusation committed to memory. I just sat there, shaking my head in disbelief. "I'd like an answer," she finally said.

"It's amazing to me how these boys can twist things to make them look exactly the way they need them to," I told her. "My assistant came to me after the second week and *asked* to be given more responsibility in the squad. I did so, on a trial basis, and he worked out well, so I allowed him to maintain his responsibilities. He probably had more interaction with the plebes than any one of his classmates in their own squads, but he did not have more interaction with them than I did. He wasn't the one in their rooms, secretly, after taps, teaching them to shine their shoes, helping them learn their knowledge or study for a test. He's a gutsy kid, but he's far from being a squad leader, and far from being one of the best yearlings in the company." (When I went to him later about this, he said, meekly, without once looking me in the face, that he "never said it was too much. Just that [he] rarely ever saw [me] in the plebes' room.")

"Actually," she said in her most authoritative voice, "there really isn't anything else on this list that is even worth mentioning." Having said that, I made the assumption that this visit would soon be considered unnecessary. "So, let's discuss what you can do to get your classmates to like you better." She was out of her mind if she thought I was even going to entertain that idea!

"Listen," I said with surprising reserve as I rose to leave, "I've had enough of this kangaroo court. This is not a popularity contest, ma'am. My record is unblemished and chock full of accolades, including glowing reports from the last all-male class. I won't sit here any further and dignify the ravings of little boys whose egos have been bruised. How dare a mere female show them up! Just who do I think I am? Well, I'll tell you. I'm a woman who has put up with more hassles and crap over the past three years than you've ever thought about. How would *you* know what one minute of cadet life is like? You're no more qualified to sit here and tell me how you think my behavior should be modified than my grandmother is! You don't run this company, those boys do. And you know it. And *they* know it! Why don't you do something really bold, ma'am, and just once, show some support for the women?"

"Cadet Peterson, sit down!" she commanded. I guess I was out of line. But I didn't give 110 percent of myself to West Point to have some ROTC female tell me that my "problem" was relating to the male classmates in my company! She said she needed time to think about our talk and asked me to come back the next day.

When I got back to my room, Leslie was waiting for me. She asked me how it went.

"How do you think it went, roommate?" My eyes were fixed in a dead stare. She began to explain that she and I had been so close but that, since her fiancé had graduated, and last semester was so busy for me, she needed someone to fill the void, and I wasn't always available. She said that she never realized Rocky had been taking notes every time she went to complain about the decreasing amounts of time I spent with her. "When I found out what they were planning to do, I begged them not to," she cried. "Is the letter going to hurt you? Oh, God! I'm so sorry. If I could take it back, I would. I just didn't know!"

All I could do was sit there and silently cry while she rambled her confession. I walked into the bathroom to get some tissue to dry my eyes and, when I returned, I spoke.

"You just don't get it, do you?" I looked at her disappointedly. "I loved you. You were like the sister I left behind. Your most intimate secrets were safe with me, until I died. I could've expected this of those guys. When they can't make it any other way they'll tear a woman down to get what they want, and we both know it. *You* are the one who told *me* that! But to be betrayed by you, because you were jealous

of the time I spent with Billy, now that your boyfriend has graduated
. . ." I was talking between sobs at this point.

"Why didn't you tell *me* how you were feeling? And why didn't
you at least have the decency to warn me once you knew what was
being planned? Not one of the women mentioned it, and you all
knew." Les and I stood silent for a moment, tears streaming down our
faces. Then I continued. "Do you know they listed my relationship
with Billy in that letter?" She was silent, but I pushed for an answer.
"Well?"

"I asked them not to," she blubbered. She was crying uncontrollably now and, for the first time since I'd met her, I had no sympathy
for her.

"They said that I was dating a 'Striper' to get close to the people
who made the summer assignments. How could you tell anyone that?
You, above all people, know that nothing could be further from the
truth. You *know*, Leslie." My roommate crumpled onto her bed.
"Damn you," I spat at her, then grabbed my hat and walked out of the
room, leaving Leslie prostrate on her bed, sobbing.

The next day in the Tac's office she asked me what I intended to
do about our talk the day before. I told her absolutely nothing. Her
phone rang. She told the party on the other end of the line that she
"would need some more time," then hung up, saying, "What's going
on here, Donna? That's the second request I've gotten to send your file
up for primary consideration this summer. What do you know about
it?" I had no answer for her. I felt that I had completely lost control of
my career.

"How big is the position you're being considered for?" she
pressed.

"The rumors say 'Queen of Beast.' At least that's what I heard last
week," I offered. "I just want a company command during Beast,
ma'am. I want to work with the new cadets."

"I don't think I can let you have that," she said, enjoying her
power over me. I was slowly being whipped. The fight was ebbing
from me as each minute passed, and she could see it. The phone rang
again.

"No," she said. "I'm keeping her in the company, where I can
keep an eye on her." After a pause she said, "I don't think it's the best
thing." It seemed like the people on the other end of the phone were
being quite persistent. "Look," she said finally, "just tell him she
doesn't get along with her classmates," and hung up the phone.

She had applied the kiss of death to my file. It was over. All that I had worked to achieve, two women had allowed seventeen boys to destroy. I was given a position as a company executive officer, second in command of a company, during Beast, and was put on staff during the academic year. No one I've ever spoken to about this incident has ever heard of anything like it occurring. Billy told me that he thought the problem started when one of his classmates saw Brigadier General and Mrs. Franklin give me a hug when Billy and I left his class' 100th Night party, celebrating 100 days before graduation. I suppose that excuse was as good as any. Of course, the Franklins hugged or shook hands with all of the cadets and their dates who had been seated at the table as we were. It's common behavior for senior military people, and I had been working closely with Mrs. Franklin on the organization of the dance team. Besides, Billy and I left the table early — that's how important it was for us to "make points."

The real truth was that there were very few of the extremely high positions available in the Corps. The guys in my company had a male classmate whom they wanted to see receive one of those positions. It was next to impossible for two cadets from the same company to receive positions like those. The Academy tries to spread them throughout the Corps, and rightly so. If I had received one, and the chances were good otherwise these guys wouldn't have gone through all that trouble, that would probably have eradicated his chances of receiving one. I believe he was the motivating force behind the letter scheme but I cannot prove it. I do know that he signed the letter.

I mentioned the incident to MaryAnn at our five-year reunion. It was the first time I had spoken of it since it happened. "You have got to be kidding," she said in disbelief. "I've never heard of such a horrible thing!"

The guys from my company still write to our female Tac. She's been promoted to major and is serving a tough assignment — in Hawaii. And so it goes.

There was a bright spot to the year's end, however. Despite the fact that the president of the United States had been shot several months earlier, he accepted the invitation to speak at the graduation ceremonies for the Class of 1981. As commander-in-chief, the president generally tries to attend at least one graduation at each service academy during his tenure. Of course, it didn't hurt that Ronald Reagan was a good friend of Edwin Meese, whose son Michael was graduating with this class. And I doubt he could have felt safer speaking outdoors anywhere in the world.

I was very impressed with the way his visit was handled, and I was very impressed with the president himself. I met him only briefly as the superintendent introduced him to a group of cadets. There is an aura that surrounds this man that is remarkable. I felt his presence five seconds before he entered the room. His handshake was firm; his manner, honest and open. He instilled pride in those who met him.

There were, of course, dozens of rumors surrounding Reagan's visit. We heard that cadets would be forced to walk through metal detectors before they would be allowed into the stadium, just as the civilian populace would be required to do, or that each company of cadets would be asked to swear, upon entrance to the stadium, that all cadets were completely unarmed. It was even rumored that the graduation exercises would be moved indoors for added security.

When I heard all of this, I was livid. So were quite a few of the cadets. This was West Point, not USC; we were soldiers, and he was our commander-in-chief. If he was going to come and insult our very way of life by insinuating that we might try to harm the symbol of the country we had sworn to lay our lives on the line for, then it would have been better for him not to come at all. For weeks prior to graduation, the cadets spoke of ways they would defend him from harm during his visit — with their lives if necessary. We all wondered which one of us would be the one to take a bullet to save him, and the idea never frightened us. Of course, as cadets have a tendency to do, we were preparing for the worst and crossing bridges unnecessarily.

Though I may never know for certain, I truly believe that the president could have briefed the Secret Service that he had complete trust in us, and to treat us with respect, for that is exactly how we were handled. Though security was extensive — surveillance helicopters in the sky, Secret Service agents with binoculars perched at intervals along the rim of the stadium, the small section of bleachers behind the speaker's platform completely cleared — no one ever asked the cadets to swear that they were not carrying weapons into the stadium, and no cadets were asked to pass through metal detectors of any kind. In fact, I tried to enter the stadium through the public gates rather than through those specifically reserved for "cadet admittance only" and was stopped by the Secret Service because I was carrying a present for a graduate.

"You'll have to unwrap that gift and let us check it," the agent said officially, pulling me off to the side of the gates. I could feel my temperature begin to rise. The agent opened his leather brief case, as if it contained a detection device to sweep the package with, then closed it abruptly, empty-handed.

"Is that a gift for a graduate?" he asked, never touching the box I was holding.

"Yes," I answered confidently as I watched a familiar look settle on his face. He was face-to-face with a female cadet for the first time.

"It must have been tough for you," he remarked, shaking his head with respect.

"Some days are better than others," I replied, as a smile replaced the scowl my face had been holding since I was first delayed.

He smiled, too, and motioned me through a different gate. "I hope he likes it," he said with a wink.

I moved into the stadium thinking that what had just happened had to be the greatest display of trust I had ever seen. Pausing, I stood near the entrance for several moments, watching the army officers and attending civilians pull change from their pockets and hand their purses over for inspection after passing through the metal detectors. And suddenly, knowing the president of the United States had this much trust in me, because of the reputation of the uniform I was wearing, it did not matter anymore what summer position I held or what those seventeen boys had tried to accomplish. All that mattered was the marvelous way I felt inside at that moment. Thanks to that day, I was reminded of my reasons for wanting to attend West Point in the first place. And I decided that I would go through it *all,* all over again, for that feeling.

# GO, ARMY

Maj. Gardner M. Nason

**The Army-Navy football game is a rivalry dating back to 1890. Its color and pageantry have made it a major event.**

Cheerleaders, like Donna Peterson, •

add to the excitement and hoopla. • One of the Army's nicknames is the Black Knights. Their mascot is a mule. The Black Knight is a cadet whose identity remains a secret, by tradition.

Soldiers Magazine *article, November 1980.*

*With Billy Hubbard before a football game, Fall '80.*

*Yell-leaders Bucky, Tony, and Brian during lunchtime football rally on steps of cadet mess hall.*

*Gen. Omar Bradley during last visit to West Point.*

*President Ronald Reagan salutes the Corps during visit to West Point.*

(U.S. Army Photo)

*Women in my company compare rings after presentation ceremony: Leslie, me, Pam.*

*Just after ring ceremony. Notice the right hand!*

*Leading the battalion at parade during senior year (I'm at far left).*

*Academy Honor Guard during pass-in-review ceremony.*

(U.S. Army Photo)

*Brigade Commander Nicholson and his staff at parade.*

*With Medal of Honor recipient M.Sgt. Roy Benavidez and brigade staff members.*
(U.S. Army Photo)

*As a senior, in dress gray.*

*Surrounded by "Zoomies" during Army–Air Force football weekend in Colorado Springs.*

*With Commander Forrington (on right) and his deputy at Royal Military College in Canada, February '82.*

*A new tradition: Women of the first three classes posed for class photos just prior to graduation.*

*With 1st Lt. David Parker at graduation dinner-dance.*

*"You bet I made it!" Accepting my diploma from the commandant of cadets.*

*Taking the commissioning oath and becoming lieutenants.*

*Caps fill the sky . . . It's all over.*

# CHAPTER 9

# Firstie Year

*". . . along a glittering path of sunlit water . . . hemmed in, besides, all 'round with memories of Washington, and the events of the Revolutionary War: is the Military School of America. It could not stand on more appropriate ground, and any ground more beautiful can hardly be."*
— Charles Dickens, *American Notes*, 1841

As I pinned the shiny black brass of a first-class cadet to the epaulettes of my white dress shirt, I made a decision: I was going to enjoy my firstie year and savor every precious moment of my last year at West Point.

To begin with, my class was in charge of the R-Day operation, and what a tremendous undertaking it was. There were three weeks of classes and training to go through before we ever even saw our first new cadet candidate. We learned about the planning for the operation, practiced teaching many of the military tasks the new cadets would be required to learn, and sat through several hours of input from the Psychology Department to prepare us to understand and deal with the mental and emotional reactions of the new cadets to this tough indoctrination.

At one such session the instructor asked some of the male cadets

214

how they would handle a situation in which a new cadet asked to quit before the end of the first week (many ask to quit the first day). After they responded satisfactorily, the instructor asked the same question, except this time the new cadet was a female, and she was crying. The response from the men was the same.

"I think your reaction would be different," the instructor cautioned them. "Could I get a female to volunteer to act this out?" he asked, addressing the group. I raised my hand.

I stood at attention in front of the company commander, tears flowing freely down my cheeks, sobbing, almost blubbering, and begging, "Please, I can't stay here anymore. I wanna get out of here!" No matter what questions he would ask, I would answer with, "I just wanna get out of here!" and cry harder until I was literally hysterical. The entire group sat silently, in shock. Finally, the commander looked at the instructor in desperation.

"Okay, that's enough. Cadet Peterson are you okay?" the instructor asked, taking me by the arm. "Can I get you something?"

"Do you have a tissue?" I responded spryly as if nothing had ever happened. He handed me a tissue, I blew my nose and wiped my eyes, and sat down. The tension in the air was thick. "Really, I'm okay," I offered, trying to bring the class back to life.

"I just hope I never have to actually go through something like that," one of my male classmates said, responding to the display. "What in the world would you do?" he asked the instructor.

"That is what we are here to learn. Every new cadet does not respond to Beast Barracks in the same manner. The problem is to evaluate the situation and offer the best solution for that situation," the instructor told us.

In addition to counseling instruction, we spent hours answering questions about the Honor Code and the need for a fourth-class system, and teaching classes about both. Even the Cadet-in-the-Red-Sash (the term "Man" could no longer be used now that there were women cadre members) had to rehearse his speech so that it would be flawless on R-Day.

As the company executive officer (XO), I was in charge of company administration. Most of my work was completed prior to R-Day — billeting of the new cadets, class scheduling — leaving me free to oversee the operation. From my room overlooking the area I could see most of the stations, and the cadre knew where to look to motion for me when necessary. There were a few problems, like cadets showing up whom we did not have on our list, or on any of the company lists, and having to rearrange room assignments because the sex of a cadet had been incorrectly noted on the master list and men and women were assigned to the same room. Basically, however, I was required to know how to perform most of the cadre positions so that I could relieve other cadets or pitch in when the flow of the cadets was the greatest.

As I stood near the yellow chalk line on the ground in front of me, preparing to give my first speech as the "Cadet-in-the-Red-Sash," I thought of the impact this encounter had on me when I was on the other end of the line. I hoped I would have a positive impact on the new cadets standing shakily in the line before me.

"New Cadet Candidate! Step up to my line!" I commanded in a voice that sounded strangely familiar. Throughout my four years I prided myself on my ability to impart the requirements of the West Point lifestyle by adding a certain flair of my own. This scene, however, I played exactly as it had been played for me in 1978.

"I said *to* my line. Not *on* my line, not *over* my line, *to* my line! Can't you understand English?" I felt just as polished as the shiny cadet who had shouted those words to me. But this situation wasn't the same. I was 5'4" tall, and the candidate standing in front of me was at least a foot taller.

"Look me in the eye when I'm talking to you, Mister!" I barked at the confused candidate. He was so tall that my hat almost slipped off my head when I tilted it back enough to be able to look at his face! I had hopes that the next opportunity to recite my speech would be better.

The next candidate who posted in front of me was only about six feet tall, but my initial reaction to him was one of déjà vu. Once again I was looking up into piercing blue eyes surrounded by sun-streaked blond hair, bronzed skin, and rippling biceps. This time, however, I was on the opposite side of the line. As I finished my speech and dismissed him from my sight, it occurred to me that these candidates were having more of an impact on me than I was probably having on them.

After the oath ceremony and dinner, when the plebes were remanded to the custody of their squad leaders, I called a friend of mine from the Class of 1979 to ask him about his feelings on R-Day and compare them with my own.

"Oh, yeah," he said, chuckling at the memory. "It was tough sometimes. I remember this little girl with big, dark, saucer-like eyes who had to raise her head to look at me. And there was a gal with long, blond hair. Every time a breeze blew her hair fanned out, exposing her bare shoulders, and I got a whiff of the sweetest perfume! And I would imagine, Donna, that whoever stood in line facing you when you were a candidate probably remembers you just as much as you remember him. After all, we're only human."

He was right. Cadets face the test of being human every day; what sets a good cadet apart is the ability to respond militarily, despite the desire to do otherwise.

Though I had a bold dislike for cadets who gave into their human nature and attempted to fraternize with the plebe women — and there were many, including my own squad leader when I was a plebe who tried to kiss me goodbye when I left for Christmas vacation! — my participation in Beast this summer made me understand the desire.

One of the benefits of being the XO was that I set up the table seating in the mess hall, and therefore got to pick my own table assignment. As I debated my selections, I remembered two incidents that had occurred during my own Beast three years earlier. First, I had been assigned to sit at a table with two cadets who were known as the biggest hazes in the company (the new cadets would "match-out" to see who would have to deliver the laundry to these two). I was scared, yet, when I got to their table, I found that they treated the pretty girls very gently. Though new cadets usually rotate their seating every day, I was required to sit next to both of them for three entire days. In addition, they asked all of us seated at the table to bring to lunch a picture of ourselves "the way we used to look" and they kept them. The pair did little to inspire respect for themselves, and I felt sorry for the male plebes who had to witness their behavior.

The second incident was when I was assigned to Tony Cucculo's table. Traditionally, if you had to sit at the CO's table, it meant that you were in trouble. "What did I do to deserve this?" I asked myself when I saw the assignment.

I can still see Tony, standing there, leaning on the back of his chair and telling us his reasoning: "As the company commander, I'm often required to be away from the table, or may not be able to attend a meal at all. I have to know that this table won't have any problems when I leave it. And when I do sit in this chair, I want to be able to eat in peace, not worrying about who's doing something wrong or who I have to reprimand next. You're all sitting here because your platoon leaders tell me you're the best in the company. Don't let me down."

You know, I hardly ever remember him even inspecting the dessert when we cut it. He'd usually just place it in the center of the table and tell us all to start eating our meal.

I selected my table for both selfish and military reasons. Actually, I was much more discreet about my selections than many of my classmates. I'd like to have a dollar for every time one of my male classmates would point out a cute female new cadet and say, "She's got great legs! Seat her at my table!" Since the company supply sergeant also sat at my table, that left eight seats for plebes. I filled the table with the best — and best-looking — new cadets, male and female, in the company. It was a great table. I gave them the same talk Tony had given his table. After only two days with this group, it was obvious that this was to be a great test for me. You see, there was this one new cadet . . .

Tom Cruise had not had his dramatic rise to stardom yet, so, at the time, I did not see the resemblance. I do now. This new cadet had the same dark hair, flashing blue eyes, and a devilish smile that I became addicted to seeing. As despicable as I thought fraternization was, because I believed it was taking advantage of innocent new cadets or plebes, I had to fight the desire to do it myself. And I think the young man probably perceived it. I had to keep telling myself that feeling this way was all right, as long as I didn't act on it.

We laughed a little at the table: I let the new cadets tell jokes in return for the privilege of "taking big bites" of their food. (Actually, this had been standard practice for many years when dealing with plebes.) These new cadets were impressive, and I wanted to reward them by letting them know that I wasn't going to harass them needlessly. It's nice to be able to relax, if only in your mind, while you're eating. That was the greatest benefit of sitting at Tony's table. It was nice to have a break from having your stomach in knots. Of course, with less stalwart new cadets, I didn't have the same option for leniency.

Because male cadets greatly outnumber the female cadre during Beast (we had only three female cadre), new cadets will, at least once, call a female "sir." I always corrected the offender, who occasionally was female, but warned against its happening again. One new cadet could not get the hang of saying "ma'am," so I took advantage of the easily intimidated nature of new cadets to play a joke on my male classmates, especially the company commander.

As the kid passed by he said, "Good afternoon, sir" to the company commander, whose room was adjacent to mine, and then "Good afternoon, sir" to me as well, as he went "pinging" down the hall. This was the last straw.

"Mister, halt!" I barked at him. He stopped, realizing what he had done. "Get in here!" I ordered. He was scared. Usually the cadre yells at a new cadet in the hallway, not inside their room. I slammed the door behind him. "Up against that locker!" He shuffled his feet as he backed up to my clothes locker then stopped with a thud when his head met the wooden door.

"Mister, do you think I look like a man?" I began.

"No, ma'am!" he replied confidently.

"Then why do you keep referring to me as 'sir'?" I asked.

"No, excuse, ma'am!" he said, hoping I'd allow him to explain that he gets caught up in saying "sir" and it comes out before he realizes it sometimes. Heck, I knew that, because it happens to all the new cadets and plebes. It even happened to me once when I was a plebe, but it bothered me so much that I made a point of never letting it happen again. And, after hearing too many male plebes let "sir" slip out over the last two years, I was going to use this guy to turn the tables, and let the guys find out what it's like to be referred to incorrectly.

"Do you have any idea how very difficult it is for a woman at this institution?" I continued.

"No, ma'am," he said finally, after surveying his four answers for the one that would best fit this question.

"It's very difficult," I said, answering my own question. "But, despite the difficulty, I still try to look like a female, and be a good cadet at the same time. Then I have to put up with insulting comments like yours!" My brow was knitted and my voice was firm as I leaned toward his face, staring into his eyes.

"You're a smart kid, so listen closely to what I'm telling you. As one of very few female firsties, if you think I have a lot of power in this company, you should see the power I have in the Corps. Push me, one more time, and I'll have you out, permanently. It would be better for you to call a male cadet 'ma'am' than to call me, or any other female, 'sir' one more time. And if you think I'm bluffing, just try me!" I sounded like Clint Eastwood. And, of course, it was a complete bluff, but it worked like a charm.

The next afternoon the new cadet was walking quickly down the hallway. The company commander, along with several cadre members, and I were standing in our doorways when I heard, "Good morning, ma'am. Good morning, ma'am," in rapid succession. I smiled at the young man as he passed my room, then smiled to myself as six cadets stopped him in his tracks and lit into him.

"Do you think I look like a girl, Mister?" one said angrily.

"I can forgive you saying the wrong thing to a female," the company commander told the kid, "but there are so many men. How could you get confused? In three years no one has ever called me that!" The kid just apologized and offered no excuse.

I'm sure the CO could forgive someone saying the wrong thing to a female, and, like he said, no one had ever called *him* the wrong thing before. Well, I didn't have to wonder how he liked experiencing something the women put up with a lot; he didn't like it one bit. It was good to see the shoe on the other foot for a change. I spoke to the new cadet at the dinner formation.

"They were pretty rough on you, huh?" I asked.

"Yes, ma'am," he replied.

"But at least you're still here," I said, raising my eyebrows and remaining in character. As we marched to dinner I overheard several of the males talking about the incident, unable to believe it had really occurred.


"Cadet Peterson, come quick! He's trying to kill himself!" a new cadet screamed into my doorway.

I grabbed my robe and headed into the hallway. My God, it was barely breaking dawn. There was a light on in one of the new cadet rooms several doors down. As I approached the door I saw that the squad leader had gotten there first. He was talking to a frightened young man who was sitting on his knees on his bed, holding a tiny pen knife to his left wrist.

"You don't want to do this," the squad leader told him. "Just give me the knife and then we can talk."

"I just want to get out of here. I have to leave," the new cadet said as tears streamed down his face, the knife still pressed against his flesh. Then he saw me standing in the doorway. He just stared at me as the squad leader moved closer to him. If there is such a thing as a "mother instinct," I was feeling it at this moment. I wanted to go to the young man, put his head in my lap, and let him cry. I wanted to scream at my classmates, "Put your arms around him. He's crying out to be hugged!" but I didn't dare. This was West Point and, though I'm certain that is what would have served him best at that moment, I kept it to myself. This was a strange, very powerful feeling, one that I had no conscious desire to have.

The new cadet continued to stare up at me, until the squad leader took the knife from him, then patted him on the shoulder, saying, "Yeah, he's just fine now," to the group that had assembled by this time. Then the CO turned to me and said, "You can leave now, you're not needed."

I walked quietly back down the hall, knowing by the young man's gaze that I had been sorely needed. The CO was just upset because the new cadet's roommate had come to get me, instead of him, and his ego was bruised. Then too, he may have been a bit embarrassed, as I was the only one who grabbed a robe when I left my room; the rest of the assemblage attended the crisis in their underwear. It didn't faze me in the least. I had grown up with two brothers.

The ambulance took the young man away moments later. He hadn't even broken the skin on his wrist. He just wanted to leave, and West Point had a new policy that you had to give Beast a try for at least two weeks before you'd be allowed to leave. He wanted out before the two-week deadline. I'd never heard of a cadet seriously attempting suicide. I thought we were too well-adjusted for that. Groups like the followers of the Reverend Moon ("Moonies") have no followers at this place. Yet this kid was attempting suicide? And this wasn't the only strange occurrence that summer.

Later that week, I was called to a new cadet's room by her platoon leader. "Could you try to talk to her, Donna? We've tried everything. The ambulance is on its way."

Not again! But this time it was different. The young female was sitting in her chair, facing the window, her ghost-white fingers gripping the wooden arms of the chair. She was completely catatonic. She wouldn't respond to anything I said or did; she wouldn't even blink. *This place can't be that bad,* I thought. *They should've been here under the Class of '79. No, then they'd all be jumping out of the windows. What's the matter with society? Are young people getting so weak that they can't adjust to some discipline and regimentation?*

In desperation, I brushed her hair with my fingers, then sat on one of the arms of the chair and put my arms around her. This was done with hesitation as I wondered what I'd do if she flipped out and attacked me. I wasn't having any instinctive feelings on this one; I was just trying anything and everything. I spoke soothingly to her, constantly stroking her skin and hair for about the next fifteen minutes.

By the time the ambulance personnel arrived, she had relaxed her grip on the chair. They helped her out of the room, and she walked down to the ambulance with them. She was processed out several days later.

I blamed these two failings on a too-lenient society. I remembered going to fifth grade and hearing some of the kids talk about their five-dollar allowances. "My goodness," I'd say as my mouth fell open. "What chores do you have to do to get that much money?" I was thinking about my own list of chores to perform before I could get my seventy-five cents every Saturday, and imagining these poor children chained to a table leg or something.

"We don't do chores," they said. "Our folks just give us an allowance." I couldn't believe it — no chores at all! I went sheepishly back to my house, thinking of how I would ask my mother for a raise.

I rose early that Saturday and performed my chores in a manner that would assure my pay increase. "Do you think I could get an increase to a dollar?" I asked my mother as I presented her with a completed list of duties.

"No," she said unemotionally, "but you can get a job if you like." Several months later I took over my brother's paper route.

If young people aren't as strong or responsible as they used to be, society needs to take a part of the blame. And certainly, they have no business at West Point. Thank goodness that Beast Barracks works; it weeds out the weakest of the new recruits immediately.


Before I knew it, the first detail was over and the second detail cadre would be taking our places. I had four weeks of leave, the longest of my cadet career, and I was going to Hawaii with my family. As I packed my gear I heard a knock on the door.

"Come on in," I responded.

There he was: Tom Cruise II. He had come to say goodbye. He wondered if he'd ever see me again. I told him that I was pretty hard to miss at this institution, whether that was good or bad. I told him a little about his new squad leader, to put him at ease about the change of detail. Then he said he had to go.

"Good idea," I said with a wink and just the hint of a smile. As he left I felt as if I had passed the test. I doubted I would ever see him again.

Four of the new cadets who sat at my table came to say goodbye that day, two men and two women. The meeting with one of the women sticks in my mind especially. She was probably the most promising female new cadet in the company, and a good runner. As she was standing in my room at a perfect position of parade rest, her eyes became misty.

"I want to be so much like you, but I don't think I'll make it. You're good, and well respected, and nice, too. Please tell me what I can do," she pleaded. I handed her a tissue and tried to explain.

"Oh, dear," I said, shaking my head. "It's not how you see it. Right now you're on the outside, thinking you know what the inside looks like. Do you know the company commander doesn't like me?" She looked startled. "Well, he doesn't. He'd never met me before, but he told his Tac he didn't want me as his XO. I'm not a wallflower, though many of my classmates wish I was, which doesn't make me popular. And I stand up for women too much, which doesn't endear me to many of the males, and makes this place even more difficult to get through. I've always believed in standing up for what's right. After all, as the saying goes, if you don't stand for something you'll fall for anything." The new cadet grinned slightly. "There are easier ways for a woman to get through West Point than the one I selected, so maybe I shouldn't be the one to give you advice."

I did not want her to feel the bitterness that had grown in me over the past year. The West Point she would spend her next four years getting to know would be very different from the one I had known, thanks to the efforts of some very courageous young women. And I wanted her to be free to face her next years without dread. "Just be the best you can be at everything you do, and don't get caught up trying to compete in this place. If somebody told you life was fair, they lied. But it can be fun. Take advantage of the programs, classes, clubs, and sports that USMA has to offer and try to leave here liking yourself and liking West Point. Just don't sweat the small stuff." She hugged me, then regained her composure and left. *I hope she makes it,* I thought as the door closed behind her.

I was reminded of the end of the first detail of my own Beast experience, when the red-headed cadet referred to my roommate as MaryAnn. As unprofessional as I thought that was, how was what had occurred on this day really any different? Beast, especially first detail, has got to be the most emotionally chaotic experience in a young person's life. That is why it was so important for me to participate in the process, and particularly first detail. This was where I thought I could make the most difference. I hope I did.


The academic year began with celebration and controversy. Ring Weekend, which had for decades been celebrated during the last semester of cow year, was now used to mark the official start of our final year at the Academy. My mother flew up for the August weekend celebration.

The "Cadets Only" ring presentation ceremony, held in the mess hall, was as exciting and thrilling as I always imagined it would be. Cadets slipped the rings they had painstakingly designed and ordered a semester before (*all* U.S. cadets are required to purchase rings) solemnly upon their fingers, then raced throughout the cavernous hall congratulating friends and comparing their symbols of achievement. The private ceremony culminated with the time-honored ritual of "ring-knocking." The echoes of 900 "brass and glass" symbols tapping the wooden mess hall tables for the first time raised chills throughout my body. The rings were now christened!

The four women in my company posed for a picture, our ring hands extended ostentatiously, before heading to the formal dance at Ike Hall. My mother met me in the huge stone foyer just inside the entrance. Before gaining access to the dance, one final ritual had to be observed: Just before the grand marble staircase leading to the ballroom sat a gigantic "ring," an exact replica of the golden rings we were now wearing. Each cadet, and his date or guest, marched down a red-carpeted aisle and stood completely inside the ring, pausing momentarily for a photographic memento, before walking through the ring and into the gala.

The rest of the evening was filled with the musical strains of a hired orchestra and the sounds of numerous eloquent "toasts." And of course, cameras flashed throughout the hall during the entire evening. In fact, one photo taken of Leslie and me (unbeknownst to us) became a fixture on a West Point poster several months later, and she and I were gifted with 8 x 10 glossy photos of the shot for our graduation! The weekend had been perfect, despite the controversy that threatened it during the week prior.

Two days before the ring presentation, I was summoned to the USMA Treasurer's Office, the office that controlled the ordering of the cadet rings. I assumed I had been called because of some matter with the Cadet Store, since I had worked with the Treasurer's Office as a member of that council. Even after I arrived, and saw the nearly 900 ring cases covering the tables and counters of the room, I still had no clue as to what was about to occur.

The familiar dark-haired man handed me a ring box. "I thought you might like to see your ring prior to the ceremony," he began. Of course I would! When I opened the box, I thought that it was the most breathtaking ring I had ever laid eyes upon! It was pale yellow gold with a shiny gold platform covering the entire head of the ring. From the center of the platform protruded six gold prongs which safely housed one single brilliant diamond. The stone, from the first wedding ring my father gave to my mother, was my graduation gift from my parents. I gasped slightly, then looked again at the man as he continued to speak.

"Donna, we have a problem." Immediately the smile left my face. "You see," he stated delicately, "our office inspects all of the rings prior to presentation and yours," he paused and swallowed hard, "yours doesn't look like a West Point ring."

I couldn't believe my ears! "Well, what does it look like?" I questioned.

"It looks more like a cocktail ring," he spurted quickly. "But don't worry. We're still going to let you have your ring for the presentation ceremony, but you'll have to come back in next week and redesign the ring along more standard lines."

It only took me a few moments to realize what was really happening here. The male cadets are free to completely cover the massive head of the ring with several carats of cut diamonds; it's done frequently by the more affluent cadets. My stone was only a $3/4$-carat diamond, but it was a solitaire, and, rather than being fully set into the head of the ring, was raised from the head about a quarter of an inch. I had requested that the stone be set into the head, but the representative for the Balfour Company, which made the rings, told me that they couldn't "set-in" a stone larger than a $1/2$-carat, though they could set-in as many of them as I liked.

"What you actually mean," I stated boldly to the man at the Cadet Store, "is that the ring looks too feminine." The man was visibly nervous at this accusation.

"Not necessarily," he replied. "But you have to admit, it looks more like a ring a woman would wear to a party than one a West Point officer would wear to the field." His argument had no credibility, and he knew it. All West Point rings were identical, except for the design of the head. And, most West Point officers don't even wear their rings to the field. "Look, Donna," he continued, "we just feel that the ring should look a bit more military."

"So, if I come back next week and decide to put several carats of diamonds into the head of the ring, that's okay with your office?" I wanted to be certain I understood the requirements.

"As long as they're set-in," he stated confidently. "In fact, several men in your class have rings just like that! I'm glad you understand."

What I understood was that, since I had never actually agreed to the reviewers' request, once I placed the ring on my finger at the Friday night ceremony, they were going to have to come and *take* it off my hand if they wanted it.

On Tuesday after the ceremony, the Treasurer's Office called: When would I be bringing the ring in? "I won't be," I stated. "Everything military is not necessarily masculine anymore, sir. And since you have no viable reason for rejecting the design of my ring, except perhaps that it looks feminine, I'm going to keep it. Besides, I like it."

He never pushed the issue. I have had the ring for almost ten years now; it's one of my most prized possessions. I was asked once, hypothetically, if I would go back to save anything if my home was on fire. I held up my right hand and told the man, "As long as this ring is on my finger and my family members are all safe, I wouldn't." I never go anywhere without it, including flying an aircraft, digging trenches on month long field exercises, or running PT, and I have never damaged the ring or even loosened the stone.

During the first half of the academic year, I lived on staff, away from the company, as the cadet activities officer. I had two female roommates, the regimental and battalion athletic officers. We lived on the sixth floor, one floor below the infamous seventh floor where I had spent so much time as a plebe. We had a phone in our room — no more waiting for a booth in the cold basement — and even an elevator, which ran so slowly that it was usually faster to walk. Best of all, there was a good group of people (eleven of us, male and female) on our floor and we all got along well. The regimental commander, who lived one floor above, was the male cadet who had been supported by my male classmates during the "letter episode," and he really had his hands full. Not only did his staff not get along well with each other, one of the females on his staff was rumored to have been counseled by the regimental Tac officer because of her reputation for promiscuity. "From now on, when you go on a date, I expect you to keep your legs closed," he reportedly ordered her. According to one of my roommates, this girl's passion during spring leave was to "get laid in the back of a limousine." Whether she was ever successful or not, I don't know. I do know that this type of female was the definite exception to the rule at West Point. Besides, she was certainly not the most promiscuous cadet at the Academy; it just wasn't as much fun to talk about male promiscuity. I had learned by now that, unfortunately, in many ways West Point mirrors society, and this was typical behavior at many educational institutions across the country.

It would be naive to think that West Point wouldn't mirror the society which supports it, at least in some ways. After all, the Academy accepts young people who are products of that society, from all walks of that society and backgrounds as diverse as those of two classmates like Billy Hubbard and Michael Meese. I suppose I had thought that cadets were demigods: members of society who were unhappy with that society and its morals and ethics. But cadets, I found out, are people who are as different from each other as their fingerprints, and who, once accepted at West Point, adopt a moral-ethical code that society has mislaid over the years but wishes it had not. West Point holds those lost virtues for the country. Were we to lose them, or demand less of our cadets, the country would lose them. Still, not surprisingly, societal vices often slip in, but (hopefully) are quickly cast out.

During the first semester of my senior year, a drug incident occurred. A couple of senior cadets were stopped by police in Cornwall, a city about twenty minutes from West Point, and were found to have marijuana in their car. There was a rumor going around the Corps that these cadets had violated regulations by leaving the Academy during the week to attend a concert, and were caught en route.

As part of my staff duties that year, I attended a "coffee call" for senior cadets at which the commandant, Brigadier General Franklin, answered questions put to him, to provide the Corps with facts rather than rampant rumors. At that meeting he informed the cadets that "the seniors picked up in Cornwall on a marijuana offense were given no option to graduate." They could resign or be separated following a full investigation by USMA. The two elected to leave, quickly.

West Point does not lend itself to drug use; without maintaining a clear head it would be impossible to make it from Beast Barracks to graduation. Of course, that does not mean that cadets don't use marijuana or drugs, only that its use is very slight. And, if cadets use drugs when they are away from the Academy, I have no definite knowledge of it. It would be very risky in either case, however, because of random drug testing.

I remember only one other drug incident during my four years at West Point. It happened just before graduation week of my plebe year. The Corps was buzzing: three senior cadets were to be dismissed from the Academy without graduating after the Military Police narcotics dogs were taken through the cadet parking lot (only seniors are allowed to have cars). All that the cadets were told was that the dogs had alerted on several cars. The total amount of marijuana found in the cars was not enough to make a complete cigarette. One of the cadets, however, also had several "joints" stashed in the garage of Mrs. Brown's house, without her knowledge, of course. The three cadets that were implicated reportedly never graduated, though it was rumored that at least one of them had to serve time in the army as an enlisted soldier to pay back the government for his education. Nothing stronger than marijuana was ever found.

After my graduation from West Point, I was informed, by two cadets, that one of my classmates had supplied barbiturates to them while at the Academy. "Uppers" were supplied to these cadets to help them stay awake to meet the demands of cadet life during certain peak periods. In addition, these cadets were members of varsity athletic teams and were concerned about maintaining their positions on their squads, especially when having to compete with fresh plebes, whose muscles hadn't yet been torn down by years of the demanding physical requirements of the Academy. To remain competitive, these cadets say that they took uppers before practice or competition. This was all news to me. I had never even heard of this occurring while I was a cadet. But, understanding the grueling demands placed on the cadets, it does not seem impossible that this could have occurred.

Also after my graduation, I was informed by a cadet in the Class of 1983, that, as a senior, one of his classmates was implicated in a co-caine-buying operation in New York City one weekend. Apparently, as the cadet drove away in his brand new 300ZX, the authorities saw the cadet parking sticker on his vehicle and gave the make, model, and color of the car to the West Point Military Police, who easily tracked down the owner. As far as my source knows, the cadet was dismissed from the Academy immediately, though no action was taken by the military courts, and no cocaine was reported to have been used or sold on the Academy grounds.

The other, very sensitive, potential problem area among the Corps of Cadets was homosexuality. I don't remember the subject even being mentioned until my second year at the Academy.

As a yearling, I returned from class one day to find my roommate in an agitated state.

"Donna, have you heard? Two women were caught kissing each other in the barracks!" The two women were members of the Class of 1980, and both were involved with the women's basketball team. Neither one was suspended after it was found that the person who caught them in the supposed act had actually only seen them hugging, one female allegedly consoling the other on the loss of a boyfriend.

I resented the hoopla that was made over this incident. It made women very afraid to comfort other women, at an institution where women often needed comforting, for fear that they would be labeled as homosexuals. Before this time, I had heard rumors about homosexual incidents involving males (who mysteriously vanished from the Academy), but no women had ever been implicated. Truthfully, though, this was the first time when women *could* be implicated in something out of the ordinary. Women had only been in attendance for a little over three years, and most of that time they were poked, prodded, analyzed and scrutinized, quizzed and queried, and observed as if under a microscope. Women had not had the privacy nor the time or opportunity to get into this sort of trouble. After four years of women in attendance at West Point, however, the first class with women were seniors, and now both men and women could be implicated in this type of behavior.

During my four years, to my knowledge, four women and two men were "allowed to resign" from the Academy for alleged homosexual or deviate behavior. A male cadet, against whom allegations of homosexuality had been waged several times (though the allegations were never proven) was allowed to resign, in lieu of being separated, when a locker inspection revealed homosexual and sadomasochism materials among his personal belongings. Even before the locker inspection, however, the cadet had to reside in a room by himself, as no other male cadet would consider being his roommate. I knew the young man and thought he was a very nice guy, but West Point males can't tolerate gay men among their ranks. A male graduate from an all-male class told me that he never personally knew of any cadet who was gay. He said there were rumors about a few guys, but most cadets just stayed away from them. The cadets knew that the system would weed out any cadet who could be proven to be homosexual, so the other men never worried about it or threatened violence against any cadet suspected of being gay. "It was never an issue," he said.

There was also a scandal alleging homosexual behavior between members of the women's basketball team and a female officer representative. The officer was immediately reassigned and, I was told by a female classmate, is now living with one of the former female team members (one of the two females implicated in the original "kissing" incident of my yearling year). The officer and the former cadet are both still in the army.

Though normal resignation procedures take one to two weeks to complete at USMA, when these offenses are alleged the cadets involved seem to disappear from the face of the earth. One of my female classmates in MaryAnn's company was implicated when she wrote a love letter to another female cadet. The news leaked out on Friday, and by Monday it was as if she had never existed. In one final case, two women were actually caught in bed together by the company CQ, who was alerted by several males who watched the two women through binoculars from a parallel barracks. Both women were moved from their barracks immediately, pending an investigation, but elected to resign in lieu of being investigated. As usual, they vanished as if they had never existed.

Regardless of what laws the Supreme Court or the Court of Appeals chooses to uphold where homosexuality in the U.S. Armed Forces is concerned, I do not believe it will ever be tolerated at the United States Military Academy. Cadets live in too close and demanding an environment. Cadets themselves will not put up with it.


In all, West Point is an idyllic academic environment. Visiting professors from other major universities wait for the opportunity to teach at an institution where no one is allowed to "cut class," all homework must be done, students are coherent in class and really want to learn, and no one *ever* threatens or harasses a teacher. For the students, there are no alcohol or substance-abuse support groups, and no gay rights doctrine or racial discrimination policy letters written. At this point, there simply is no need for any of it. The only real problem area the Academy had a difficult time monitoring while I was there was the type of reading material cadets obtained through the mail.

During my plebe year, freshmen still delivered all of the mail (cadets had individual post office boxes by the time I graduated). Once a month each company would receive stacks of magazines with plain brown wrappers covering them. Anyone could see through the open ends that these were *Playboy* and *Penthouse* subscriptions the cadets were receiving. I *always* refused to deliver any of them — my personal feelings about that type of propaganda were strong — but many of the male plebes would slide out a copy from its wrapping and skim through it before delivering it to the addressee. I never saw a male cadet refuse to deliver these magazines, but quite a few male cadets found that type of magazine distasteful and had no use for other cadets who did. I had no use for the *Playgirl* subscription one of my summer roommates at Camp Buckner received, either. Of all the male cadets I came to care about during my four years as a cadet, only Dave — not Tony, David, or Billy — had any interest in those types of magazines.

What I considered the largest "scandal" of my cadet career occurred because of the Academy's inability to monitor what cadets receive through the mail. Apparently, some male cadets were watching pornographic movies, the kind that were specially ordered and mailed in plain brown wrappers. They used the football team's movie projector in the barracks. Their only crime, according to the hierarchy at the Academy, was that they were teasing some female cadets about the movies while seated in the mess hall the next day. One of the females, who had previously decided to leave the Academy, reported their activities on her way out. Had she never mentioned the incident, no one would have found out about it.

I was upset. If cadets want to participate in those types of activities, let them do it when they go away from the Academy, not there, using government equipment, and staying up after taps to do it!

I did not determine the punishments at the Academy, and there was no specific regulation against such behavior, except their being out of their rooms after taps, so I waited to see the punishments handed down for what I considered "conduct unbecoming an officer." It never came. "Boys will be boys" was the unofficial Academy ruling. A contact of mine from the commandant's office said that it was impossible to punish these cadets under the statute for "conduct unbecoming an officer" because, if they searched the Bachelor Officer's Quarters on post, they were sure they would find much worse than a few bad movies. Besides, how could the Academy explain to the members of the

Association of Graduates around the world that male cadets were being punished for being "all-male"? Of course, I found it particularly interesting that a male cadet on an organized trip-section to New York City one evening urinated on the steps of the United Nations and was severely punished under "conduct unbecoming an officer," but these cadets could not be.

I was disappointed with the Academy leadership. *Boys will be boys* . . . What kind of a cop-out was that? West Point had real "criminals" out walking the area: cadets who left a dull ceremonial bayonet sitting on their beds for five minutes longer than they were told to after a weapons check, and cadets who received too many monthly demerits for dust on their windowsills. Yet these male cadets had committed no wrongdoing? In the end, the cadets were reprimanded with slaps on their hands, and the cadet who ordered the tapes, and who I later found out lived in *my* company, was told to keep his toys under wraps. If any punishments were handed down, they were for abuse of the fourth-class system, because plebe females were seated at the mess hall table when the discussion about the movies occurred.

I spoke to Billy about the incident and he said, unfortunately, that cadets frequently watch those types of films at the Academy, only none of them had ever been caught before by women who objected. (At about the same time that this was occurring, rumors were flying that cadets at the Naval Academy had been expelled for *making* a pornographic movie. I guess that really stretched the "boys will be boys" theory.)


There were very few women in the highest positions of authority during my senior year. This was probably due, at least in part, to the fact that men who were the "leaders" of the class were not known to the Corps as supporters of women at West Point. When these cadets were questioned by the selection committees who assigned the highest leadership positions, many of them expressed the feeling that, though they didn't personally feel that women belonged here, Congress had mandated it, and therefore they supported it. I guess that *perhaps* that type of an answer can be turned into a vote of support. The truth was, the male leadership of my class acted more anti-women than the two classes that preceded them. So, the absence of any women in direct positions of authority pleased many of my male classmates. What didn't please them was that the classmate selected as the brigade commander had not been a classmate of ours for all four years.

Cadet "Mick" Nicholson was a cadet from the Class of 1979, who left the Academy after two years, got a degree in history from George-town, and returned to the Academy, having decided that he really did wish to pursue a military career after all. The fact that he was origi-nally part of the class that ran our Beast was seen as a slap in the face to the class, as if no member of our own class was qualified enough to lead us. Instead, they had to go back to the last all-male class to find some-one qualified enough. Many of my classmates appeared to support Mick as the commander, but there was great dissension in the ranks.

I approved of Mick as the commander of the Corps. Not only did he look the epitome of a brigade commander, he was older than most of our classmates and was one of the few cadets who already had a col-lege degree. And I had great affinity toward the masculinity of the men in the Class of 1979. I can't explain the aura that so many of them were able to exude, but so many cadets since have been unable to re-create it. I do not mean to imply that Cadet Nicholson approved of women at West Point. In fact, I do not believe that he did. But then, most of my male classmates who were contenders for his job didn't either.

I had two run-ins with Mick and his staff in the fall of my senior year. The first encounter was due to a simple case of bruised egos. A special friend of mine, M.Sgt. Roy Benavidez, became this country's latest Medal of Honor winner while I was a cadet. The Academy paid tribute to this great American with a parade in his honor during the fall of 1981. The morning of the parade, as I was preparing for my cheerleading duties, I received a phone call from the superintendent's office requesting my presence at the Supe's parade box. Sergeant Ben-avidez had requested a seat for me. I quickly changed clothes and headed to the parade field.

Several photographers were on hand to capture the event. Before the parade began, the country's latest hero posed for pictures with the commandant and members of the brigade staff. I stood, quietly observ-ing, on the sidelines until Sergeant Benavidez asked me to step into the photo beside him. The commandant nodded his approval, and a group photo was taken.

Mick was not in any of the photos, but his staff was, and they were not happy. From the moment I arrived at the parade field I was questioned: "What are *you* doing here?" and "Who authorized you to be here?" The reception I received had been cool, but steam rose from their heads after I was allowed into the picture with them. After all, who was I? I certainly didn't carry the rank they did. Seventeen boys had ensured that, and they knew it. But I wasn't personally offended. They treated most cadets like that. They reminded me of typical politicians: they were "of the corps and by the corps," but after they were selected to positions of great leadership, they felt they were "above" the Corps.

The second confrontation occurred about ten days later. Just prior to the Thayer Awards banquet held in the mess hall, the uniform was announced as "full dress gray over white trousers." Several of my female classmates and I had planned to wear our skirts. Since there was no regulation prohibiting females from wearing skirts at this function, I called Central Guard Room. The cadet who made the announcement said that it was announced just as it was received from the brigade staff. So, I called the staff. "Because we think it'll look better," came the reply. Because *they* think?

"You can't just arbitrarily change the regulations because you feel like it," I reminded them. But they did, and hung up on me. Because I had worked with the officers on the uniform committee, I called the head of the group at home and explained the situation.

"They can't do that," he told me. "Those boys are getting too big for their britches. I'll take care of it." Soon another announcement came over the public address system repeating the uniform for the dinner, then adding, "Women may wear skirts." Normally, the announcement never includes a delineation as to the wearing of skirts or trousers. The regs are clearly written as to when the uniform is optional, and when it is not. Announcements simply say, "The uniform is white over gray." Why these men decided that it mattered whether we wore skirts or trousers when seated at our tables in the mess hall was a puzzlement to me. Of course, when they couldn't get away with it, I heard about it. Word filtered back through the regimental commander to the battalion commander that the staff was mad and they weren't going to speak to me. Did anyone ever say they spoke to me, or fifty percent of my classmates, male or female, in the first place?

The next opportunity I had to speak to any of them was in February of the next semester when I attended a trip-section to visit the Royal Military College (RMC) of Canada, with which we had a thriving annual hockey rivalry going. As a plebe I dated one of their cadets who was visiting for the match-up. We had corresponded over the years, and dated again when he returned for the match-up my cow year. I promised him during that visit that I would make the trip to visit his Academy the following year. Shortly after that visit he was selected to be the wing commander at RMC, equivalent to our brigade commander at USMA. (He is now an officer in the Canadian Navy.)

I was treated like royalty at RMC. "You're Mr. Forrington's friend, aren't you?" the RMC cadets would say, almost in awe. John had told everyone he could think of that I was coming. He was so proud of my accomplishments at West Point. This was the first year that RMC had accepted women, but it was quickly obvious, probably due in part to the fact that John was the commander, that RMC treated their women in a much more decent manner than West Point had during the initial years. I recall thinking that American men should be ashamed that these Canadian men had outclassed them. But I got the feeling that, on the average, Canadian men just generally treated women with greater respect than did American men.

John left me a note saying to meet him at his room after I got settled. When I arrived at his room, Mick was standing near the door. "What do you need, Donna?" he asked me.

"John," I answered. John finished tying his shoes then welcomed me with a huge hug and a soft kiss, while Mick stood there, surprised and confused that the commander of the college would choose to date a cadet. Mick's date for the weekend was the daughter of one of the college's professors. I suppose he was not too excited at the prospect of having to spend his weekend double-dating with a female cadet, standing in receiving lines, and sitting at head tables with her. It must have been excruciating for him. But, in true Class of '79 fashion, he was not openly rude about it, as I was certain members of his staff — my classmates — would have been.

Actually, I had little time to notice how Mick was reacting to me. John and I were great friends and we always had a great time together, especially when we got an opportunity to dance. Both John and I *loved* to ballroom dance. I could fall asleep on his shoulder while he was whirling me around the floor, and never miss a step.

The favorite winter pastime for generations of seniors has been to stand on the mess hall steps and watch the plebes slip on the ice. This was always guaranteed amusement. Many plebes from warmer climates had never seen snow or had to negotiate ice from a New York winter. Even those who had experienced both hadn't been forced to negotiate them while maneuvering about like West Point plebes were required to do. If the upperclassmen didn't have a class before lunch, they would gather on the steps at high noon. As the plebes left their 11:00 classes, they hurried back to their companies to perform duties or change their shoes before formation, and they were always heavily laden with books. As they came "pinging" across the apron, several of them would lose their footing and go sprawling on the ice, arms and legs flailing, their saucer caps rolling away from them like spare tires. If one plebe falls, unless he fails to get up immediately, none of those behind him stop to help, for fear that falling is contagious. Usually, the plebe is back up just as quickly as he fell, the look on his face saying, "Who fell? Not me," as he scurries away.

If a plebe, when he realizes a fall is imminent, would just allow himself to fall, he would be able to reclaim his dignity much sooner. The humor is in watching the plebe try to prevent himself from falling, then seeing him fall anyway, slipping, sliding, and sprawling along ten feet of ice. Then his classmates have to help him chase his papers across the Plain. What really makes the show worthwhile is if, when several classmates assist the plebe and finally get him composed, all of them hit the pavement again.

It sounds cruel to laugh at the plebes' pain, but generally it's only their pride that is wounded.

The remainder of my senior year was a fairly happy time for my class, filled with parties celebrating 100 days before graduation and the traditional role-reversal, where plebes assumed the role of seniors for two hours, and seniors were hazed by the plebes, to include having to perform mess hall duties. Since the reversal ended after "brigade rise" in the mess hall, plebes left when the first-class light came on, indicating that first-class cadets could leave the meal, and *ran* to the library, fearful of the repercussions that could be heaped upon them if they remained in the company area.

It was a time for enjoying the Academy, picking wild blackberries along the road near the lower level of Eisenhower Hall, sunbathing on the gymnasium roof or at the athletic courts ("River Courts") down near the river. We used to play frisbee there and, if the frisbee drifted into the Hudson, we let it go. There was a fear that the river was too polluted to put a human limb into, even if it meant the game had to end.

When I first got to the Academy, cadets could not sunbathe in civilian swimming suits (our Academy suits were one-piece, maillotstyle suits). Most cadets just wore their shorts, or shorts and T-shirts if they were female. By the time I graduated, suits had to be "in good taste," which I suppose meant no string bikinis, though I often observed some men wearing very skimpy suits — and looking great in them.

There was very little harassment from the males during my senior year. The harassment during my yearling year had been a hassle to deal with, but after surviving the trials of my junior year, I doubted there was much they could have done to shock or upset me.

During my cow year the harassment had graduated from the mischievous sexual expressions and playful jokes of yearling year to vicious and harmful acts. It seemed as if, once we were welcomed to the "profession of arms" at lunchtime during the first academic day of cow year (signifying our commitment to the Academy and to the military), we were a threat to the male cadets.

When my roommates and I indicated a desire to attend the Helen Reddy concert at Eisenhower Hall, we were "warned" by our male company-mates not to go. We purchased tickets and went anyway, and found our room ransacked upon our return. We knew who destroyed our room that night, but proving it, as our female Tac required, was impossible. When I played Helen Reddy's "I Am Woman" on my stereo, the senior cadets (Class of 1981) threatened to take away my stereo for "playing it too disruptively." When Leslie and I were particularly mad at any of our male classmates, we would play "I Am Woman," point the speakers toward the open door of our room, and crank up the volume. As seniors, we could get away with this type of behavior, on occasion.

Across the Corps, the harassment was similar that year. Females would return from classes to find that someone had put trash in their waste baskets during inspection hours (rooms were inspected every morning and no trash could be placed in the trash can until after lunch), and they would receive demerits for the violation. At times, a female's best inspection shoes would be scuffed just prior to the weekly lunchtime inspection, with no time to repolish. Demerits were almost always awarded.

During the last semester of cow year, as competition for leadership positions increased, some of my male classmates began exercising their leadership styles early. I would find academic books, those which we had to pay for, and homework assignments mysteriously missing from my desk. On one occasion I found a paper that I had stayed up all night typing for an elective history course torn to shreds and left sitting on the desk.

"Just prove who did it," was all my Tac would say or do.

My senior year, however, most of the cadets were too preoccupied with other things to play those kinds of games, or to invent new ones, but I could see that my classmates had passed some of their tactics down to the men in the Class of 1983, who were now cows. For the most part, those cadets who didn't want women in the class could see how futile their harassment would be at this point in time and just ignored the women. There were many men who had no problem with our presence, some of whom had been converted to that attitude after having served beside us for four years, and many were our friends. When we stayed around them, life was enjoyable.


I remember going out to the Plain on Saturday afternoons during my last semester and looking back at the Academy buildings and mess hall. I would take deep breaths of the clean, cool air and try to freeze the moment in my mind — the scenery, the smell, and the awe. Then I would take one step forward, look down at my foot upon the earth, and wonder who in our nation's great history had placed his foot upon the very same spot I was now placing mine. George Washington had fought here, and even Benedict Arnold, before his name came to be synonymous with treachery and deceit. Robert E. Lee and Douglas MacArthur were trained here, and even Edgar Allan Poe spent a year of his life here (cadets are the first to say that it was his year here that made him so crazy).

Who could have placed his foot in that spot? How close was I to the many masters of the universe? I took one last trip down Flirtation Walk, scrambled down the side of a hill to where a piece of the "great chain" lay partially exposed in the water, reached out my hand and touched it softly, so as not to damage any of America's great history. Then, realizing that the huge iron links were impregnable, I placed both my palms on a part of the exposed link and squeezed firmly, as if I expected the history of America to filter from the chain into my hands. Actually, it filtered into my heart.

I did not want to forget — anything — and for cadets, that isn't normal.

Just as the trees filled with leaves again and the dress gray uniform gave way to the short-sleeved white shirt over gray, I sat on a stone wall at the Cadet Chapel overlooking the Academy barracks. A person could see for miles from this spot, and it was breathtaking. My eyes filled with tears as I surveyed "the little boys' school on the Hudson," and I smiled.

"Well, it's sure been tough," I said, probably talking to both the Academy itself and to God. "But I have to tell you the truth: For me, West Point has been everything I needed it to be, and more. I don't regret one day of it." A car full of tourists pulled up and went inside the majestic old chapel as I sat, quietly, with my back to the entrance.

"It's all over very quickly, isn't it?" I asked, continuing my confession out loud. "It seems like only yesterday I stepped boldly up to the Man-in-the-Red-Sash, and hoped I would make it at this place at least until dinner!" I chuckled and smiled. "Thank you, Lord, for giving me a great young life, and for allowing me to wear dress gray for four short years of it."

My prayer was concluded by the sound of an eager voice from behind me. "Miss, can you direct us to a place called Trophy Point?" the woman asked. I wiped my face quickly with my hands before turning around, hopped off of my perch, and smiled, "Yes, ma'am."

The only milestone left in my cadet career was graduation: May 26, 1982.

The graduation of the Class of 1982 was not remarkable, except that it was mine, and that made it very special to me. As I stood solemnly in the tunnel beneath the stadium, awaiting the bugler's call to commencement, dressed in my shiniest, crispest, full-dress uniform, I reflected on my last four years.

I recalled the innocence of the spunky young lady who stepped boldly up to the "Man-in-the-Red-Sash" and saluted proudly, though improperly, in the summer of '78. I lamented the shattered dreams and disillusioned ideals of a youthful cadet which molded the secure, but cautious, woman I could hear breathing inside my head. And I chased away the bitter feelings that had grown silently inside of me like a cancer over the last year and a half. This was my graduation day! I didn't want to feel bitter. Yet, I couldn't quite bring myself to feel elated, either.

"What is the matter with you, Peterson?" I asked, scolding myself softly. I felt so confused, when I should have been so very happy. How could I be feeling like this now? Wasn't this what I had shed blood for four years to obtain? The sacrifices I'd made. The injustices I'd endured. The pain, the anguish, the tears . . . tears that were flowing today. I excused myself from the view of my classmates.

This was *not* the West Point way. Cadets did not shed tears at the thought of leaving the institution. All of our belongings were packed. Our cars, filled with fuel, were parked strategically for the fastest escape possible after the sea of white caps filled the sky. My tears would not be acceptable today, not to the other 861 starched souls lining the tunnel walls, awaiting the call to graduate.

Well, here's another one for the history books! How many West Point graduates have had to worry about their mascara running on graduation day? Or getting makeup on their bleached-white gloves while trying to catch the tears rolling off their chins before the lightly salted drops dulled the shine of the forty-four brass buttons of the traditional dress coat? I know that the answer is "at least one."

Our graduation mirrored those of the past years, a solemn but symbolic ceremony held under blue skies, the day too hot for the wool dress uniforms we wore. The graduating cadets took their cue from the band and marched onto the field in a single-file line; I hadn't marched that way since Beast. The cadets strode neatly from opposite ends of the field into alternate rows of chairs to attend the final ceremony of their unique college lives.

Our graduation speaker was Senator John Tower of Texas, chairman of the Senate Armed Services Committee, and the man who had my vote on any ballot! I had kept in contact with the senator who had nominated me, and sent him an invitation to my graduation. When he was chosen by a committee of class representatives and Academy officers to be the graduation speaker, he told the new superintendent, Lieutenant General Scott, that I had already invited him. I got a phone call telling me to report to the superintendent's office. "Cadet Peterson," he said, "from now on, if you're going to invite senators to speak at the graduation I wish you'd inform me first!" Of course, he was only kidding, and I thought the choice of speakers that year was excellent.

The line of graduates leading to the podium seemed endless. But, almost before I was ready, loudspeakers called my name, and I ascended the ramp. Ten steps and a crisp facing movement to the right placed me directly in front of the commandant of cadets, who was holding in his hands my prize.

"Congratulations, Donna. You made it!" I can still hear Brigadier General Franklin say as he pressed the cardboard tube into my left hand.

"You bet I did, sir!" I replied with a smile, the platform camera capturing the frozen moment.

I stood shaking the commandant's hand for several seconds afterward. I felt his hand on mine and the diploma in the other, but I had no desire to move. I kept thinking, *When I step from this spot, it's all over. I can never go back!* And I did not want to leave.

I stepped forward only because West Point had taught me to "choose the harder right," and I knew I had to accept the diploma and step into my future.

I left the sanctuary of that sacred spot and turned immediately toward Senator Tower. I shook his extended hand and thanked him for making this day possible. I felt so lucky. My parents and my sponsor were in the audience, both Senator Tower and General Goodpaster were in attendance (I had spoken to both the retired general and Mrs. Goodpaster the day prior to the graduation so I knew they would be present), and I held the hard-earned diploma of a West Point graduate in my left hand.

I descended the ramp at the back of the stage, looked into the audience gathered in the stands, raised both arms above my head and yelled, "Yes!" Then I raised my face to the heavens and whispered, "Thank you," as tears began to roll from my eyes.

A nosy newswoman quickly shoved a camera in my face and a microphone near my mouth and said, "It must be a relief to be leaving a place that put you through such hell."

My heart was in my throat, so it was impossible for me to answer her before several of my female classmates embraced me and hustled me out of camera range. It's just as well, though, for the answer I would've given her would never have made the evening news. I was smiling because it was all over and because that is what was expected of me. But I wasn't jubilant, and I really didn't feel relieved.

My sponsor threw a huge party at her home that afternoon. I excused myself for about ten minutes to have a good cry, then I presented my saber to my very proud father, and he excused himself to shed a few tears. I had never seen my father cry before that day.

Later we loaded into the car and headed for Texas. As we passed through the gates into the town of Highland Falls, I turned around in my seat and watched until West Point was out of sight. I said goodbye to my past. Then I turned on the radio and heard strains of a recently released song that reminded me that I was ready for my future:

*Step back, get out of the way, she's coming.*
*She's an eighties modern girl.*
*There's no more crawling for her, she's running.*
*And she's taking on the world.*
*Step back, get out of the way, she's coming . . .*
*Step back!*

# Epilogue

*". . . come walk these storied acres. Your heart will beat stronger, your step will gain extra spring, your head will tilt higher — for you will have savored a return to the very source of the values on which our Nation was built."*

— Lt. Gen. Dave Palmer, superintendent
of West Point, 1987

"Ladies and gentlemen," the master of ceremonies began, "I am proud to introduce the next congresswoman from the state of Texas, our own Captain Donna Peterson!"

As I ascended to the podium, I was honored by a standing ovation from the several hundred citizens gathered before me. I began this speech just as I begin every speech, by talking about the place where my adult life began — West Point.

"In 1978, a young girl from East Texas applied for a nomination to the United States Military Academy at West Point. Part of the nomination process required an essay to be written on 'Why I want to attend West Point.' I was as honest as I could be in my short paper, telling Senator John Tower that I was privileged to live in the greatest country in the world and that I wanted to give something back to a country that had given me so much in my young life. I didn't know

243

how I would one day serve my country or in what capacity, but I knew
that I would serve her. When I did, I knew I would have to be the best
trained, the best educated, and have the best background so that,
whatever I decided to do, I would never embarrass my country." The
crowd cheered in thunderous applause.

"Thank you," I began again. "I guess John Tower liked it, too,
because I ended up at West Point!"

I guess I really have come a long way since R-Day . . .

After graduation from the Officer's Basic Course, I went immediately to Fort Rucker, Alabama, for helicopter flight training. I was
school-trained in the UH-1 Huey helicopter and took twenty-five
hours of unit time in the AH-1 Cobra helicopter. I asked for, and received, a position at Fort Hood, Texas, where all of the military's latest
advances in equipment and technology were being fielded, including
the $11 million per copy AH-64 Apache helicopter. I was a helicopter
pilot, maintenance test pilot, and finally, chief of protocol for the free
world's largest military installation, Fort Hood.

In July 1987 I accepted a commission in the U.S. Army Reserve
and returned to my home in East Texas. In November of 1987 I was
selected Outstanding Young Career Woman by the local Business and
Professional Women's organization. In 1988 I was honored in the
Houston Astrodome as one of five Outstanding Female Veterans in the
State of Texas. By 1989 I had completed four years of effort on the
pages you are reading, and in 1990, the year I turned thirty, I was the
Republican candidate for U.S. representative from my home in East
Texas. And I've had a wonderful time throughout all of it.

Along the way, some prophecies were fulfilled, while others never
can be. Dave departed active duty and is working in California, the
land with plenty of sun and scantily clad women. Tony is a married
captain working with Special Forces and Special Operations teams. It's
all very secret and hush-hush, and Tony does it very well. We still
keep up with each other.

Speaking of secret operations, David Parker was a successful commander in the army's most elite helicopter unit and found himself "on
alert" for operations as sensitive as the hijacking of the *Achille Lauro*
and the bombing of Quadafy's headquarters. David and I were together
for many years after my graduation from West Point. Today David is a
student at Edwards Air Force Base, on his way to the Naval Experimental Test Pilot School in Maryland. David and I logged many hours
flying together over the years, and it has been one of my life's greatest

joys. He will always be my dearest friend.

And, of all of the hundreds of paragraphs in this book, this is the only one I dreaded penning. I was awakened in the middle of the night by the very phone call that anyone who has ever loved someone who wears a uniform fears the most. On July 22, 1984, the greatest love of my young life was killed in a tragic helicopter accident. Lt. Billy Dean Hubbard died that day, and a part of me died with him. I doubt that I will ever stop mourning his loss in some way. In the last card I received from Billy, just two weeks earlier for my birthday, he said some things that made we wonder if he knew his time would be coming soon. He wrote: "I have had a wonderful life. I've had the love of an Angel, and the career I've always dreamed of. And if I die tomorrow, I want you to know that you are the greatest gift of my life."

He went on to say that if he couldn't die in my arms, he hoped he'd die "behind the stick." Then he signed it as he always did, with the word "Love" and a big "B."

I miss you, Billy.


As for the Academy, it survives as it has for almost 200 years. Women have been in attendance now since 1976, and the bricks haven't crumbled yet. In fact, in 1990, the first female was selected to be the brigade commander. Even I doubted I'd actually live to see that one. She was joined that year by West Point's two female Rhodes Scholars. Women are not only maintaining the "reputation of the Corps untarnished" but are enhancing it as well. Of course, it's hard to believe it could actually be that rosy, right? Not as long as male graduates have something to say about it.

I overheard a group of older graduates who were talking about their recent trip to West Point and what they thought of a female brigade commander. "Oh, come on," one said, his face turning red. "None of the cadets respects her. They call her 'First Pussy' and laugh when she squeaks commands to the brigade. She belongs in the back seat of a car, not leading the Corps." The man had no idea that I had entered the room to hear his diatribe.

"Is that the way you really feel about us? I thought you were the one who was so upset when I didn't get one of the highest leadership positions," I said as I stared dead into his eyes.

"Oh, she's not you," he spouted nervously trying to talk his way out of this one. "You've got a great command voice. You deserved a

position like that. We all know it! The new Supe just put this girl in
to make a name for himself."

This year, 1990, is one of the first years since my graduation that
I haven't gone back to the Academy to visit, so I haven't met this con-
troversial woman. I have seen her on the television news, however, and
found no reason why these men should object so vociferously to her appointment, except for the obvious.

If I thought the attitude of the men at the Academy was bad, it
pales in comparison to the attitudes of the graduates I met after I left
West Point. I couldn't help but wonder if there would come a day
when I would *not* meet people who felt they had justification to be rude
to me because of the school I attended.

As the only female from Southeast Texas to graduate from West
Point, I sat at the head table at an annual West Point Founder's Day
Dinner in Houston in 1985. The man seated next to me was the president of the local West Point Parents Club. The alumni association
president had just finished reading off a list of the head table and
dinner was being served as this tasteless man leaned over to me and
asked, "You don't really believe women belong at West Point, do
you?" He was serious. By this time, there were women from the Houston area attending West Point as cadets, and, as I heard this man's
question, I felt sorry for them.

At a similar dinner in Dallas that same year, my mother and I
walked into the club where the function was being held and, though
many heads turned, no one came over to meet us. The group had been
told that a female graduate would be attending, but I had never met
any of the members, nor had they met me. After about five minutes,
two beautifully dressed officers' wives came over, introduced themselves, and said, "Aren't you Miss Texas?"

I couldn't help but feel flattered. I explained my presence to
them, and one of the women replied, "But you don't look like a female
cadet. I met some of 'them' when my husband took me on a visit last
year, and they're hideous. Yew!" she said, wrinkling her nose as if
she'd smelled a dead animal along the roadside. "You're much too
glamorous to be a cadet. Who are you, really?"

My mother must have known how steamed I was becoming because, before I could respond, I felt her stroke me from behind. I'd
heard this comment often enough over the years, however, that I was
prepared for the answer.

"Actually, ma'am, you're mistaken. There are a lot of pretty girls at West Point, and NCAA athletes, and Rhodes Scholars, and women with a great deal of courage who are lovely, inside and out. I hope you'll give them a second chance the next time you visit."

Regardless of the accomplishments of women, they are still measured by their physical presence. A male doesn't have to look like the man on the evening news to be considered successful. In contrast, if a women is striking in face or figure, she has to work extremely hard to prove that she also has intelligence. But, hopefully, when people who carry around those types of attitudes meet me, I'm able to change their feelings, or at least open up their minds.

That same evening, I met the parents of a classmate who had died during Christmas break of my senior year. I had spent the entire semester before Christmas break sitting next to the cadet in one of my classes, every other day. We used to enjoy bowling together, and he was always making me laugh. He had a marvelous attitude about life. I offered my condolences to his parents, and told them how I remembered their son.

"That's impossible," his father barked at me. "He wouldn't have acted that way at all. He never approved of women attending West Point!" Then he stormed off. The mother was terribly embarrassed, and she apologized for her husband.

"I'm used to it by now," I told the cadet's mother. "Your son was a much nicer person than his father."

At an Army–Navy football weekend function in 1987, I sat, as an invited guest, at dinner with friends and graduates, several of whom were now retired army officers. During the meal, a retired general officer who still harbored resentment at not having been chosen as superintendent of the Military Academy while he was on active duty, said to me, out of the blue, "I realize you may not agree with this, but I don't approve of women at West Point."

My face was completely expressionless. One of the colonels seated at the table turned ghost-white when he heard the comment. I continued eating my dinner in silence, when the general's wife, placing her hand over his on the table, corrected her husband, announcing, "*We* don't approve of women at West Point."

I couldn't believe my ears. At least the general, having graduated from the institution, was entitled to have an opinion. But a wife, who hadn't the faintest idea what life at USMA is really all about, had no right to voice that opinion as far as I was concerned! Having been a protocol officer after graduation from West Point, and accustomed to being placed in this awkward position, I made no comment. When the other retired officers at the table attempted to rally to the defense of my feelings, my only comment was, "Believe it or not, gentlemen, I *have* met ruder graduates."

For the most part, however, my experiences with graduates reluctant to accept women at West Point generally end much the same as in a scenario I went through in Houston, Texas.

When I was a yearling, I agreed to attend a seminar for prospective candidates in Houston, during my Christmas leave and at my own expense. The Houston area had no women attending West Point. I drove almost three hours to attend the seminar. After I arrived, I was introduced to the president of the West Point Society, the association sponsoring the seminar. Not only did the president refuse to shake my hand, he just looked at me and walked away in a huff. And I was doing his group the favor!

I didn't let his reaction upset me. I gave my speech, which was primarily along a humorous vein, and this man was the first one to step forward afterward to offer his hand and say thanks.

"It's just that I had never actually met a female cadet before," he told me.

The USMA Class of '51 graduate had amassed quite a fortune since his days in dress gray, and was exuberantly willing to expend it all to prevent the matriculation of women. Today, his friends and fellow graduates are amazed at the tremendous change in this man, and I'm proud to say that he is one of my dearest friends. In a letter written to me just prior to my graduation, he states: "You've done a splendid job and it is my respect for that which — among so many high qualities — makes me respect you so. You are as good as any male, and the greatest female I have ever known. I'm proud of you."

This man credits his change of attitude to finally meeting and conversing with not just me but *many* female cadets since our meeting in 1979. That's probably the comment I hear graduates make most often: "I don't feel quite as resentful, now that I've met some female cadets." So many graduates walk around bemoaning women at West Point, having never laid eyes on one, having never sat down and spoken to one. I don't know what they expect, but I'm glad they seem pleasantly surprised when they meet me. Of course, some people will never change their attitude, and that's okay. One thing that makes America great is that people are entitled to their opinions, even where women at West Point are concerned. I do believe, however, that freedom of speech does not give people the right to be rude and to hurt others' feelings unnecessarily.

So, are women any better off at the Military Academy today? I had a chance to speak to a dozen or so male and female cadets when I returned to West Point for my five-year reunion in the fall of 1987. Comments were varied, but, basically, I was pleased that the female cadets feel very little resentment these days. What I was not as pleased about, however, was the females' lack of reverence for the price women paid so that these females could feel as they do.

One female yearling, who graduated in May 1990, was asked by me if she had any feelings for what the first classes of women went through. She responded quite unemotionally, "Oh, I don't know. I guess it was pretty tough."

"Do you feel any kinship or obligation to them at all?" I pushed.

"We don't know what you went through. It doesn't seem that tough emotionally. The guys accept us," she responded.

I suppose I was a little hurt by the uninvolved nature of her response. I remembered reading those admissions brochures and memorizing the names and the faces of as many of the first women as I possibly could. And I couldn't wait to finally meet some of them. The females I was speaking to today were not at all inspired by the struggles of the pioneer women.

"So, how are women being treated today?" I asked another female from the same class.

"Fine. It's about time the Academy let us wear earrings like the other two academies. And we're trying to get the Academy to let us grow our hair longer before graduation. They'll have to let us. The other academies do."

*Wow, they just take it all for granted,* I thought. I remember biting on a washcloth every night while my roommate repierced my ears which had closed during the day, since we were not allowed to wear earrings of any kind. I'd sleep with them in, take them out in the morning, and repierce my ears each night with a muffled scream of pain. It should have taken my ears three weeks to remain open; it was three weeks before yellow fluid stopped shooting from my ears as they were repierced, and four months before the holes remained open. As for the haircuts, after my first barber shop cut I thought I looked remarkably like my brother: short hair, parted on one side, barely over the ears, my neck shaved in the back.

At the Army–Navy game in 1986 (I attend every year), I was fortunate enough to be introduced to the newest superintendent of the Military Academy, Lieutenant General Dave Palmer. When he asked, "What do you think?" I replied, "The women's hair is so long!" Of course, he was asking about the score of the game (which we were soundly winning), not the haircut standards.

Yes, many things have changed for the women. But when I asked the question, I expected to hear about the successes of the changes that needed to be made to promote the degree of equality that was sorely lacking when I graduated. Instead, all I heard from these young cadets were trivialities about hair and earrings and privileges! And there was absolutely no thought of making contributions to assist future females entering the Academy. My ears burned with the shallowness of their responses, and my heart ached at the comparison of West Point to the other service academies.

USMA had always maintained the reputation for being the strictest on its cadets; the most demanding physically, emotionally, and militarily; having the strictest Honor Code; offering the fewest privileges; and being the most prestigious. Who cares about the leniency of the other service academies? They've always had those reputations. That's what sets West Point apart. It is the lack of leniency that has enabled the Military Academy to maintain its reputation, throughout the world, as the most prestigious military institution. Accepting women put great strain on the Academy, but it did not change the basic standards of excellence. In fact, in 1988, the United States Military Academy was determined to be the "most selective" educational institution in the country, as evaluated by the publication *USA Today*. The decision was based on evaluation criteria such as SAT scores, number of applicants completing files (around 15,000 in 1990), and number actually admitted (less than 1,400). Too many trivial changes will produce "happier" West Point graduates, but not "better" ones. It's time now for the Academy to stabilize and look toward the future. And perhaps that is what these female cadets were attempting to do, by ignoring the struggles of the past.

As for women feeling they are accepted, I hope they are. At least, I'm glad that they live each day feeling that they are, for living each day knowing that you aren't was painful. My younger brother left the Academy after two years as a cadet. He loved West Point and the "fabulous people" he came to know, but, having had a sister attend the Academy, it hurt him to see how the women were treated by the majority of male cadets. "To their faces the men would be nice, but behind their backs they ripped the women to shreds!" he said. "They would be nice to the women and could get the females to do anything for them, and they lost all respect for those women."

It was hard for me to convince my brother that women had progressed, and that they were probably not as naive as they pretended to be.

"If it's like this now," he said, shaking his head in disbelief, "it must have been *hell* for you back in '78! I don't understand how a woman could let herself go through that!"

One of his classmates (Class of 1987) from Texas was nodding his head in agreement. Then the cadet added, "You know, ma'am, I don't see why people are still making this such a big deal. If the women couldn't handle it, they wouldn't be here. The Academy doesn't care what sex you are — if you fail, they kick you out. It's the immaturity of some of the male cadets that causes the problems." If only he knew of the immaturity of former cadets old enough to be his grandfather!

Basically, though, by 1987 the men, just like the women I spoke to, were more preoccupied with being cadets than with being either male or female. The hatred and bitterness of the past was evolving away, and cadets were looking toward the future. Soon the struggles the Academy faced in the seventies would be remembered only in history books, and the hearts of the second decade of male and female cadets would be unencumbered with the painful baggage of the first decade.

Though I was disappointed during my reunion that the struggles of the first women seemed unappreciated by the newest generation of female cadets, I am no longer. In the past three years since leaving active duty, I have spent a great deal of time speaking publicly on behalf of West Point and its women. During that time I have received over a dozen letters from cadets — three from women in the Class of 1990 — who "just wanted me to know" how much they appreciated what my female classmates and I must have gone through during those tumultuous times and to say "Thank you" for being "an outstanding role model and representative for women at West Point." Their endorsement means more to me than any accolade I've received during my entire military career.

Being a pioneer is never easy. But you don't concentrate on the difficulty: you focus on the brass ring. And if the reward is worth the pain, you persevere. The very fact that the harassment is no longer blatant says that the Academy has applied enough pressure that things are changing. Progress takes time, and it takes the perseverance of women — and men — of courage.

It was unrealistic to think that two centuries of tradition could be changed in half a decade. Change doesn't move that quickly. Today, however, women have been in attendance at U.S. service academies for fourteen years, and evidence of their acceptance is all around — in the attitudes of the male and female cadets, graduates, senior military officers, and the American public. If I were ever to have a daughter, I would be honored to have her join the legacy of the Long Gray Line.

# The Long Gray Line

The impressive Long Gray Line, living and dead, does not number in total the graduates from one single class at the University of Texas. Yet, this historic record of graduates boasts a collection of the nation's most revered warriors, statesmen, and legends. At West Point, "much of the history we teach was made by people we taught."

West Point's impressive list of graduates includes familiar national heroes: Jefferson Davis (1828), Robert E. Lee (1829), William T. Sherman (1840), Ulysses S. Grant (1843), George McClellan (1846), George Pickett (1846), Philip Sheridan (1853), George Custer (1861), John J. Pershing (1886), Douglas MacArthur (1903), George S. Patton, Jr. (1909), Dwight D. Eisenhower (1915), James Van Fleet (1915), Omar N. Bradley (1915), Matthew Ridgway (1917), Lucius D. Clay (1918), Maxwell Taylor (1922), William C. Westmoreland (1936), and Colin P. Kelly, Jr. (1937). Very few Americans would find any of the names on this list surprising. There are, however, additional graduate names, many of whom the American public might be surprised to learn graduated from West Point. These include:

Abner Doubleday, the "Father of Baseball" (1842);

Frank Dow Merrill, "Merrill's Marauders" (1929);

Henry M. Robert, author of *Robert's Rules of Order* (1857);

Thomas E. Selfridge, first man killed in an airplane crash, September 17, 1908, with Orville Wright (1903);

James Allen, discovered the source of the Mississippi River (1883);

George Washington Goethals, headed the building of the Panama Canal (1880);

Henry A. DuPont, grandson of the founder of E. I. Du Pont de Nemours, U.S. senator from Delaware, Congressional Medal of Honor winner (1861);

Leslie R. Groves, commanding general of the U.S. atomic program (1918);

Glenn W. Davis, Heisman Trophy winner, pro football player, he was the first grown-up love interest of young Elizabeth Taylor (1947);

Felix "Doc" Blanchard, Heisman Trophy winner (1947);

Peter M. Dawkins, Heisman Trophy candidate, Rhodes Scholarship recipient (1959);

Frank Borman, NASA astronaut, commander of the first spacecraft in circumlunar orbit (1950);

Edward H. White, NASA astronaut, first man to walk in space (1952);

Edwin Aldrin, Jr., NASA astronaut, first manned flight to the moon, participated in first manned landing on the moon with Neil Armstrong (1951);

Michael Collins, NASA astronaut, participated in first manned landing on the moon (*Apollo 11*) with Neil Armstrong and Edwin Aldrin (1952);

Anastasio Somoza, Jr., general, president of Nicaragua until he was overthrown in 1979 (1946);

Edgar Allan Poe, author, mystery writer, left the Academy without graduating (1834).